PILOT/CON[illegible]
GLOSSARY

PURPOSE

a. This Glossary was compiled to promote a common understanding of the terms used in the Air Traffic Control system. It includes those terms which are intended for pilot/controller communications. Those terms most frequently used in pilot/controller communications are printed in ***bold italics***. The definitions are primarily defined in an operational sense applicable to both users and operators of the National Airspace System. Use of the Glossary will preclude any misunderstandings concerning the system's design, function, and purpose.

b. Because of the international nature of flying, terms used in the Lexicon, published by the International Civil Aviation Organization (ICAO), are included when they differ from FAA definitions. These terms are followed by "[ICAO]." For the reader's convenience, there are also cross references to related terms in other parts of the Glossary and to other documents, such as the Code of Federal Regulations (CFR) and the Aeronautical Information Manual (AIM).

c. Terms used in this glossary that apply to flight service station (FSS) roles are included when they differ from air traffic control functions. These terms are followed by "[FSS]."

d. This Glossary will be revised, as necessary, to maintain a common understanding of the system.

EXPLANATION OF CHANGES

e. Terms Added:
SPECIAL MILITARY ACTIVITY ROUTE (SMAR)
WEATHER RADAR PRECIPITATION INTENSITY

f. Terms Deleted:
PRECIPITATION RADAR WEATHER DESCRIPTIONS

g. Terms Modified:
ADAPTED ROUTES
DEVIATIONS

h. Editorial/format changes were made where necessary. Revision bars were not used due to the insignificant nature of the changes.

ADR–
(See ADAPTED ROUTES.)
(See AIRPORT DEPARTURE RATE.)

ADS [ICAO]–
(See ICAO term AUTOMATIC DEPENDENT SURVEILLANCE.)

ADS–B–
(See AUTOMATIC DEPENDENT SURVEILLANCE–BROADCAST.)

ADS–C–
(See AUTOMATIC DEPENDENT SURVEILLANCE–CONTRACT.)

ADVANCED AIR MOBILITY (AAM)–A transportation system that transports people and property by air between two points in the NAS using aircraft with advanced technologies, including electric aircraft or electric vertical takeoff and landing aircraft, in both controlled and uncontrolled airspace.

ADVISE INTENTIONS– Tell me what you plan to do.

ADVISORY– Advice and information provided to assist pilots in the safe conduct of flight and aircraft movement.
(See ADVISORY SERVICE.)

ADVISORY CIRCULAR (AC)– An FAA publication, advisory and descriptive in nature, which is not regulatory.

ADVISORY FREQUENCY– The appropriate frequency to be used for Airport Advisory Service.
(See LOCAL AIRPORT ADVISORY.)
(See UNICOM.)
(Refer to ADVISORY CIRCULAR NO. 90-66.)
(Refer to AIM.)

ADVISORY SERVICE– Advice and information provided by a facility to assist pilots in the safe conduct of flight and aircraft movement.
(See ADDITIONAL SERVICES.)
(See LOCAL AIRPORT ADVISORY.)
(See RADAR ADVISORY.)
(See SAFETY ALERT.)
(See TRAFFIC ADVISORIES.)
(Refer to AIM.)

ADW–
(See ARRIVAL DEPARTURE WINDOW)

AERIAL REFUELING– A procedure used by the military to transfer fuel from one aircraft to another during flight.
(Refer to VFR/IFR Wall Planning Charts.)

AERODROME– A defined area on land or water (including any buildings, installations and equipment) intended to be used either wholly or in part for the arrival, departure, and movement of aircraft.

AERODROME BEACON [ICAO]– Aeronautical beacon used to indicate the location of an aerodrome from the air.

AERODROME CONTROL SERVICE [ICAO]– Air traffic control service for aerodrome traffic.

AERODROME CONTROL TOWER [ICAO]– A unit established to provide air traffic control service to aerodrome traffic.

AERODROME ELEVATION [ICAO]– The elevation of the highest point of the landing area.

AERODROME TRAFFIC CIRCUIT [ICAO]– The specified path to be flown by aircraft operating in the vicinity of an aerodrome.

AERONAUTICAL BEACON– A visual NAVAID displaying flashes of white and/or colored light to indicate the location of an airport, a heliport, a landmark, a certain point of a Federal airway in mountainous terrain, or an obstruction.

(See AIRPORT ROTATING BEACON.)
(Refer to AIM.)

AERONAUTICAL CHART– A map used in air navigation containing all or part of the following: topographic features, hazards and obstructions, navigation aids, navigation routes, designated airspace, and airports. Commonly used aeronautical charts are:

a. Sectional Aeronautical Charts (1:500,000)– Designed for visual navigation of slow or medium speed aircraft. Topographic information on these charts features the portrayal of relief and a judicious selection of visual check points for VFR flight. Aeronautical information includes visual and radio aids to navigation, airports, controlled airspace, permanent special use airspace (SUA), obstructions, and related data.

b. VFR Terminal Area Charts (1:250,000)– Depict Class B airspace which provides for the control or segregation of all the aircraft within Class B airspace. The chart depicts topographic information and aeronautical information which includes visual and radio aids to navigation, airports, controlled airspace, permanent SUA, obstructions, and related data.

c. En Route Low Altitude Charts– Provide aeronautical information for en route instrument navigation (IFR) in the low altitude stratum. Information includes the portrayal of airways, limits of controlled airspace, position identification and frequencies of radio aids, selected airports, minimum en route and minimum obstruction clearance altitudes, airway distances, reporting points, permanent SUA, and related data. Area charts, which are a part of this series, furnish terminal data at a larger scale in congested areas.

d. En Route High Altitude Charts– Provide aeronautical information for en route instrument navigation (IFR) in the high altitude stratum. Information includes the portrayal of jet routes, identification and frequencies of radio aids, selected airports, distances, time zones, special use airspace, and related information.

e. Instrument Approach Procedure (IAP) Charts– Portray the aeronautical data which is required to execute an instrument approach to an airport. These charts depict the procedures, including all related data, and the airport diagram. Each procedure is designated for use with a specific type of electronic navigation system including NDB, TACAN, VOR, ILS RNAV and GLS. These charts are identified by the type of navigational aid(s)/equipment required to provide final approach guidance.

f. Instrument Departure Procedure (DP) Charts– Designed to expedite clearance delivery and to facilitate transition between takeoff and en route operations. Each DP is presented as a separate chart and may serve a single airport or more than one airport in a given geographical location.

g. Standard Terminal Arrival (STAR) Charts– Designed to expedite air traffic control arrival procedures and to facilitate transition between en route and instrument approach operations. Each STAR procedure is presented as a separate chart and may serve a single airport or more than one airport in a given geographical location.

h. Airport Taxi Charts– Designed to expedite the efficient and safe flow of ground traffic at an airport. These charts are identified by the official airport name; e.g., Ronald Reagan Washington National Airport.

(See ICAO term AERONAUTICAL CHART.)

AERONAUTICAL CHART [ICAO]– A representation of a portion of the earth, its culture and relief, specifically designated to meet the requirements of air navigation.

AERONAUTICAL INFORMATION MANUAL (AIM)– A primary FAA publication whose purpose is to instruct airmen about operating in the National Airspace System of the U.S. It provides basic flight information, ATC Procedures and general instructional information concerning health, medical facts, factors affecting flight safety, accident and hazard reporting, and types of aeronautical charts and their use.

AAM–
(See ADVANCED AIR MOBILITY.)

AAR–
(See AIRPORT ARRIVAL RATE.)
(See ADAPTED ROUTES.)

ABBREVIATED IFR FLIGHT PLANS– An authorization by ATC requiring pilots to submit only that information needed for the purpose of ATC. It includes only a small portion of the usual IFR flight plan information. In certain instances, this may be only aircraft identification, location, and pilot request. Other information may be requested if needed by ATC for separation/control purposes. It is frequently used by aircraft which are airborne and desire an instrument approach or by aircraft which are on the ground and desire a climb to VFR-on-top.
(See VFR-ON-TOP.)
(Refer to AIM.)

ABEAM– An aircraft is "abeam" a fix, point, or object when that fix, point, or object is approximately 90 degrees to the right or left of the aircraft track. Abeam indicates a general position rather than a precise point.

ABORT– To terminate a preplanned aircraft maneuver; e.g., an aborted takeoff.

ABRR–
(See AIRBORNE REROUTE)

AC–
(See ADVISORY CIRCULAR.)

ACC [ICAO]–
(See ICAO term AREA CONTROL CENTER.)

ACCELERATE-STOP DISTANCE AVAILABLE– The runway plus stopway length declared available and suitable for the acceleration and deceleration of an airplane aborting a takeoff.

ACCELERATE-STOP DISTANCE AVAILABLE [ICAO]– The length of the take-off run available plus the length of the stopway if provided.

ACDO–
(See AIR CARRIER DISTRICT OFFICE.)

ACKNOWLEDGE– Let me know that you have received and understood this message.

ACL–
(See AIRCRAFT LIST.)

ACLS–
(See AUTOMATIC CARRIER LANDING SYSTEM.)

ACROBATIC FLIGHT– An intentional maneuver involving an abrupt change in an aircraft's attitude, an abnormal attitude, or abnormal acceleration not necessary for normal flight.
(See ICAO term ACROBATIC FLIGHT.)
(Refer to 14 CFR Part 91.)

ACROBATIC FLIGHT [ICAO]– Maneuvers intentionally performed by an aircraft involving an abrupt change in its attitude, an abnormal attitude, or an abnormal variation in speed.

ACTIVE RUNWAY–
(See RUNWAY IN USE/ACTIVE RUNWAY/DUTY RUNWAY.)

ACTUAL NAVIGATION PERFORMANCE (ANP)−
(See REQUIRED NAVIGATION PERFORMANCE.)

ADAPTED ROUTES− Departure and/or arrival routes that are adapted in ARTCC ERAM computers to accomplish inter/intrafacility controller coordination and to ensure that flight data is posted at the proper control positions. Adapted routes are automatically applied to flight plans where appropriate. When the workload or traffic situation permits, controllers may provide radar vectors or assign requested routes to minimize circuitous routing. Adapted routes are usually confined to one ARTCC's area and are referred to by the following names or abbreviations:

a. Adapted Arrival Route (AAR). A specific arrival route from an appropriate en route point to an airport or terminal area. A Standard Terminal Arrival (STAR) and/or a partial Preferred IFR Route may be included in an AAR.

b. Adapted Departure Route (ADR). A specific departure route from an airport or terminal area to an en route point where there is no further need for flow control. An Instrument Departure Procedure (DP) and/or a partial Preferred IFR Route may be included in an ADR.

c. Adapted Departure and Arrival Route (ADAR). A route between two terminals which are within or immediately adjacent to one ARTCC's area. ADARs are similar to Preferred IFR Routes and may share components, but they are not synonymous.
(See PREFFERED IFR ROUTES.)

ADAR−
(See ADAPTED ROUTES.)

ADDITIONAL SERVICES− Advisory information provided by ATC which includes but is not limited to the following:

a. Traffic advisories.

b. Vectors, when requested by the pilot, to assist aircraft receiving traffic advisories to avoid observed traffic.

c. Altitude deviation information of 300 feet or more from an assigned altitude as observed on a verified (reading correctly) automatic altitude readout (Mode C).

d. Advisories that traffic is no longer a factor.

e. Weather and chaff information.

f. Weather assistance.

g. Bird activity information.

h. Holding pattern surveillance. Additional services are provided to the extent possible contingent only upon the controller's capability to fit them into the performance of higher priority duties and on the basis of limitations of the radar, volume of traffic, frequency congestion, and controller workload. The controller has complete discretion for determining if he/she is able to provide or continue to provide a service in a particular case. The controller's reason not to provide or continue to provide a service in a particular case is not subject to question by the pilot and need not be made known to him/her.
(See TRAFFIC ADVISORIES.)
(Refer to AIM.)

ADF−
(See AUTOMATIC DIRECTION FINDER.)

ADIZ−
(See AIR DEFENSE IDENTIFICATION ZONE.)

ADLY−
(See ARRIVAL DELAY.)

ADMINISTRATOR− The Federal Aviation Administrator or any person to whom he/she has delegated his/her authority in the matter concerned.

AERONAUTICAL INFORMATION PUBLICATION (AIP) [ICAO]- A publication issued by or with the authority of a State and containing aeronautical information of a lasting character essential to air navigation.

(See CHART SUPPLEMENT.)

AERONAUTICAL INFORMATION SERVICES (AIS)- A facility in Silver Spring, MD, established by FAA to operate a central aeronautical information service for the collection, validation, and dissemination of aeronautical data in support of the activities of government, industry, and the aviation community. The information is published in the National Flight Data Digest.

(See NATIONAL FLIGHT DATA DIGEST.)

AFFIRMATIVE- Yes.

AFIS-

(See AUTOMATIC FLIGHT INFORMATION SERVICE - ALASKA FSSs ONLY.)

AFP-

(See AIRSPACE FLOW PROGRAM.)

AHA-

(See AIRCRAFT HAZARD AREA.)

AIM-

(See AERONAUTICAL INFORMATION MANUAL.)

AIP [ICAO]-

(See ICAO term AERONAUTICAL INFORMATION PUBLICATION.)

AIR CARRIER DISTRICT OFFICE- An FAA field office serving an assigned geographical area, staffed with Flight Standards personnel serving the aviation industry and the general public on matters related to the certification and operation of scheduled air carriers and other large aircraft operations.

AIR DEFENSE EMERGENCY- A military emergency condition declared by a designated authority. This condition exists when an attack upon the continental U.S., Alaska, Canada, or U.S. installations in Greenland by hostile aircraft or missiles is considered probable, is imminent, or is taking place.

(Refer to AIM.)

AIR DEFENSE IDENTIFICATION ZONE (ADIZ)- An area of airspace over land or water in which the ready identification, location, and control of all aircraft (except for Department of Defense and law enforcement aircraft) is required in the interest of national security.

Note: ADIZ locations and operating and flight plan requirements for civil aircraft operations are specified in 14 CFR Part 99.

(Refer to AIM.)

AIR NAVIGATION FACILITY- Any facility used in, available for use in, or designed for use in, aid of air navigation, including landing areas, lights, any apparatus or equipment for disseminating weather information, for signaling, for radio-directional finding, or for radio or other electrical communication, and any other structure or mechanism having a similar purpose for guiding or controlling flight in the air or the landing and takeoff of aircraft.

(See NAVIGATIONAL AID.)

AIR ROUTE SURVEILLANCE RADAR- Air route traffic control center (ARTCC) radar used primarily to detect and display an aircraft's position while en route between terminal areas. The ARSR enables controllers to provide radar air traffic control service when aircraft are within the ARSR coverage. In some instances, ARSR may enable an ARTCC to provide terminal radar services similar to but usually more limited than those provided by a radar approach control.

AIR ROUTE TRAFFIC CONTROL CENTER (ARTCC)- A facility established to provide air traffic control service to aircraft operating on IFR flight plans within controlled airspace and principally during the en route phase of flight. When equipment capabilities and controller workload permit, certain advisory/assistance services may be provided to VFR aircraft.

(See EN ROUTE AIR TRAFFIC CONTROL SERVICES.)
(Refer to AIM.)

AIR TAXI– Used to describe a helicopter/VTOL aircraft movement conducted above the surface but normally not above 100 feet AGL. The aircraft may proceed either via hover taxi or flight at speeds more than 20 knots. The pilot is solely responsible for selecting a safe airspeed/altitude for the operation being conducted.

(See HOVER TAXI.)
(Refer to AIM.)

AIR TRAFFIC– Aircraft operating in the air or on an airport surface, exclusive of loading ramps and parking areas.

(See ICAO term AIR TRAFFIC.)

AIR TRAFFIC [ICAO]– All aircraft in flight or operating on the maneuvering area of an aerodrome.

AIR TRAFFIC CLEARANCE– An authorization by air traffic control for the purpose of preventing collision between known aircraft, for an aircraft to proceed under specified traffic conditions within controlled airspace. The pilot-in-command of an aircraft may not deviate from the provisions of a visual flight rules (VFR) or instrument flight rules (IFR) air traffic clearance except in an emergency or unless an amended clearance has been obtained. Additionally, the pilot may request a different clearance from that which has been issued by air traffic control (ATC) if information available to the pilot makes another course of action more practicable or if aircraft equipment limitations or company procedures forbid compliance with the clearance issued. Pilots may also request clarification or amendment, as appropriate, any time a clearance is not fully understood, or considered unacceptable because of safety of flight. Controllers should, in such instances and to the extent of operational practicality and safety, honor the pilot's request. 14 CFR Part 91.3(a) states: "The pilot in command of an aircraft is directly responsible for, and is the final authority as to, the operation of that aircraft." THE PILOT IS RESPONSIBLE TO REQUEST AN AMENDED CLEARANCE if ATC issues a clearance that would cause a pilot to deviate from a rule or regulation, or in the pilot's opinion, would place the aircraft in jeopardy.

(See ATC INSTRUCTIONS.)
(See ICAO term AIR TRAFFIC CONTROL CLEARANCE.)

AIR TRAFFIC CONTROL– A service operated by appropriate authority to promote the safe, orderly and expeditious flow of air traffic.

(See ICAO term AIR TRAFFIC CONTROL SERVICE.)

AIR TRAFFIC CONTROL CLEARANCE [ICAO]– Authorization for an aircraft to proceed under conditions specified by an air traffic control unit.

Note 1: For convenience, the term air traffic control clearance is frequently abbreviated to clearance when used in appropriate contexts.

Note 2: The abbreviated term clearance may be prefixed by the words taxi, takeoff, departure, en route, approach or landing to indicate the particular portion of flight to which the air traffic control clearance relates.

AIR TRAFFIC CONTROL SERVICE–

(See AIR TRAFFIC CONTROL.)

AIR TRAFFIC CONTROL SERVICE [ICAO]– A service provided for the purpose of:

a. Preventing collisions:

1. Between aircraft; and

2. On the maneuvering area between aircraft and obstructions.

b. Expediting and maintaining an orderly flow of air traffic.

AIR TRAFFIC CONTROL SPECIALIST– A person authorized to provide air traffic control service.

(See AIR TRAFFIC CONTROL.)
(See FLIGHT SERVICE STATION.)
(See ICAO term CONTROLLER.)

AIR TRAFFIC CONTROL SYSTEM COMMAND CENTER (ATCSCC)– An Air Traffic Tactical Operations facility responsible for monitoring and managing the flow of air traffic throughout the NAS, producing a safe, orderly, and expeditious flow of traffic while minimizing delays. The following functions are located at the ATCSCC:

a. Central Altitude Reservation Function (CARF). Responsible for coordinating, planning, and approving special user requirements under the Altitude Reservation (ALTRV) concept.
(See ALTITUDE RESERVATION.)

b. Airport Reservation Office (ARO). Monitors the operation and allocation of reservations for unscheduled operations at airports designated by the Administrator as High Density Airports. These airports are generally known as slot controlled airports. The ARO allocates reservations on a first come, first served basis determined by the time the request is received at the ARO.
(Refer to 14 CFR Part 93.)
(See CHART SUPPLEMENT.)

c. U.S. Notice to Air Missions (NOTAM) Office. Responsible for collecting, maintaining, and distributing NOTAMs for the U.S. civilian and military, as well as international aviation communities.
(See NOTICE TO AIR MISSIONS.)

d. Weather Unit. Monitor all aspects of weather for the U.S. that might affect aviation including cloud cover, visibility, winds, precipitation, thunderstorms, icing, turbulence, and more. Provide forecasts based on observations and on discussions with meteorologists from various National Weather Service offices, FAA facilities, airlines, and private weather services.

e. Air Traffic Organization (ATO) Space Operations and Unmanned Aircraft System (UAS); the Office of Primary Responsibility (OPR) for all space and upper class E tactical operations in the National Airspace System (NAS).

AIR TRAFFIC SERVICE– A generic term meaning:

a. Flight Information Service.

b. Alerting Service.

c. Air Traffic Advisory Service.

d. Air Traffic Control Service:

1. Area Control Service,

2. Approach Control Service, or

3. Airport Control Service.

AIR TRAFFIC ORGANIZATION (ATO) – The FAA line of business responsible for providing safe and efficient air navigation services in the national airspace system.

AIR TRAFFIC SERVICE (ATS) ROUTES – The term "ATS Route" is a generic term that includes "VOR Federal airways," "colored Federal airways," "jet routes," and "RNAV routes." The term "ATS route" does not replace these more familiar route names, but serves only as an overall title when listing the types of routes that comprise the United States route structure.

AIRBORNE– An aircraft is considered airborne when all parts of the aircraft are off the ground.

AIRBORNE DELAY– Amount of delay to be encountered in airborne holding.

AIRBORNE REROUTE (ABRR)– A capability within the Traffic Flow Management System used for the timely development and implementation of tactical reroutes for airborne aircraft. This capability defines a set of aircraft–specific reroutes that address a certain traffic flow problem and then electronically transmits them to En Route Automation Modernization (ERAM) for execution by the appropriate sector controllers.

AIRCRAFT– Device(s) that are used or intended to be used for flight in the air, and when used in air traffic control terminology, may include the flight crew.
(See ICAO term AIRCRAFT.)

AIRCRAFT [ICAO]– Any machine that can derive support in the atmosphere from the reactions of the air other than the reactions of the air against the earth's surface.

AIRCRAFT APPROACH CATEGORY– A grouping of aircraft based on a speed of 1.3 times the stall speed in the landing configuration at maximum gross landing weight. An aircraft must fit in only one category. If it is necessary to maneuver at speeds in excess of the upper limit of a speed range for a category, the minimums for the category for that speed must be used. For example, an aircraft which falls in Category A, but is circling to land at a speed in excess of 91 knots, must use the approach Category B minimums when circling to land. The categories are as follows:

a. Category A– Speed less than 91 knots.

b. Category B– Speed 91 knots or more but less than 121 knots.

c. Category C– Speed 121 knots or more but less than 141 knots.

d. Category D– Speed 141 knots or more but less than 166 knots.

e. Category E– Speed 166 knots or more.

(Refer to 14 CFR Part 97.)

AIRCRAFT CLASSES– For the purposes of Wake Turbulence Separation Minima, ATC classifies aircraft as Super, Heavy, Large, and Small as follows:

a. Super. The Airbus A-380-800 (A388) and the Antonov An-225 (A225) are classified as super.

b. Heavy– Aircraft capable of takeoff weights of 300,000 pounds or more whether or not they are operating at this weight during a particular phase of flight.

c. Large– Aircraft of more than 41,000 pounds, maximum certificated takeoff weight, up to but not including 300,000 pounds.

d. Small– Aircraft of 41,000 pounds or less maximum certificated takeoff weight.

(Refer to AIM.)

AIRCRAFT CONFLICT– Predicted conflict, within EDST of two aircraft, or between aircraft and airspace. A Red alert is used for conflicts when the predicted minimum separation is 5 nautical miles or less. A Yellow alert is used when the predicted minimum separation is between 5 and approximately 12 nautical miles. A Blue alert is used for conflicts between an aircraft and predefined airspace.

(See EN ROUTE DECISION SUPPORT TOOL.)

AIRCRAFT LIST (ACL)– A view available with EDST that lists aircraft currently in or predicted to be in a particular sector's airspace. The view contains textual flight data information in line format and may be sorted into various orders based on the specific needs of the sector team.

(See EN ROUTE DECISION SUPPORT TOOL.)

AIRCRAFT SURGE LAUNCH AND RECOVERY– Procedures used at USAF bases to provide increased launch and recovery rates in instrument flight rules conditions. ASLAR is based on:

a. Reduced separation between aircraft which is based on time or distance. Standard arrival separation applies between participants including multiple flights until the DRAG point. The DRAG point is a published location on an ASLAR approach where aircraft landing second in a formation slows to a predetermined airspeed. The DRAG point is the reference point at which MARSA applies as expanding elements effect separation within a flight or between subsequent participating flights.

b. ASLAR procedures shall be covered in a Letter of Agreement between the responsible USAF military ATC facility and the concerned Federal Aviation Administration facility. Initial Approach Fix spacing requirements are normally addressed as a minimum.

AIRCRAFT HAZARD AREA (AHA)– Used by ATC to segregate air traffic from a launch vehicle, reentry vehicle, amateur rocket, jettisoned stages, hardware, or falling debris generated by failures associated with any of these activities. An AHA is designated via NOTAM as either a TFR or stationary ALTRV. Unless otherwise specified, the vertical limits of an AHA are from the surface to unlimited.

(See CONTINGENCY HAZARD AREA.)
(See REFINED HAZARD AREA.)
(See TRANSITIONAL HAZARD AREA.)

AIRCRAFT WAKE TURBULENCE CATEGORIES– For the purpose of Wake Turbulence Recategorization (RECAT) Separation Minima, ATC groups aircraft into categories ranging from Category A through Category I, dependent upon the version of RECAT that is applied. Specific category assignments vary and are listed in the RECAT Orders.

AIRMEN'S METEOROLOGICAL INFORMATION (AIRMET)– A concise description of an occurrence or expected occurrence of specified en route weather phenomena that may affect the safety of aircraft operations, but at intensities lower than those that require the issuance of a SIGMET. An AIRMET may be issued when any of the following weather phenomena are occurring or expected to occur:

a. Moderate turbulence

b. Low-level windshear

c. Strong surface winds greater than 30 knots

d. Moderate icing

e. Freezing level

f. Mountain obscuration

g. IFR

(See CONVECTIVE SIGMET.)
(See CWA.)
(See GRAPHICAL AIRMEN'S METEOROLOGICAL INFORMATION.)
(See SAW.)
(See SIGMET.)
(Refer to AIM.)

AIRPORT– An area on land or water that is used or intended to be used for the landing and takeoff of aircraft and includes its buildings and facilities, if any.

AIRPORT ADVISORY AREA– The area within ten miles of an airport without a control tower or where the tower is not in operation, and on which a Flight Service Station is located.

(See LOCAL AIRPORT ADVISORY.)
(Refer to AIM.)

AIRPORT ARRIVAL RATE (AAR)– A dynamic input parameter specifying the number of arriving aircraft which an airport or airspace can accept from the ARTCC per hour. The AAR is used to calculate the desired interval between successive arrival aircraft.

AIRPORT DEPARTURE RATE (ADR)– A dynamic parameter specifying the number of aircraft which can depart an airport and the airspace can accept per hour.

AIRPORT ELEVATION– The highest point of an airport's usable runways measured in feet from mean sea level.

(See TOUCHDOWN ZONE ELEVATION.)
(See ICAO term AERODROME ELEVATION.)

AIRPORT LIGHTING– Various lighting aids that may be installed on an airport. Types of airport lighting include:

a. Approach Light System (ALS)– An airport lighting facility which provides visual guidance to landing aircraft by radiating light beams in a directional pattern by which the pilot aligns the aircraft with the extended centerline of the runway on his/her final approach for landing. Condenser-Discharge Sequential Flashing Lights/Sequenced Flashing Lights may be installed in conjunction with the ALS at some airports. Types of Approach Light Systems are:

1. ALSF-1– Approach Light System with Sequenced Flashing Lights in ILS Cat-I configuration.

2. ALSF-2– Approach Light System with Sequenced Flashing Lights in ILS Cat-II configuration. The ALSF-2 may operate as an SSALR when weather conditions permit.

3. SSALF– Simplified Short Approach Light System with Sequenced Flashing Lights.

4. SSALR– Simplified Short Approach Light System with Runway Alignment Indicator Lights.

5. MALSF– Medium Intensity Approach Light System with Sequenced Flashing Lights.

6. MALSR– Medium Intensity Approach Light System with Runway Alignment Indicator Lights.

7. RLLS– Runway Lead-in Light System Consists of one or more series of flashing lights installed at or near ground level that provides positive visual guidance along an approach path, either curving or straight, where special problems exist with hazardous terrain, obstructions, or noise abatement procedures.

8. RAIL– Runway Alignment Indicator Lights– Sequenced Flashing Lights which are installed only in combination with other light systems.

9. ODALS– Omnidirectional Approach Lighting System consists of seven omnidirectional flashing lights located in the approach area of a nonprecision runway. Five lights are located on the runway centerline extended with the first light located 300 feet from the threshold and extending at equal intervals up to 1,500 feet from the threshold. The other two lights are located, one on each side of the runway threshold, at a lateral distance of 40 feet from the runway edge, or 75 feet from the runway edge when installed on a runway equipped with a VASI.

(Refer to FAA Order JO 6850.2, Visual Guidance Lighting Systems.)

b. Runway Lights/Runway Edge Lights– Lights having a prescribed angle of emission used to define the lateral limits of a runway. Runway lights are uniformly spaced at intervals of approximately 200 feet, and the intensity may be controlled or preset.

c. Touchdown Zone Lighting– Two rows of transverse light bars located symmetrically about the runway centerline normally at 100 foot intervals. The basic system extends 3,000 feet along the runway.

d. Runway Centerline Lighting– Flush centerline lights spaced at 50-foot intervals beginning 75 feet from the landing threshold and extending to within 75 feet of the opposite end of the runway.

e. Threshold Lights– Fixed green lights arranged symmetrically left and right of the runway centerline, identifying the runway threshold.

f. Runway End Identifier Lights (REIL)– Two synchronized flashing lights, one on each side of the runway threshold, which provide rapid and positive identification of the approach end of a particular runway.

g. Visual Approach Slope Indicator (VASI)– An airport lighting facility providing vertical visual approach slope guidance to aircraft during approach to landing by radiating a directional pattern of high intensity red and white focused light beams which indicate to the pilot that he/she is "on path" if he/she sees red/white, "above path" if white/white, and "below path" if red/red. Some airports serving large aircraft have three-bar VASIs which provide two visual glide paths to the same runway.

h. Precision Approach Path Indicator (PAPI)– An airport lighting facility, similar to VASI, providing vertical approach slope guidance to aircraft during approach to landing. PAPIs consist of a single row of either two or four lights, normally installed on the left side of the runway, and have an effective visual range of about 5 miles during the day and up to 20 miles at night. PAPIs radiate a directional pattern of high intensity red and white focused light beams which indicate that the pilot is "on path" if the pilot sees an equal number of white lights and red lights, with white to the left of the red; "above path" if the pilot sees more white than red lights; and "below path" if the pilot sees more red than white lights.

i. Boundary Lights– Lights defining the perimeter of an airport or landing area.

(Refer to AIM.)

AIRPORT MARKING AIDS– Markings used on runway and taxiway surfaces to identify a specific runway, a runway threshold, a centerline, a hold line, etc. A runway should be marked in accordance with its present usage such as:

a. Visual.

b. Nonprecision instrument.

c. Precision instrument.

(Refer to AIM.)

AIRPORT REFERENCE POINT (ARP)− The approximate geometric center of all usable runway surfaces.

AIRPORT RESERVATION OFFICE− Office responsible for monitoring the operation of slot controlled airports. It receives and processes requests for unscheduled operations at slot controlled airports.

AIRPORT ROTATING BEACON− A visual NAVAID operated at many airports. At civil airports, alternating white and green flashes indicate the location of the airport. At military airports, the beacons flash alternately white and green, but are differentiated from civil beacons by dualpeaked (two quick) white flashes between the green flashes.

(See INSTRUMENT FLIGHT RULES.)
(See SPECIAL VFR OPERATIONS.)
(See ICAO term AERODROME BEACON.)
(Refer to AIM.)

AIRPORT SURFACE DETECTION EQUIPMENT (ASDE)− Surveillance equipment specifically designed to detect aircraft, vehicular traffic, and other objects, on the surface of an airport, and to present the image on a tower display. Used to augment visual observation by tower personnel of aircraft and/or vehicular movements on runways and taxiways. There are three ASDE systems deployed in the NAS:

a. ASDE−3− a Surface Movement Radar.

b. ASDE−X− a system that uses an X−band Surface Movement Radar, multilateration, and ADS−B.

c. Airport Surface Surveillance Capability (ASSC)− A system that uses Surface Movement Radar, multilateration, and ADS−B.

AIRPORT SURVEILLANCE RADAR− Approach control radar used to detect and display an aircraft's position in the terminal area. ASR provides range and azimuth information but does not provide elevation data. Coverage of the ASR can extend up to 60 miles.

AIRPORT TAXI CHARTS−
(See AERONAUTICAL CHART.)

AIRPORT TRAFFIC CONTROL SERVICE− A service provided by a control tower for aircraft operating on the movement area and in the vicinity of an airport.

(See MOVEMENT AREA.)
(See TOWER.)
(See ICAO term AERODROME CONTROL SERVICE.)

AIRPORT TRAFFIC CONTROL TOWER−
(See TOWER.)

AIRSPACE CONFLICT− Predicted conflict of an aircraft and active Special Activity Airspace (SAA).

AIRSPACE FLOW PROGRAM (AFP)− AFP is a Traffic Management (TM) process administered by the Air Traffic Control System Command Center (ATCSCC) where aircraft are assigned an Expect Departure Clearance Time (EDCT) in order to manage capacity and demand for a specific area of the National Airspace System (NAS). The purpose of the program is to mitigate the effects of en route constraints. It is a flexible program and may be implemented in various forms depending upon the needs of the air traffic system.

AIRSPACE HIERARCHY− Within the airspace classes, there is a hierarchy and, in the event of an overlap of airspace: Class A preempts Class B, Class B preempts Class C, Class C preempts Class D, Class D preempts Class E, and Class E preempts Class G.

AIRSPEED− The speed of an aircraft relative to its surrounding air mass. The unqualified term "airspeed" means one of the following:

a. Indicated Airspeed− The speed shown on the aircraft airspeed indicator. This is the speed used in pilot/controller communications under the general term "airspeed."

(Refer to 14 CFR Part 1.)

b. True Airspeed− The airspeed of an aircraft relative to undisturbed air. Used primarily in flight planning and en route portion of flight. When used in pilot/controller communications, it is referred to as "true airspeed" and not shortened to "airspeed."

AIRSPACE RESERVATION− The term used in oceanic ATC for airspace utilization under prescribed conditions normally employed for the mass movement of aircraft or other special user requirements which cannot otherwise be accomplished. Airspace reservations must be classified as either "moving" or "stationary."

(See MOVING AIRSPACE RESERVATION)
(See STATIONARY AIRSPACE RESERVATION.)
(See ALTITUDE RESERVATION.)

AIRSTART− The starting of an aircraft engine while the aircraft is airborne, preceded by engine shutdown during training flights or by actual engine failure.

AIRWAY− A Class E airspace area established in the form of a corridor, the centerline of which is defined by radio navigational aids.

(See FEDERAL AIRWAYS.)
(See ICAO term AIRWAY.)
(Refer to 14 CFR Part 71.)
(Refer to AIM.)

AIRWAY [ICAO]− A control area or portion thereof established in the form of corridor equipped with radio navigational aids.

AIRWAY BEACON− Used to mark airway segments in remote mountain areas. The light flashes Morse Code to identify the beacon site.

(Refer to AIM.)

AIS−

(See AERONAUTICAL INFORMATION SERVICES.)

AIT−

(See AUTOMATED INFORMATION TRANSFER.)

ALERFA (Alert Phase) [ICAO]− A situation wherein apprehension exists as to the safety of an aircraft and its occupants.

ALERT− A notification to a position that there is an aircraft-to-aircraft or aircraft-to-airspace conflict, as detected by Automated Problem Detection (APD).

ALERT AREA−

(See SPECIAL USE AIRSPACE.)

ALERT NOTICE (ALNOT)− A request originated by a flight service station (FSS) or an air route traffic control center (ARTCC) for an extensive communication search for overdue, unreported, or missing aircraft.

ALERTING SERVICE− A service provided to notify appropriate organizations regarding aircraft in need of search and rescue aid and assist such organizations as required.

ALNOT−

(See ALERT NOTICE.)

ALONG−TRACK DISTANCE (ATD)− The horizontal distance between the aircraft's current position and a fix measured by an area navigation system that is not subject to slant range errors.

ALPHANUMERIC DISPLAY− Letters and numerals used to show identification, altitude, beacon code, and other information concerning a target on a radar display.

ALTERNATE AERODROME [ICAO]– An aerodrome to which an aircraft may proceed when it becomes either impossible or inadvisable to proceed to or to land at the aerodrome of intended landing.

Note: The aerodrome from which a flight departs may also be an en-route or a destination alternate aerodrome for the flight.

ALTERNATE AIRPORT– An airport at which an aircraft may land if a landing at the intended airport becomes inadvisable.

(See ICAO term ALTERNATE AERODROME.)

ALTIMETER SETTING– The barometric pressure reading used to adjust a pressure altimeter for variations in existing atmospheric pressure or to the standard altimeter setting (29.92).

(Refer to 14 CFR Part 91.)
(Refer to AIM.)

ALTITUDE– The height of a level, point, or object measured in feet Above Ground Level (AGL) or from Mean Sea Level (MSL).

(See FLIGHT LEVEL.)

a. MSL Altitude– Altitude expressed in feet measured from mean sea level.

b. AGL Altitude– Altitude expressed in feet measured above ground level.

c. Indicated Altitude– The altitude as shown by an altimeter. On a pressure or barometric altimeter it is altitude as shown uncorrected for instrument error and uncompensated for variation from standard atmospheric conditions.

(See ICAO term ALTITUDE.)

ALTITUDE [ICAO]– The vertical distance of a level, a point or an object considered as a point, measured from mean sea level (MSL).

ALTITUDE READOUT– An aircraft's altitude, transmitted via the Mode C transponder feature, that is visually displayed in 100-foot increments on a radar scope having readout capability.

(See ALPHANUMERIC DISPLAY.)
(Refer to AIM.)

ALTITUDE RESERVATION (ALTRV)– Airspace utilization under prescribed conditions normally employed for the mass movement of aircraft or other special user requirements which cannot otherwise be accomplished. ALTRVs are approved by the appropriate FAA facility. ALTRVs must be classified as either "moving" or "stationary."

(See MOVING ALTITUDE RESERVATION.)
(See STATIONARY ALTITUDE RESERVATION.)
(See AIR TRAFFIC CONTROL SYSTEM COMMAND CENTER.)

ALTITUDE RESTRICTION– An altitude or altitudes, stated in the order flown, which are to be maintained until reaching a specific point or time. Altitude restrictions may be issued by ATC due to traffic, terrain, or other airspace considerations.

ALTITUDE RESTRICTIONS ARE CANCELED– Adherence to previously imposed altitude restrictions is no longer required during a climb or descent.

ALTRV–

(See ALTITUDE RESERVATION.)

AMVER–

(See AUTOMATED MUTUAL-ASSISTANCE VESSEL RESCUE SYSTEM.)

APB–

(See AUTOMATED PROBLEM DETECTION BOUNDARY.)

APD–

(See AUTOMATED PROBLEM DETECTION.)

APDIA–
(See AUTOMATED PROBLEM DETECTION INHIBITED AREA.)

APPROACH CLEARANCE– Authorization by ATC for a pilot to conduct an instrument approach. The type of instrument approach for which a clearance and other pertinent information is provided in the approach clearance when required.
(See CLEARED APPROACH.)
(See INSTRUMENT APPROACH PROCEDURE.)
(Refer to AIM.)
(Refer to 14 CFR Part 91.)

APPROACH CONTROL FACILITY– A terminal ATC facility that provides approach control service in a terminal area.
(See APPROACH CONTROL SERVICE.)
(See RADAR APPROACH CONTROL FACILITY.)

APPROACH CONTROL SERVICE– Air traffic control service provided by an approach control facility for arriving and departing VFR/IFR aircraft and, on occasion, en route aircraft. At some airports not served by an approach control facility, the ARTCC provides limited approach control service.
(See ICAO term APPROACH CONTROL SERVICE.)
(Refer to AIM.)

APPROACH CONTROL SERVICE [ICAO]– Air traffic control service for arriving or departing controlled flights.

APPROACH GATE– An imaginary point used within ATC as a basis for vectoring aircraft to the final approach course. The gate will be established along the final approach course 1 mile from the final approach fix on the side away from the airport and will be no closer than 5 miles from the landing threshold.

APPROACH/DEPARTURE HOLD AREA– The locations on taxiways in the approach or departure areas of a runway designated to protect landing or departing aircraft. These locations are identified by signs and markings.

APPROACH LIGHT SYSTEM–
(See AIRPORT LIGHTING.)

APPROACH SEQUENCE– The order in which aircraft are positioned while on approach or awaiting approach clearance.
(See LANDING SEQUENCE.)
(See ICAO term APPROACH SEQUENCE.)

APPROACH SEQUENCE [ICAO]– The order in which two or more aircraft are cleared to approach to land at the aerodrome.

APPROACH SPEED– The recommended speed contained in aircraft manuals used by pilots when making an approach to landing. This speed will vary for different segments of an approach as well as for aircraft weight and configuration.

APPROACH WITH VERTICAL GUIDANCE (APV)– A term used to describe RNAV approach procedures that provide lateral and vertical guidance but do not meet the requirements to be considered a precision approach.

APPROPRIATE ATS AUTHORITY [ICAO]– The relevant authority designated by the State responsible for providing air traffic services in the airspace concerned. In the United States, the "appropriate ATS authority" is the Program Director for Air Traffic Planning and Procedures, ATP-1.

APPROPRIATE AUTHORITY–

a. Regarding flight over the high seas: the relevant authority is the State of Registry.

b. Regarding flight over other than the high seas: the relevant authority is the State having sovereignty over the territory being overflown.

APPROPRIATE OBSTACLE CLEARANCE MINIMUM ALTITUDE– Any of the following:

(See MINIMUM EN ROUTE IFR ALTITUDE.)
(See MINIMUM IFR ALTITUDE.)
(See MINIMUM OBSTRUCTION CLEARANCE ALTITUDE.)
(See MINIMUM VECTORING ALTITUDE.)

APPROPRIATE TERRAIN CLEARANCE MINIMUM ALTITUDE– Any of the following:

(See MINIMUM EN ROUTE IFR ALTITUDE.)
(See MINIMUM IFR ALTITUDE.)
(See MINIMUM OBSTRUCTION CLEARANCE ALTITUDE.)
(See MINIMUM VECTORING ALTITUDE.)

APRON– A defined area on an airport or heliport intended to accommodate aircraft for purposes of loading or unloading passengers or cargo, refueling, parking, or maintenance. With regard to seaplanes, a ramp is used for access to the apron from the water.

(See ICAO term APRON.)

APRON [ICAO]– A defined area, on a land aerodrome, intended to accommodate aircraft for purposes of loading or unloading passengers, mail or cargo, refueling, parking or maintenance.

ARC– The track over the ground of an aircraft flying at a constant distance from a navigational aid by reference to distance measuring equipment (DME).

AREA CONTROL CENTER [ICAO]– An air traffic control facility primarily responsible for ATC services being provided IFR aircraft during the en route phase of flight. The U.S. equivalent facility is an air route traffic control center (ARTCC).

AREA NAVIGATION (RNAV)– A method of navigation which permits aircraft operation on any desired flight path within the coverage of ground– or space–based navigation aids or within the limits of the capability of self-contained aids, or a combination of these.

Note: Area navigation includes performance–based navigation as well as other operations that do not meet the definition of performance–based navigation.

AREA NAVIGATION (RNAV) APPROACH CONFIGURATION:

a. STANDARD T– An RNAV approach whose design allows direct flight to any one of three initial approach fixes (IAF) and eliminates the need for procedure turns. The standard design is to align the procedure on the extended centerline with the missed approach point (MAP) at the runway threshold, the final approach fix (FAF), and the initial approach/intermediate fix (IAF/IF). The other two IAFs will be established perpendicular to the IF.

b. MODIFIED T– An RNAV approach design for single or multiple runways where terrain or operational constraints do not allow for the standard T. The “T” may be modified by increasing or decreasing the angle from the corner IAF(s) to the IF or by eliminating one or both corner IAFs.

c. STANDARD I– An RNAV approach design for a single runway with both corner IAFs eliminated. Course reversal or radar vectoring may be required at busy terminals with multiple runways.

d. TERMINAL ARRIVAL AREA (TAA)– The TAA is controlled airspace established in conjunction with the Standard or Modified T and I RNAV approach configurations. In the standard TAA, there are three areas: straight-in, left base, and right base. The arc boundaries of the three areas of the TAA are published portions of the approach and allow aircraft to transition from the en route structure direct to the nearest IAF. TAAs will also eliminate or reduce feeder routes, departure extensions, and procedure turns or course reversal.

1. STRAIGHT-IN AREA– A 30 NM arc centered on the IF bounded by a straight line extending through the IF perpendicular to the intermediate course.

2. LEFT BASE AREA– A 30 NM arc centered on the right corner IAF. The area shares a boundary with the straight-in area except that it extends out for 30 NM from the IAF and is bounded on the other side by a line extending from the IF through the FAF to the arc.

3. RIGHT BASE AREA– A 30 NM arc centered on the left corner IAF. The area shares a boundary with the straight-in area except that it extends out for 30 NM from the IAF and is bounded on the other side by a line extending from the IF through the FAF to the arc.

AREA NAVIGATION (RNAV) GLOBAL POSITIONING SYSTEM (GPS) PRECISION RUNWAY MONITORING (PRM) APPROACH–
A GPS approach, which requires vertical guidance, used in lieu of another type of PRM approach to conduct approaches to parallel runways whose extended centerlines are separated by less than 4,300 feet and at least 3,000 feet, where simultaneous close parallel approaches are permitted. Also used in lieu of an ILS PRM and/or LDA PRM approach to conduct Simultaneous Offset Instrument Approach (SOIA) operations.

ARMY AVIATION FLIGHT INFORMATION BULLETIN– A bulletin that provides air operation data covering Army, National Guard, and Army Reserve aviation activities.

ARO–
(See AIRPORT RESERVATION OFFICE.)

ARRESTING SYSTEM– A safety device consisting of two major components, namely, engaging or catching devices and energy absorption devices for the purpose of arresting both tailhook and/or nontailhook-equipped aircraft. It is used to prevent aircraft from overrunning runways when the aircraft cannot be stopped after landing or during aborted takeoff. Arresting systems have various names; e.g., arresting gear, hook device, wire barrier cable.
(See ABORT.)
(Refer to AIM.)

ARRIVAL CENTER– The ARTCC having jurisdiction for the impacted airport.

ARRIVAL DELAY– A parameter which specifies a period of time in which no aircraft will be metered for arrival at the specified airport.

ARRIVAL/DEPARTURE WINDOW (ADW)– A depiction presented on an air traffic control display, used by the controller to prevent possible conflicts between arrivals to, and departures from, a runway. The ADW identifies that point on the final approach course by which a departing aircraft must have begun takeoff.

ARRIVAL SECTOR (En Route)– An operational control sector containing one or more meter fixes on or near the TRACON boundary.

ARRIVAL TIME– The time an aircraft touches down on arrival.

ARSR–
(See AIR ROUTE SURVEILLANCE RADAR.)

ARTCC–
(See AIR ROUTE TRAFFIC CONTROL CENTER.)

ASDA–
(See ACCELERATE-STOP DISTANCE AVAILABLE.)

ASDA [ICAO]–
(See ICAO Term ACCELERATE-STOP DISTANCE AVAILABLE.)

ASDE–
(See AIRPORT SURFACE DETECTION EQUIPMENT.)

ASLAR–
(See AIRCRAFT SURGE LAUNCH AND RECOVERY.)

ASR–
(See AIRPORT SURVEILLANCE RADAR.)

ASR APPROACH–
(See SURVEILLANCE APPROACH.)

ASSOCIATED– A radar target displaying a data block with flight identification and altitude information.
(See UNASSOCIATED.)

ATC–
(See AIR TRAFFIC CONTROL.)

ATC ADVISES– Used to prefix a message of noncontrol information when it is relayed to an aircraft by other than an air traffic controller.
(See ADVISORY.)

ATC ASSIGNED AIRSPACE– Airspace of defined vertical/lateral limits, assigned by ATC, for the purpose of providing air traffic segregation between the specified activities being conducted within the assigned airspace and other IFR air traffic.
(See SPECIAL USE AIRSPACE.)

ATC CLEARANCE–
(See AIR TRAFFIC CLEARANCE.)

ATC CLEARS– Used to prefix an ATC clearance when it is relayed to an aircraft by other than an air traffic controller.

ATC INSTRUCTIONS– Directives issued by air traffic control for the purpose of requiring a pilot to take specific actions; e.g., "Turn left heading two five zero," "Go around," "Clear the runway."
(Refer to 14 CFR Part 91.)

ATC PREFERRED ROUTE NOTIFICATION– EDST notification to the appropriate controller of the need to determine if an ATC preferred route needs to be applied, based on destination airport.
(See ROUTE ACTION NOTIFICATION.)
(See EN ROUTE DECISION SUPPORT TOOL.)

ATC PREFERRED ROUTES– Preferred routes that are not automatically applied by Host.

ATC REQUESTS– Used to prefix an ATC request when it is relayed to an aircraft by other than an air traffic controller.

ATC SECURITY SERVICES– Communications and security tracking provided by an ATC facility in support of the DHS, the DoD, or other Federal security elements in the interest of national security. Such security services are only applicable within designated areas. ATC security services do not include ATC basic radar services or flight following.

ATC SECURITY SERVICES POSITION– The position responsible for providing ATC security services as defined. This position does not provide ATC, IFR separation, or VFR flight following services, but is responsible for providing security services in an area comprising airspace assigned to one or more ATC operating sectors. This position may be combined with control positions.

ATC SECURITY TRACKING– The continuous tracking of aircraft movement by an ATC facility in support of the DHS, the DoD, or other security elements for national security using radar (i.e., radar tracking) or other means (e.g., manual tracking) without providing basic radar services (including traffic advisories) or other ATC services not defined in this section.

ATS SURVEILLANCE SERVICE [ICAO]– A term used to indicate a service provided directly by means of an ATS surveillance system.

ATC SURVEILLANCE SOURCE– Used by ATC for establishing identification, control and separation using a target depicted on an air traffic control facility's video display that has met the relevant safety standards for operational use and received from one, or a combination, of the following surveillance sources:

a. Radar (See RADAR.)

b. ADS-B (See AUTOMATIC DEPENDENT SURVEILLANCE–BROADCAST.)

c. WAM (See WIDE AREA MULTILATERATION.)
(See INTERROGATOR.)
(See TRANSPONDER.)
(See ICAO term RADAR.)
(Refer to AIM.)

ATS SURVEILLANCE SYSTEM [ICAO]– A generic term meaning variously, ADS–B, PSR, SSR or any comparable ground–based system that enables the identification of aircraft.

Note: A comparable ground–based system is one that has been demonstrated, by comparative assessment or other methodology, to have a level of safety and performance equal to or better than monopulse SSR.

ATCAA–
(See ATC ASSIGNED AIRSPACE.)

ATCRBS–
(See RADAR.)

ATCSCC–
(See AIR TRAFFIC CONTROL SYSTEM COMMAND CENTER.)

ATCT–
(See TOWER.)

ATD–
(See ALONG–TRACK DISTANCE.)

ATIS–
(See AUTOMATIC TERMINAL INFORMATION SERVICE.)

ATIS [ICAO]–
(See ICAO Term AUTOMATIC TERMINAL INFORMATION SERVICE.)

ATO–
(See AIR TRAFFIC ORGANIZATION.)

ATPA–
(See AUTOMATED TERMINAL PROXIMITY ALERT.)

ATS ROUTE [ICAO]– A specified route designed for channeling the flow of traffic as necessary for the provision of air traffic services.

Note: The term "ATS Route" is used to mean variously, airway, advisory route, controlled or uncontrolled route, arrival or departure, etc.

ATTENTION ALL USERS PAGE (AAUP)- The AAUP provides the pilot with additional information relative to conducting a specific operation, for example, PRM approaches and RNAV departures.

AUTOLAND APPROACH–An autoland system aids by providing control of aircraft systems during a precision instrument approach to at least decision altitude and possibly all the way to touchdown, as well as in some cases, through the landing rollout. The autoland system is a sub-system of the autopilot system from which control surface management occurs. The aircraft autopilot sends instructions to the autoland system and monitors the autoland system performance and integrity during its execution.

AUTOMATED EMERGENCY DESCENT–
(See EMERGENCY DESCENT MODE.)

AUTOMATED INFORMATION TRANSFER (AIT)– A precoordinated process, specifically defined in facility directives, during which a transfer of altitude control and/or radar identification is accomplished without verbal coordination between controllers using information communicated in a full data block.

AUTOMATED MUTUAL-ASSISTANCE VESSEL RESCUE SYSTEM– A facility which can deliver, in a matter of minutes, a surface picture (SURPIC) of vessels in the area of a potential or actual search and rescue incident, including their predicted positions and their characteristics.
(See FAA Order JO 7110.65, Para 10–6–4, INFLIGHT CONTINGENCIES.)

AUTOMATED PROBLEM DETECTION (APD)– An Automation Processing capability that compares trajectories in order to predict conflicts.

AUTOMATED PROBLEM DETECTION BOUNDARY (APB)– The adapted distance beyond a facilities boundary defining the airspace within which EDST performs conflict detection.

(See EN ROUTE DECISION SUPPORT TOOL.)

AUTOMATED PROBLEM DETECTION INHIBITED AREA (APDIA)– Airspace surrounding a terminal area within which APD is inhibited for all flights within that airspace.

AUTOMATED SERVICES–Services delivered via an automated system (that is, without human interaction). For example, flight plans, Notices to Air Missions (NOTAM), interactive maps, computer–generated text–to–speech messages, short message service, or email.

AUTOMATED TERMINAL PROXIMITY ALERT (ATPA)– Monitors the separation of aircraft on the Final Approach Course (FAC), displaying a graphical notification (cone and/or mileage) when a potential loss of separation is detected. The warning cone (Yellow) will display at 45 seconds and the alert cone (Red) will display at 24 seconds prior to predicted loss of separation. Current distance between two aircraft on final will be displayed in line 3 of the full data block of the trailing aircraft in corresponding colors.

AUTOMATED WEATHER SYSTEM– Any of the automated weather sensor platforms that collect weather data at airports and disseminate the weather information via radio and/or landline. The systems currently consist of the Automated Surface Observing System (ASOS) and Automated Weather Observation System (AWOS).

AUTOMATED UNICOM– Provides completely automated weather, radio check capability and airport advisory information on an Automated UNICOM system. These systems offer a variety of features, typically selectable by microphone clicks, on the UNICOM frequency. Availability will be published in the Chart Supplement and approach charts.

AUTOMATIC ALTITUDE REPORT–

(See ALTITUDE READOUT.)

AUTOMATIC ALTITUDE REPORTING– That function of a transponder which responds to Mode C interrogations by transmitting the aircraft's altitude in 100-foot increments.

AUTOMATIC CARRIER LANDING SYSTEM– U.S. Navy final approach equipment consisting of precision tracking radar coupled to a computer data link to provide continuous information to the aircraft, monitoring capability to the pilot, and a backup approach system.

AUTOMATIC DEPENDENT SURVEILLANCE (ADS) [ICAO]– A surveillance technique in which aircraft automatically provide, via a data link, data derived from on–board navigation and position fixing systems, including aircraft identification, four dimensional position and additional data as appropriate.

AUTOMATIC DEPENDENT SURVEILLANCE–BROADCAST (ADS-B)– A surveillance system in which an aircraft or vehicle to be detected is fitted with cooperative equipment in the form of a data link transmitter. The aircraft or vehicle periodically broadcasts its GNSS–derived position and other required information such as identity and velocity, which is then received by a ground–based or space–based receiver for processing and display at an air traffic control facility, as well as by suitably equipped aircraft.

(See AUTOMATIC DEPENDENT SURVEILLANCE–BROADCAST IN.)
(See AUTOMATIC DEPENDENT SURVEILLANCE–BROADCAST OUT.)
(See COOPERATIVE SURVEILLANCE.)
(See GLOBAL POSITIONING SYSTEM.)
(See SPACE–BASED ADS–B.)

AUTOMATIC DEPENDENT SURVEILLANCE–BROADCAST IN (ADS–B In)– Aircraft avionics capable of receiving ADS–B Out transmissions directly from other aircraft, as well as traffic or weather information transmitted from ground stations.

(See AUTOMATIC DEPENDENT SURVEILLANCE–BROADCAST OUT.)
(See AUTOMATIC DEPENDENT SURVEILLANCE–REBROADCAST.)
(See FLIGHT INFORMATION SERVICE–BROADCAST.)
(See TRAFFIC INFORMATION SERVICE–BROADCAST.)

AUTOMATIC DEPENDENT SURVEILLANCE–BROADCAST OUT (ADS–B Out)– The transmitter onboard an aircraft or ground vehicle that periodically broadcasts its GNSS–derived position along with other required information, such as identity, altitude, and velocity.

(See AUTOMATIC DEPENDENT SURVEILLANCE–BROADCAST.)
(See AUTOMATIC DEPENDENT SURVEILLANCE–BROADCAST IN.)

AUTOMATIC DEPENDENT SURVEILLANCE–CONTRACT (ADS–C)– A data link position reporting system, controlled by a ground station, that establishes contracts with an aircraft's avionics that occur automatically whenever specific events occur, or specific time intervals are reached.

AUTOMATIC DEPENDENT SURVEILLANCE- REBROADCAST (ADS-R)– A datalink translation function of the ADS–B ground system required to accommodate the two separate operating frequencies (978 MHz and 1090 MHz). The ADS–B system receives the ADS–B messages transmitted on one frequency and ADS–R translates and reformats the information for rebroadcast and use on the other frequency. This allows ADS–B In equipped aircraft to see nearby ADS–B Out traffic regardless of the operating link of the other aircraft. Aircraft operating on the same ADS–B frequency exchange information directly and do not require the ADS–R translation function.

AUTOMATIC DIRECTION FINDER– An aircraft radio navigation system which senses and indicates the direction to a L/MF nondirectional radio beacon (NDB) ground transmitter. Direction is indicated to the pilot as a magnetic bearing or as a relative bearing to the longitudinal axis of the aircraft depending on the type of indicator installed in the aircraft. In certain applications, such as military, ADF operations may be based on airborne and ground transmitters in the VHF/UHF frequency spectrum.

(See BEARING.)
(See NONDIRECTIONAL BEACON.)

AUTOMATIC FLIGHT INFORMATION SERVICE (AFIS) – ALASKA FSSs ONLY– The continuous broadcast of recorded non–control information at airports in Alaska where a FSS provides local airport advisory service. The AFIS broadcast automates the repetitive transmission of essential but routine information such as weather, wind, altimeter, favored runway, braking action, airport NOTAMs, and other applicable information. The information is continuously broadcast over a discrete VHF radio frequency (usually the ASOS/AWOS frequency).

AUTOMATIC TERMINAL INFORMATION SERVICE– The continuous broadcast of recorded noncontrol information in selected terminal areas. Its purpose is to improve controller effectiveness and to relieve frequency congestion by automating the repetitive transmission of essential but routine information; e.g., "Los Angeles information Alfa. One three zero zero Coordinated Universal Time. Weather, measured ceiling two thousand overcast, visibility three, haze, smoke, temperature seven one, dew point five seven, wind two five zero at five, altimeter two niner niner six. I-L-S Runway Two Five Left approach in use, Runway Two Five Right closed, advise you have Alfa."

(See ICAO term AUTOMATIC TERMINAL INFORMATION SERVICE.)
(Refer to AIM.)

AUTOMATIC TERMINAL INFORMATION SERVICE [ICAO]– The provision of current, routine information to arriving and departing aircraft by means of continuous and repetitive broadcasts throughout the day or a specified portion of the day.

AUTOROTATION– A rotorcraft flight condition in which the lifting rotor is driven entirely by action of the air when the rotorcraft is in motion.

a. Autorotative Landing/Touchdown Autorotation. Used by a pilot to indicate that the landing will be made without applying power to the rotor.

b. Low Level Autorotation. Commences at an altitude well below the traffic pattern, usually below 100 feet AGL and is used primarily for tactical military training.

c. 180 degrees Autorotation. Initiated from a downwind heading and is commenced well inside the normal traffic pattern. "Go around" may not be possible during the latter part of this maneuver.

AVAILABLE LANDING DISTANCE (ALD)– The portion of a runway available for landing and roll-out for aircraft cleared for LAHSO. This distance is measured from the landing threshold to the hold-short point.

AVIATION WATCH NOTIFICATION MESSAGE– The Storm Prediction Center (SPC) issues Aviation Watch Notification Messages (SAW) to provide an area threat alert for the aviation meteorology community to forecast organized severe thunderstorms that may produce tornadoes, large hail, and/or convective damaging winds as indicated in Public Watch Notification Messages within the Continental U.S. A SAW message provides a description of the type of watch issued by SPC, a valid time, an approximation of the area in a watch, and primary hazard(s).

AVIATION WEATHER SERVICE– A service provided by the National Weather Service (NWS) and FAA which collects and disseminates pertinent weather information for pilots, aircraft operators, and ATC. Available aviation weather reports and forecasts are displayed at each NWS office and FAA FSS.

(See TRANSCRIBED WEATHER BROADCAST.)
(See WEATHER ADVISORY.)
(Refer to AIM.)

B

B4UFLY– A free downloadable application, which allows operators to check airspace and local advisories before flying.

BACK-TAXI– A term used by air traffic controllers to taxi an aircraft on the runway opposite to the traffic flow. The aircraft may be instructed to back-taxi to the beginning of the runway or at some point before reaching the runway end for the purpose of departure or to exit the runway.

BASE LEG–
(See TRAFFIC PATTERN.)

BEACON–
(See AERONAUTICAL BEACON.)
(See AIRPORT ROTATING BEACON.)
(See AIRWAY BEACON.)
(See MARKER BEACON.)
(See NONDIRECTIONAL BEACON.)
(See RADAR.)

BEARING– The horizontal direction to or from any point, usually measured clockwise from true north, magnetic north, or some other reference point through 360 degrees.
(See NONDIRECTIONAL BEACON.)

BELOW MINIMUMS– Weather conditions below the minimums prescribed by regulation for the particular action involved; e.g., landing minimums, takeoff minimums.

BEYOND VISUAL LINE OF SIGHT (BVLOS)– The operation of a UAS beyond the visual capability of the flight crew members (i.e., remote pilot in command [RPIC], the person manipulating the controls, and visual observer [VO]), if used to see the aircraft with vision unaided by any device other than corrective lenses, spectacles, and contact lenses.

BLAST FENCE– A barrier that is used to divert or dissipate jet or propeller blast.

BLAST PAD– A surface adjacent to the ends of a runway provided to reduce the erosive effect of jet blast and propeller wash.

BLIND SPEED– The rate of departure or closing of a target relative to the radar antenna at which cancellation of the primary radar target by moving target indicator (MTI) circuits in the radar equipment causes a reduction or complete loss of signal.
(See ICAO term BLIND VELOCITY.)

BLIND SPOT– An area from which radio transmissions and/or radar echoes cannot be received. The term is also used to describe portions of the airport not visible from the control tower.

BLIND TRANSMISSION–
(See TRANSMITTING IN THE BLIND.)

BLIND VELOCITY [ICAO]– The radial velocity of a moving target such that the target is not seen on primary radars fitted with certain forms of fixed echo suppression.

BLIND ZONE–
(See BLIND SPOT.)

BLOCKED– Phraseology used to indicate that a radio transmission has been distorted or interrupted due to multiple simultaneous radio transmissions.

BOTTOM ALTITUDE– In reference to published altitude restrictions on a STAR or STAR runway transition, the lowest altitude authorized.

BOUNDARY LIGHTS−
(See AIRPORT LIGHTING.)

BRAKING ACTION (GOOD, GOOD TO MEDIUM, MEDIUM, MEDIUM TO POOR, POOR, OR NIL)− A report of conditions on the airport movement area providing a pilot with a degree/quality of braking to expect. Braking action is reported in terms of good, good to medium, medium, medium to poor, poor, or nil.
(See RUNWAY CONDITION READING.)
(See RUNWAY CONDITION REPORT.)
(See RUNWAY CONDITION CODES.)

BRAKING ACTION ADVISORIES− When tower controllers receive runway braking action reports which include the terms "medium," "poor," or "nil," or whenever weather conditions are conducive to deteriorating or rapidly changing runway braking conditions, the tower will include on the ATIS broadcast the statement, "Braking Action Advisories are in Effect." During the time braking action advisories are in effect, ATC will issue the most current braking action report for the runway in use to each arriving and departing aircraft. Pilots should be prepared for deteriorating braking conditions and should request current runway condition information if not issued by controllers. Pilots should also be prepared to provide a descriptive runway condition report to controllers after landing.

BREAKOUT− A technique to direct aircraft out of the approach stream. In the context of simultaneous (independent) parallel operations, a breakout is used to direct threatened aircraft away from a deviating aircraft.

BROADCAST− Transmission of information for which an acknowledgement is not expected.
(See ICAO term BROADCAST.)

BROADCAST [ICAO]− A transmission of information relating to air navigation that is not addressed to a specific station or stations.

BUFFER AREA− As applied to an MVA or MIA chart, a depicted 3 NM or 5 NM radius MVA/MIA sector isolating a displayed obstacle for which the sector is established. A portion of a buffer area can also be inclusive of a MVA/MIA sector polygon boundary.

BVLOS−
(See BEYOND VISUAL LINE OF SIGHT.)

C

CALCULATED LANDING TIME– A term that may be used in place of tentative or actual calculated landing time, whichever applies.

CALIBRATED AIRSPEED (CAS) – The indicated airspeed of an aircraft, corrected for position and instrument error. Calibrated airspeed is equal to true airspeed in standard atmosphere at sea level.

CALL FOR RELEASE– Wherein the overlying ARTCC requires a terminal facility to initiate verbal coordination to secure ARTCC approval for release of a departure into the en route environment.

CALL UP– Initial voice contact between a facility and an aircraft, using the identification of the unit being called and the unit initiating the call.

(Refer to AIM.)

CANADIAN MINIMUM NAVIGATION PERFORMANCE SPECIFICATION AIRSPACE– That portion of Canadian domestic airspace within which MNPS separation may be applied.

CARDINAL ALTITUDES– "Odd" or "Even" thousand-foot altitudes or flight levels; e.g., 5,000, 6,000, 7,000, FL 250, FL 260, FL 270.

(See ALTITUDE.)
(See FLIGHT LEVEL.)

CARDINAL FLIGHT LEVELS–

(See CARDINAL ALTITUDES.)

CAT–

(See CLEAR-AIR TURBULENCE.)

CATCH POINT– A fix/waypoint that serves as a transition point from the high altitude waypoint navigation structure to an arrival procedure (STAR) or the low altitude ground–based navigation structure.

CBO–

(See COMMUNITY–BASED ORGANIZATION.)

CEILING– The heights above the earth's surface of the lowest layer of clouds or obscuring phenomena that is reported as "broken," "overcast," or "obscuration," and not classified as "thin" or "partial."

(See ICAO term CEILING.)

CEILING [ICAO]– The height above the ground or water of the base of the lowest layer of cloud below 6,000 meters (20,000 feet) covering more than half the sky.

CENTER–

(See AIR ROUTE TRAFFIC CONTROL CENTER.)

CENTER'S AREA– The specified airspace within which an air route traffic control center (ARTCC) provides air traffic control and advisory service.

(See AIR ROUTE TRAFFIC CONTROL CENTER.)
(Refer to AIM.)

CENTER WEATHER ADVISORY– An unscheduled weather advisory issued by Center Weather Service Unit meteorologists for ATC use to alert pilots of existing or anticipated adverse weather conditions within the next 2 hours. A CWA may modify or redefine a SIGMET.

(See AIRMET.)
(See CONVECTIVE SIGMET.)
(See GRAPHICAL AIRMEN'S METEOROLOGICAL INFORMATION.)
(See SAW.)
(See SIGMET.)
(Refer to AIM.)

CENTRAL EAST PACIFIC– An organized route system between the U.S. West Coast and Hawaii.

CEP–
(See CENTRAL EAST PACIFIC.)

CERAP–
(See COMBINED CENTER‐RAPCON.)

CERTIFICATE OF WAIVER OR AUTHORIZATION (COA)– An FAA grant of approval for a specific flight operation or airspace authorization or waiver.

CERTIFIED TOWER RADAR DISPLAY (CTRD)– An FAA radar display certified for use in the NAS.

CFR–
(See CALL FOR RELEASE.)

CHA
(See CONTINGENCY HAZARD AREA)

CHAFF– Thin, narrow metallic reflectors of various lengths and frequency responses, used to reflect radar energy. These reflectors, when dropped from aircraft and allowed to drift downward, result in large targets on the radar display.

CHART SUPPLEMENT– A series of civil/military flight information publications issued by FAA every 56 days consisting of the Chart Supplement U.S., Chart Supplement Alaska, and Chart Supplement Pacific.

CHART SUPPLEMENT ALASKA– A flight information publication designed for use with appropriate IFR or VFR charts which contains data on all airports, seaplane bases, and heliports open to the public including communications data, navigational facilities, airport diagrams, certain special notices, and non–regulatory procedures. Also included in this publication are selected entries needed to support the unique geographical operational conditions of Alaska. This publication is issued in one volume for the state of Alaska.

CHART SUPPLEMENT PACIFIC– A flight information publication designed for use with appropriate IFR or VFR charts which contains data on all airports, seaplane bases, and heliports open to the public including communications data, navigational facilities, airport diagrams, certain special notices, and non–regulatory procedures. Also included in this publication are Instrument Approach Procedures (IAP), Departure Procedures (DP), and Standard Terminal Arrival (STAR) charts, along with selected entries needed to support the unique geographical operational conditions of the Pacific Oceanic region. This publication is issued in one volume for the Hawaiian Islands and other selected Pacific Islands.

CHART SUPPLEMENT U.S.– A flight information publication designed for use with appropriate IFR or VFR charts which contains data on all airports, seaplane bases, and heliports open to the public including communications data, navigational facilities, airport diagrams, certain special notices, and non–regulatory procedures. This publication is issued for the conterminous U.S., Puerto Rico, and the Virgin Islands in seven volumes according to geographical area.

CHARTED VFR FLYWAYS– Charted VFR Flyways are flight paths recommended for use to bypass areas heavily traversed by large turbine‐powered aircraft. Pilot compliance with recommended flyways and associated altitudes is strictly voluntary. VFR Flyway Planning charts are published on the back of existing VFR Terminal Area charts.

CHARTED VISUAL FLIGHT PROCEDURE APPROACH– An approach conducted while operating on an instrument flight rules (IFR) flight plan which authorizes the pilot of an aircraft to proceed visually and clear of clouds to the airport via visual landmarks and other information depicted on a charted visual flight procedure. This approach must be authorized and under the control of the appropriate air traffic control facility. Weather minimums required are depicted on the chart.

CHASE– An aircraft flown in proximity to another aircraft normally to observe its performance during training or testing.

CHASE AIRCRAFT−
(See CHASE.)

CHOP− A form of turbulence.

a. Light Chop− Turbulence that causes slight, rapid and somewhat rhythmic bumpiness without appreciable changes in altitude or attitude.

b. Moderate Chop− Turbulence similar to Light Chop but of greater intensity. It causes rapid bumps or jolts without appreciable changes in aircraft altitude or attitude.
(See TURBULENCE.)

CIRCLE-TO-LAND MANEUVER− A maneuver initiated by the pilot to align the aircraft with a runway for landing when a straight-in landing from an instrument approach is not possible or is not desirable. At tower controlled airports, this maneuver is made only after ATC authorization has been obtained and the pilot has established required visual reference to the airport.
(See CIRCLE TO RUNWAY.)
(See LANDING MINIMUMS.)
(Refer to AIM.)

CIRCLE TO RUNWAY (RUNWAY NUMBER)− Used by ATC to inform the pilot that he/she must circle to land because the runway in use is other than the runway aligned with the instrument approach procedure. When the direction of the circling maneuver in relation to the airport/runway is required, the controller will state the direction (eight cardinal compass points) and specify a left or right downwind or base leg as appropriate; e.g., "Cleared VOR Runway Three Six Approach circle to Runway Two Two," or "Circle northwest of the airport for a right downwind to Runway Two Two."
(See CIRCLE-TO-LAND MANEUVER.)
(See LANDING MINIMUMS.)
(Refer to AIM.)

CIRCLING APPROACH−
(See CIRCLE-TO-LAND MANEUVER.)

CIRCLING MANEUVER−
(See CIRCLE-TO-LAND MANEUVER.)

CIRCLING MINIMA−
(See CONTROLLED AIRSPACE.)

CIVIL AIRCRAFT OPERATION (CAO)− Aircraft operations other than public use.

CLASS A AIRSPACE−
(See CONTROLLED AIRSPACE.)

CLASS B AIRSPACE−
(See CONTROLLED AIRSPACE.)

CLASS C AIRSPACE−
(See CONTROLLED AIRSPACE.)

CLASS D AIRSPACE−
(See CONTROLLED AIRSPACE.)

CLASS E AIRSPACE−
(See CONTROLLED AIRSPACE.)

CLASS G AIRSPACE− Airspace that is not designated in 14 CFR Part 71 as Class A, Class B, Class C, Class D, or Class E controlled airspace is Class G (uncontrolled) airspace.
(See UNCONTROLLED AIRSPACE.)

CLEAR AIR TURBULENCE (CAT)– Turbulence encountered in air where no clouds are present. This term is commonly applied to high-level turbulence associated with wind shear. CAT is often encountered in the vicinity of the jet stream.
(See WIND SHEAR.)
(See JET STREAM.)

CLEAR OF THE RUNWAY–

a. Taxiing aircraft, which is approaching a runway, is clear of the runway when all parts of the aircraft are held short of the applicable runway holding position marking.

b. A pilot or controller may consider an aircraft, which is exiting or crossing a runway, to be clear of the runway when all parts of the aircraft are beyond the runway edge and there are no restrictions to its continued movement beyond the applicable runway holding position marking.

c. Pilots and controllers shall exercise good judgment to ensure that adequate separation exists between all aircraft on runways and taxiways at airports with inadequate runway edge lines or holding position markings.

CLEARANCE–
(See AIR TRAFFIC CLEARANCE.)

CLEARANCE LIMIT– The fix, point, or location to which an aircraft is cleared when issued an air traffic clearance.
(See ICAO term CLEARANCE LIMIT.)

CLEARANCE LIMIT [ICAO]– The point to which an aircraft is granted an air traffic control clearance.

CLEARANCE VOID IF NOT OFF BY (TIME)– Used by ATC to advise an aircraft that the departure release is automatically canceled if takeoff is not made prior to a specified time. The expiration of a clearance void time does not cancel the departure clearance or IFR flight plan. It withdraws the pilot's authority to depart IFR until a new departure release/release time has been issued by ATC. Pilots who choose to depart VFR after their clearance void time has expired should not depart using the previously assigned IFR transponder code.
(See ICAO term CLEARANCE VOID TIME.)

CLEARANCE VOID TIME [ICAO]– A time specified by an air traffic control unit at which a clearance ceases to be valid unless the aircraft concerned has already taken action to comply therewith.

CLEARED APPROACH– ATC authorization for an aircraft to execute any standard or special instrument approach procedure for that airport. Normally, an aircraft will be cleared for a specific instrument approach procedure.
(See CLEARED (Type of) APPROACH.)
(See INSTRUMENT APPROACH PROCEDURE.)
(Refer to 14 CFR Part 91.)
(Refer to AIM.)

CLEARED (Type of) APPROACH– ATC authorization for an aircraft to execute a specific instrument approach procedure to an airport; e.g., "Cleared ILS Runway Three Six Approach."
(See APPROACH CLEARANCE.)
(See INSTRUMENT APPROACH PROCEDURE.)
(Refer to 14 CFR Part 91.)
(Refer to AIM.)

CLEARED AS FILED– Means the aircraft is cleared to proceed in accordance with the route of flight filed in the flight plan. This clearance does not include the altitude, DP, or DP Transition.
(See REQUEST FULL ROUTE CLEARANCE.)
(Refer to AIM.)

CLEARED FOR TAKEOFF– ATC authorization for an aircraft to depart. It is predicated on known traffic and known physical airport conditions.

CLEARED FOR THE OPTION– ATC authorization for an aircraft to make a touch-and-go, low approach, missed approach, stop and go, or full stop landing at the discretion of the pilot. It is normally used in training so that an instructor can evaluate a student's performance under changing situations. Pilots should advise ATC if they decide to remain on the runway, of any delay in their stop and go, delay clearing the runway, or are unable to comply with the instruction(s).

(See OPTION APPROACH.)

(Refer to AIM.)

CLEARED THROUGH– ATC authorization for an aircraft to make intermediate stops at specified airports without refiling a flight plan while en route to the clearance limit.

CLEARED TO LAND– ATC authorization for an aircraft to land. It is predicated on known traffic and known physical airport conditions.

CLEARWAY– An area beyond the takeoff runway under the control of airport authorities within which terrain or fixed obstacles may not extend above specified limits. These areas may be required for certain turbine-powered operations and the size and upward slope of the clearway will differ depending on when the aircraft was certificated.

(Refer to 14 CFR Part 1.)

CLIMB TO VFR– ATC authorization for an aircraft to climb to VFR conditions within Class B, C, D, and E surface areas when the only weather limitation is restricted visibility. The aircraft must remain clear of clouds while climbing to VFR.

(See SPECIAL VFR CONDITIONS.)

(Refer to AIM.)

CLIMBOUT– That portion of flight operation between takeoff and the initial cruising altitude.

CLIMB VIA– An abbreviated ATC clearance that requires compliance with the procedure lateral path, associated speed restrictions, and altitude restrictions along the cleared route or procedure.

CLOSE PARALLEL RUNWAYS– Two parallel runways whose extended centerlines are separated by less than 4,300 feet and at least 3000 feet (750 feet for SOIA operations) for which ATC is authorized to conduct simultaneous independent approach operations. PRM and simultaneous close parallel appear in approach title. Dual communications, special pilot training, an Attention All Users Page (AAUP), NTZ monitoring by displays that have aural and visual alerting algorithms are required. A high update rate surveillance sensor is required for certain runway or approach course spacing.

CLOSED LOOP CLEARANCE– A vector or reroute clearance that includes a return to route point and updates ERAM to accurately reflect the anticipated route (e.g., a QU route pick that anticipates length of vector and includes the next fix that ties into the route of flight.)

CLOSED RUNWAY– A runway that is unusable for aircraft operations. Only the airport management/military operations office can close a runway.

CLOSED TRAFFIC– Successive operations involving takeoffs and landings or low approaches where the aircraft does not exit the traffic pattern.

CLOUD– A cloud is a visible accumulation of minute water droplets and/or ice particles in the atmosphere above the Earth's surface. Cloud differs from ground fog, fog, or ice fog only in that the latter are, by definition, in contact with the Earth's surface.

CLT–

(See CALCULATED LANDING TIME.)

CLUTTER– In radar operations, clutter refers to the reception and visual display of radar returns caused by precipitation, chaff, terrain, numerous aircraft targets, or other phenomena. Such returns may limit or preclude ATC from providing services based on radar.
(See CHAFF.)
(See GROUND CLUTTER.)
(See PRECIPITATION.)
(See TARGET.)
(See ICAO term RADAR CLUTTER.)

CMNPS–
(See CANADIAN MINIMUM NAVIGATION PERFORMANCE SPECIFICATION AIRSPACE.)

COA–
(See CERTIFICATE OF WAIVER OR AUTHORIZATION.)

COASTAL FIX– A navigation aid or intersection where an aircraft transitions between the domestic route structure and the oceanic route structure.

CODES– The number assigned to a particular multiple pulse reply signal transmitted by a transponder.
(See DISCRETE CODE.)

COLD TEMPERATURE CORRECTION– A correction in feet, based on height above airport and temperature, that is added to the aircraft's indicated altitude to offset the effect of cold temperature on true altitude.

COLLABORATIVE TRAJECTORY OPTIONS PROGRAM (CTOP)– CTOP is a traffic management program administered by the Air Traffic Control System Command Center (ATCSCC) that manages demand through constrained airspace, while considering operator preference with regard to both route and delay as defined in a Trajectory Options Set (TOS).

COMBINED CENTER-RAPCON– An air traffic facility which combines the functions of an ARTCC and a radar approach control facility.
(See AIR ROUTE TRAFFIC CONTROL CENTER.)
(See RADAR APPROACH CONTROL FACILITY.)

COMMON POINT– A significant point over which two or more aircraft will report passing or have reported passing before proceeding on the same or diverging tracks. To establish/maintain longitudinal separation, a controller may determine a common point not originally in the aircraft's flight plan and then clear the aircraft to fly over the point.
(See SIGNIFICANT POINT.)

COMMON PORTION–
(See COMMON ROUTE.)

COMMON ROUTE– That segment of a North American Route between the inland navigation facility and the coastal fix.

OR

COMMON ROUTE–
(See SEGMENTS OF A SID/STAR)

COMMON TRAFFIC ADVISORY FREQUENCY (CTAF)– A frequency designed for the purpose of carrying out airport advisory practices while operating to or from an airport without an operating control tower. The CTAF may be a UNICOM, Multicom, FSS, or tower frequency and is identified in appropriate aeronautical publications.
(See DESIGNATED COMMON TRAFFIC ADVISORY FREQUENCY (CTAF) AREA.)
(Refer to AC 90-66, Non–Towered Airport Flight Operations.)

COMMUNITY–BASED ORGANIZATION (CBO)– A membership–based entity, described under Section 501(a,c), whose mission is the furtherance of model aviation. (see also, 49 United States Code (USC) §44809 (h) and Advisory Circular (AC) 91–57).

COMPASS LOCATOR– A low power, low or medium frequency (L/MF) radio beacon installed at the site of the outer or middle marker of an instrument landing system (ILS). It can be used for navigation at distances of approximately 15 miles or as authorized in the approach procedure.

a. Outer Compass Locator (LOM)– A compass locator installed at the site of the outer marker of an instrument landing system.

(See OUTER MARKER.)

b. Middle Compass Locator (LMM)– A compass locator installed at the site of the middle marker of an instrument landing system.

(See MIDDLE MARKER.)
(See ICAO term LOCATOR.)

COMPASS ROSE– A circle, graduated in degrees, printed on some charts or marked on the ground at an airport. It is used as a reference to either true or magnetic direction.

COMPLY WITH RESTRICTIONS– An ATC instruction that requires an aircraft being vectored back onto an arrival or departure procedure to comply with all altitude and/or speed restrictions depicted on the procedure. This term may be used in lieu of repeating each remaining restriction that appears on the procedure.

COMPOSITE FLIGHT PLAN– A flight plan which specifies VFR operation for one portion of flight and IFR for another portion. It is used primarily in military operations.

(Refer to AIM.)

COMPULSORY REPORTING POINTS– Reporting points which must be reported to ATC. They are designated on aeronautical charts by solid triangles or filed in a flight plan as fixes selected to define direct routes. These points are geographical locations which are defined by navigation aids/fixes. Pilots should discontinue position reporting over compulsory reporting points when informed by ATC that their aircraft is in "radar contact."

COMPUTER NAVIGATION FIX (CNF)– A Computer Navigation Fix is a point defined by a latitude/longitude coordinate and is required to support Performance–Based Navigation (PBN) operations. A five–letter identifier denoting a CNF can be found next to an "x" on en route charts and on some approach charts. Eventually, all CNFs will be labeled and begin with the letters "CF" followed by three consonants (e.g., 'CFWBG'). CNFs are not recognized by ATC, are not contained in ATC fix or automation databases, and are not used for ATC purposes. Pilots should not use CNFs for point–to–point navigation (e.g., proceed direct), filing a flight plan, or in aircraft/ATC communications. Use of CNFs has not been adopted or recognized by the International Civil Aviation Organization (ICAO).

(REFER to AIM 1–1–17b5(i)(2), Global Positioning System (GPS).

CONDITIONS NOT MONITORED– When an airport operator cannot monitor the condition of the movement area or airfield surface area, this information is issued as a NOTAM. Usually necessitated due to staffing, operating hours or other mitigating factors associated with airport operations.

CONFIDENCE MANEUVER– A confidence maneuver consists of one or more turns, a climb or descent, or other maneuver to determine if the pilot in command (PIC) is able to receive and comply with ATC instructions.

CONFLICT ALERT– A function of certain air traffic control automated systems designed to alert radar controllers to existing or pending situations between tracked targets (known IFR or VFR aircraft) that require his/her immediate attention/action.

(See MODE C INTRUDER ALERT.)

CONFLICT RESOLUTION– The resolution of potential conflictions between aircraft that are radar identified and in communication with ATC by ensuring that radar targets do not touch. Pertinent traffic advisories shall be issued when this procedure is applied.

Note: This procedure shall not be provided utilizing mosaic radar systems.

CONFORMANCE– The condition established when an aircraft's actual position is within the conformance region constructed around that aircraft at its position, according to the trajectory associated with the aircraft's Current Plan.

CONFORMANCE REGION– A volume, bounded laterally, vertically, and longitudinally, within which an aircraft must be at a given time in order to be in conformance with the Current Plan Trajectory for that aircraft. At a given time, the conformance region is determined by the simultaneous application of the lateral, vertical, and longitudinal conformance bounds for the aircraft at the position defined by time and aircraft's trajectory.

CONSOLAN– A low frequency, long-distance NAVAID used principally for transoceanic navigations.

CONSOLIDATED WAKE TURBULENCE (CWT)– A version of RECAT that has nine categories, A through I, that refines the grouping of aircraft while optimizing wake turbulence separation.

CONSTRAINT SATISFACTION POINT (CSP)– Meter Reference Elements (MREs) that are actively scheduled by TBFM. Constraint satisfaction occurs when the Scheduled Time of Arrival generated for each metered flight conforms to all the scheduling constraints specified at all the applicable CSPs.

CONTACT–

a. Establish communication with (followed by the name of the facility and, if appropriate, the frequency to be used).

b. A flight condition wherein the pilot ascertains the attitude of his/her aircraft and navigates by visual reference to the surface.

(See CONTACT APPROACH.)
(See RADAR CONTACT.)

CONTACT APPROACH– An approach wherein an aircraft on an IFR flight plan, having an air traffic control authorization, operating clear of clouds with at least 1 mile flight visibility and a reasonable expectation of continuing to the destination airport in those conditions, may deviate from the instrument approach procedure and proceed to the destination airport by visual reference to the surface. This approach will only be authorized when requested by the pilot and the reported ground visibility at the destination airport is at least 1 statute mile.

(Refer to AIM.)

CONTAMINATED RUNWAY– A runway is considered contaminated whenever standing water, ice, snow, slush, frost in any form, heavy rubber, or other substances are present. A runway is contaminated with respect to rubber deposits or other friction-degrading substances when the average friction value for any 500-foot segment of the runway within the ALD fails below the recommended minimum friction level and the average friction value in the adjacent 500-foot segments falls below the maintenance planning friction level.

CONTERMINOUS U.S.– The 48 adjoining States and the District of Columbia.

CONTINENTAL UNITED STATES– The 49 States located on the continent of North America and the District of Columbia.

CONTINGENCY HAZARD AREA (CHA)– Used by ATC. Areas of airspace that are defined and distributed in advance of a launch or reentry operation and are activated in response to a failure.

(See AIRCRAFT HAZARD AREA.)
(See REFINED HAZARD AREA.)
(See TRANSITIONAL HAZARD AREA.)

CONTINUE– When used as a control instruction should be followed by another word or words clarifying what is expected of the pilot. Example: "continue taxi," "continue descent," "continue inbound," etc.

CONTROL AREA [ICAO]– A controlled airspace extending upwards from a specified limit above the earth.

CONTROL SECTOR– An airspace area of defined horizontal and vertical dimensions for which a controller or group of controllers has air traffic control responsibility, normally within an air route traffic control center or an approach control facility. Sectors are established based on predominant traffic flows, altitude strata, and controller workload. Pilot communications during operations within a sector are normally maintained on discrete frequencies assigned to the sector.

(See DISCRETE FREQUENCY.)

CONTROL SLASH− A radar beacon slash representing the actual position of the associated aircraft. Normally, the control slash is the one closest to the interrogating radar beacon site. When ARTCC radar is operating in narrowband (digitized) mode, the control slash is converted to a target symbol.

CONTROLLED AIRSPACE− An airspace of defined dimensions within which air traffic control service is provided to IFR flights and to VFR flights in accordance with the airspace classification.

a. Controlled airspace is a generic term that covers Class A, Class B, Class C, Class D, and Class E airspace.

b. Controlled airspace is also that airspace within which all aircraft operators are subject to certain pilot qualifications, operating rules, and equipment requirements in 14 CFR Part 91 (for specific operating requirements, please refer to 14 CFR Part 91). For IFR operations in any class of controlled airspace, a pilot must file an IFR flight plan and receive an appropriate ATC clearance. Each Class B, Class C, and Class D airspace area designated for an airport contains at least one primary airport around which the airspace is designated (for specific designations and descriptions of the airspace classes, please refer to 14 CFR Part 71).

c. Controlled airspace in the United States is designated as follows:

1. CLASS A− Generally, that airspace from 18,000 feet MSL up to and including FL 600, including the airspace overlying the waters within 12 nautical miles of the coast of the 48 contiguous States and Alaska. Unless otherwise authorized, all persons must operate their aircraft under IFR.

2. CLASS B− Generally, that airspace from the surface to 10,000 feet MSL surrounding the nation's busiest airports in terms of airport operations or passenger enplanements. The configuration of each Class B airspace area is individually tailored and consists of a surface area and two or more layers (some Class B airspace areas resemble upside-down wedding cakes), and is designed to contain all published instrument procedures once an aircraft enters the airspace. An ATC clearance is required for all aircraft to operate in the area, and all aircraft that are so cleared receive separation services within the airspace. The cloud clearance requirement for VFR operations is "clear of clouds."

3. CLASS C− Generally, that airspace from the surface to 4,000 feet above the airport elevation (charted in MSL) surrounding those airports that have an operational control tower, are serviced by a radar approach control, and that have a certain number of IFR operations or passenger enplanements. Although the configuration of each Class C area is individually tailored, the airspace usually consists of a surface area with a 5 NM radius, a circle with a 10 NM radius that extends no lower than 1,200 feet up to 4,000 feet above the airport elevation, and an outer area that is not charted. Each person must establish two-way radio communications with the ATC facility providing air traffic services prior to entering the airspace and thereafter maintain those communications while within the airspace. VFR aircraft are only separated from IFR aircraft within the airspace.

(See OUTER AREA.)

4. CLASS D− Generally, that airspace from the surface to 2,500 feet above the airport elevation (charted in MSL) surrounding those airports that have an operational control tower. The configuration of each Class D airspace area is individually tailored and when instrument procedures are published, the airspace will normally be designed to contain the procedures. Arrival extensions for instrument approach procedures may be Class D or Class E airspace. Unless otherwise authorized, each person must establish two-way radio communications with the ATC facility providing air traffic services prior to entering the airspace and thereafter maintain those communications while in the airspace. No separation services are provided to VFR aircraft.

5. CLASS E− Generally, if the airspace is not Class A, Class B, Class C, or Class D, and it is controlled airspace, it is Class E airspace. Class E airspace extends upward from either the surface or a designated altitude to the overlying or adjacent controlled airspace. When designated as a surface area, the airspace will be configured to contain all instrument procedures. Also in this class are Federal airways, airspace beginning at either 700 or 1,200 feet AGL used to transition to/from the terminal or en route environment, en route domestic, and offshore airspace areas designated below 18,000 feet MSL. Unless designated at a lower altitude, Class E airspace begins at 14,500 MSL over the United States, including that airspace overlying the waters within 12 nautical miles of the coast of the 48 contiguous States and Alaska, up to, but not including 18,000 feet MSL, and the airspace above FL 600.

CONTROLLED AIRSPACE [ICAO]– An airspace of defined dimensions within which air traffic control service is provided to IFR flights and to VFR flights in accordance with the airspace classification.

Note: Controlled airspace is a generic term which covers ATS airspace Classes A, B, C, D, and E.

CONTROLLED TIME OF ARRIVAL– Arrival time assigned during a Traffic Management Program. This time may be modified due to adjustments or user options.

CONTROLLER–
(See AIR TRAFFIC CONTROL SPECIALIST.)

CONTROLLER [ICAO]– A person authorized to provide air traffic control services.

CONTROLLER PILOT DATA LINK COMMUNICATIONS (CPDLC)– A two–way digital communications system that conveys textual air traffic control messages between controllers and pilots using ground or satellite-based radio relay stations.

CONVECTIVE SIGMET– A weather advisory concerning convective weather significant to the safety of all aircraft. Convective SIGMETs are issued for tornadoes, lines of thunderstorms, embedded thunderstorms of any intensity level, areas of thunderstorms greater than or equal to VIP level 4 with an area coverage of $^{4}/_{10}$ (40%) or more, and hail $^{3}/_{4}$ inch or greater.
(See AIRMET.)
(See CWA.)
(See GRAPHICAL AIRMEN'S METEOROLOGICAL INFORMATION.)
(See SAW.)
(See SIGMET.)
(Refer to AIM.)

CONVECTIVE SIGNIFICANT METEOROLOGICAL INFORMATION–
(See CONVECTIVE SIGMET.)

COOPERATIVE SURVEILLANCE– Any surveillance system, such as secondary surveillance radar (SSR), wide–area multilateration (WAM), or ADS–B, that is dependent upon the presence of certain equipment onboard the aircraft or vehicle to be detected.
(See AUTOMATIC DEPENDENT SURVEILLANCE–BROADCAST.)
(See NON–COOPERATIVE SURVEILLANCE.)
(See RADAR.)
(See WIDE AREA MULTILATERATION.)

COORDINATES– The intersection of lines of reference, usually expressed in degrees/minutes/seconds of latitude and longitude, used to determine position or location.

COORDINATION FIX– The fix in relation to which facilities will handoff, transfer control of an aircraft, or coordinate flight progress data. For terminal facilities, it may also serve as a clearance for arriving aircraft.

COPTER–
(See HELICOPTER.)

CORRECTION– An error has been made in the transmission and the correct version follows.

COUPLED APPROACH– An instrument approach performed by the aircraft autopilot, and/or visually depicted on the flight director, which is receiving position information and/or steering commands from onboard navigational equipment. In general, coupled non-precision approaches must be flown manually (autopilot disengaged) at altitudes lower than 50 feet AGL below the minimum descent altitude, and coupled precision approaches must be flown manually (autopilot disengaged) below 50 feet AGL unless authorized to conduct autoland operations. Coupled instrument approaches are commonly flown to the allowable IFR weather minima established by the operator or PIC, or flown VFR for training and safety.

COUPLED SCHEDULING (CS)/ EXTENDED METERING (XM)– Adds additional Constraint Satisfaction Points for metered aircraft along their route. This provides the ability to merge flows upstream from the meter fix and results in a more optimal distribution of delays over a greater distance from the airport, increased meter list accuracy, and more accurate delivery to the meter fix.

COURSE–

a. The intended direction of flight in the horizontal plane measured in degrees from north.

b. The ILS localizer signal pattern usually specified as the front course or the back course.

(See BEARING.)
(See INSTRUMENT LANDING SYSTEM.)
(See RADIAL.)

CPDLC–

(See CONTROLLER PILOT DATA LINK COMMUNICATIONS.)

CPL [ICAO]–

(See ICAO term CURRENT FLIGHT PLAN.)

CREWMEMBER (UAS)– A person assigned to perform an operational duty. A UAS crewmember includes the remote pilot in command, the person manipulating the controls, and visual observers but may also include other persons as appropriate or required to ensure the safe operation of the UAS (e.g., sensor operator, ground control station operator).

CRITICAL ENGINE– The engine which, upon failure, would most adversely affect the performance or handling qualities of an aircraft.

CROSS (FIX) AT (ALTITUDE)– Used by ATC when a specific altitude restriction at a specified fix is required.

CROSS (FIX) AT OR ABOVE (ALTITUDE)– Used by ATC when an altitude restriction at a specified fix is required. It does not prohibit the aircraft from crossing the fix at a higher altitude than specified; however, the higher altitude may not be one that will violate a succeeding altitude restriction or altitude assignment.

(See ALTITUDE RESTRICTION.)
(Refer to AIM.)

CROSS (FIX) AT OR BELOW (ALTITUDE)– Used by ATC when a maximum crossing altitude at a specific fix is required. It does not prohibit the aircraft from crossing the fix at a lower altitude; however, it must be at or above the minimum IFR altitude.

(See ALTITUDE RESTRICTION.)
(See MINIMUM IFR ALTITUDES.)
(Refer to 14 CFR Part 91.)

CROSSWIND–

a. When used concerning the traffic pattern, the word means "crosswind leg."

(See TRAFFIC PATTERN.)

b. When used concerning wind conditions, the word means a wind not parallel to the runway or the path of an aircraft.

(See CROSSWIND COMPONENT.)

CROSSWIND COMPONENT– The wind component measured in knots at 90 degrees to the longitudinal axis of the runway.

CRUISE– Used in an ATC clearance to authorize a pilot to conduct flight at any altitude from the minimum IFR altitude up to and including the altitude specified in the clearance. The pilot may level off at any intermediate altitude within this block of airspace. Climb/descent within the block is to be made at the discretion of the pilot. However, once the pilot starts descent and verbally reports leaving an altitude in the block, he/she may not return to that altitude without additional ATC clearance. Further, it is approval for the pilot to proceed to and make an approach at destination airport and can be used in conjunction with:

a. An airport clearance limit at locations with a standard/special instrument approach procedure. The CFRs require that if an instrument letdown to an airport is necessary, the pilot shall make the letdown in accordance with a standard/special instrument approach procedure for that airport, or

b. An airport clearance limit at locations that are within/below/outside controlled airspace and without a standard/special instrument approach procedure. Such a clearance is NOT AUTHORIZATION for the pilot to descend under IFR conditions below the applicable minimum IFR altitude nor does it imply that ATC is exercising control over aircraft in Class G airspace; however, it provides a means for the aircraft to proceed to destination airport, descend, and land in accordance with applicable CFRs governing VFR flight operations. Also, this provides search and rescue protection until such time as the IFR flight plan is closed.

(See INSTRUMENT APPROACH PROCEDURE.)

CRUISE CLIMB– A climb technique employed by aircraft, usually at a constant power setting, resulting in an increase of altitude as the aircraft weight decreases.

CRUISING ALTITUDE– An altitude or flight level maintained during en route level flight. This is a constant altitude and should not be confused with a cruise clearance.

(See ALTITUDE.)
(See ICAO term CRUISING LEVEL.)

CRUISING LEVEL–
(See CRUISING ALTITUDE.)

CRUISING LEVEL [ICAO]– A level maintained during a significant portion of a flight.

CSP–
(See CONSTRAINT SATISFACTION POINT)

CT MESSAGE– An EDCT time generated by the ATCSCC to regulate traffic at arrival airports. Normally, a CT message is automatically transferred from the traffic management system computer to the NAS en route computer and appears as an EDCT. In the event of a communication failure between the traffic management system computer and the NAS, the CT message can be manually entered by the TMC at the en route facility.

CTA–
(See CONTROLLED TIME OF ARRIVAL.)
(See ICAO term CONTROL AREA.)

CTAF–
(See COMMON TRAFFIC ADVISORY FREQUENCY.)

CTOP–
(See COLLABORATIVE TRAJECTORY OPTIONS PROGRAM)

CTRD–
(See CERTIFIED TOWER RADAR DISPLAY.)

CURRENT FLIGHT PLAN [ICAO]– The flight plan, including changes, if any, brought about by subsequent clearances.

CVFP APPROACH–
(See CHARTED VISUAL FLIGHT PROCEDURE APPROACH.)

CWA–
(See CENTER WEATHER ADVISORY and WEATHER ADVISORY.)

CWT–
(See CONSOLIDATED WAKE TURBULENCE.)

D

D–ATIS–

(See DIGITAL-AUTOMATIC TERMINAL INFORMATION SERVICE.)

D–ATIS [ICAO]–

(See ICAO Term DATA LINK AUTOMATIC TERMINAL INFORMATION SERVICE.)

DA [ICAO]–

(See ICAO Term DECISION ALTITUDE/DECISION HEIGHT.)

DAIR–

(See DIRECT ALTITUDE AND IDENTITY READOUT.)

DANGER AREA [ICAO]– An airspace of defined dimensions within which activities dangerous to the flight of aircraft may exist at specified times.

Note: The term "Danger Area" is not used in reference to areas within the United States or any of its possessions or territories.

DAS–

(See DELAY ASSIGNMENT.)

DATA BLOCK–

(See ALPHANUMERIC DISPLAY.)

DATA LINK AUTOMATIC TERMINAL INFORMATION SERVICE (D–ATIS) [ICAO]– The provision of ATIS via data link.

DCT–

(See DELAY COUNTDOWN TIMER.)

DEAD RECKONING– Dead reckoning, as applied to flying, is the navigation of an airplane solely by means of computations based on airspeed, course, heading, wind direction, and speed, groundspeed, and elapsed time.

DEBRIS RESPONSE AREA (DRA)– Used by ATC. Areas of airspace that may be activated in response to unplanned falling debris in the NAS.

DECISION ALTITUDE/DECISION HEIGHT [ICAO Annex 6]- A specified altitude or height (A/H) in the precision approach at which a missed approach must be initiated if the required visual reference to continue the approach has not been established.

1. Decision altitude (DA) is referenced to mean sea level and decision height (DH) is referenced to the threshold elevation.

2. Category II and III minima are expressed as a DH and not a DA. Minima is assessed by reference to a radio altimeter and not a barometric altimeter, which makes the minima a DH.

3. The required visual reference means that section of the visual aids or of the approach area which should have been in view for sufficient time for the pilot to have made an assessment of the aircraft position and rate of change of position, in relation to the desired flight path.

DECISION ALTITUDE (DA)– A specified altitude (mean sea level (MSL)) on an instrument approach procedure (ILS, GLS, vertically guided RNAV) at which the pilot must decide whether to continue the approach or initiate an immediate missed approach if the pilot does not see the required visual references.

DECISION HEIGHT (DH)– With respect to the operation of aircraft, means the height at which a decision must be made during an ILS or PAR instrument approach to either continue the approach or to execute a missed approach.

(See ICAO term DECISION ALTITUDE/DECISION HEIGHT.)

DECODER– The device used to decipher signals received from ATCRBS transponders to effect their display as select codes.
(See CODES.)
(See RADAR.)

DEFENSE AREA– Any airspace of the contiguous United States that is not an ADIZ in which the control of aircraft is required for reasons of national security.

DEFENSE VISUAL FLIGHT RULES– Rules applicable to flights within an ADIZ conducted under the visual flight rules in 14 CFR Part 91.
(See AIR DEFENSE IDENTIFICATION ZONE.)
(Refer to 14 CFR Part 91.)
(Refer to 14 CFR Part 99.)

DELAY ASSIGNMENT (DAS)– Delays are distributed to aircraft based on the traffic management program parameters. The delay assignment is calculated in 15–minute increments and appears as a table in Traffic Flow Management System (TFMS).

DELAY COUNTDOWN TIMER (DCT)– The display of the delay that must be absorbed by a flight prior to crossing a Meter Reference Element (MRE) to meet the TBFM Scheduled Time of Arrival (STA). It is calculated by taking the difference between the frozen STA and the Estimated Time of Arrival (ETA).

DELAY INDEFINITE (REASON IF KNOWN) EXPECT FURTHER CLEARANCE (TIME)– Used by ATC to inform a pilot when an accurate estimate of the delay time and the reason for the delay cannot immediately be determined; e.g., a disabled aircraft on the runway, terminal or center area saturation, weather below landing minimums, etc.
(See EXPECT FURTHER CLEARANCE (TIME).)

DEPARTURE CENTER– The ARTCC having jurisdiction for the airspace that generates a flight to the impacted airport.

DEPARTURE CONTROL– A function of an approach control facility providing air traffic control service for departing IFR and, under certain conditions, VFR aircraft.
(See APPROACH CONTROL FACILITY.)
(Refer to AIM.)

DEPARTURE SEQUENCING PROGRAM– A program designed to assist in achieving a specified interval over a common point for departures.

DEPARTURE TIME– The time an aircraft becomes airborne.

DEPARTURE VIEWER– A capability within the Traffic Flow Management System (TFMS) that provides combined displays for monitoring departure by fixes and departure airports. Traffic management personnel can customize the displays by selecting the departure airports and fixes of interest. The information displayed is the demand for the resource (fix or departure airport) in time bins with the flight list and a flight history for one flight at a time. From the display, flights can be selected for route amendment, one or more at a time, and the Route Amendment Dialogue (RAD) screen automatically opens for easy route selection and execution. Reroute options are based on Coded Departure Route (CDR) database and Trajectory Options Set (TOS) (when available).

DESCEND VIA– An abbreviated ATC clearance that requires compliance with a published procedure lateral path and associated speed restrictions and provides a pilot-discretion descent to comply with published altitude restrictions.

DESCENT SPEED ADJUSTMENTS– Speed deceleration calculations made to determine an accurate VTA. These calculations start at the transition point and use arrival speed segments to the vertex.

DESIGNATED COMMON TRAFFIC ADVISORY FREQUENCY (CTAF) AREA– In Alaska, in addition to being designated for the purpose of carrying out airport advisory practices while operating to or from an airport without an operating airport traffic control tower, a CTAF may also be designated for the purpose of carrying out advisory practices for operations in and through areas with a high volume of VFR traffic.

DESIRED COURSE–

a. True– A predetermined desired course direction to be followed (measured in degrees from true north).

b. Magnetic– A predetermined desired course direction to be followed (measured in degrees from local magnetic north).

DESIRED TRACK– The planned or intended track between two waypoints. It is measured in degrees from either magnetic or true north. The instantaneous angle may change from point to point along the great circle track between waypoints.

DETRESFA (DISTRESS PHASE) [ICAO]– The code word used to designate an emergency phase wherein there is reasonable certainty that an aircraft and its occupants are threatened by grave and imminent danger or require immediate assistance.

DEVIATION–

a. A departure from a current clearance, such as an off course maneuver to avoid weather or turbulence.

b. Where specifically authorized in the CFRs and requested by the pilot, ATC may permit pilots to deviate from certain regulations.

DH–
(See DECISION HEIGHT.)

DH [ICAO]–
(See ICAO Term DECISION ALTITUDE/ DECISION HEIGHT.)

DIGITAL-AUTOMATIC TERMINAL INFORMATION SERVICE (D-ATIS)– The service provides text messages to aircraft, airlines, and other users outside the standard reception range of conventional ATIS via landline and data link communications to the cockpit. Also, the service provides a computer–synthesized voice message that can be transmitted to all aircraft within range of existing transmitters. The Terminal Data Link System (TDLS) D-ATIS application uses weather inputs from local automated weather sources or manually entered meteorological data together with preprogrammed menus to provide standard information to users. Airports with D-ATIS capability are listed in the Chart Supplement U.S.

DIGITAL TARGET– A computer–generated symbol representing an aircraft's position, based on a primary return or radar beacon reply, shown on a digital display.

DIGITAL TERMINAL AUTOMATION SYSTEM (DTAS)– A system where digital radar and beacon data is presented on digital displays and the operational program monitors the system performance on a real–time basis.

DIGITIZED TARGET– A computer–generated indication shown on an analog radar display resulting from a primary radar return or a radar beacon reply.

DIRECT– Straight line flight between two navigational aids, fixes, points, or any combination thereof. When used by pilots in describing off-airway routes, points defining direct route segments become compulsory reporting points unless the aircraft is under radar contact.

DIRECTLY BEHIND– An aircraft is considered to be operating directly behind when it is following the actual flight path of the lead aircraft over the surface of the earth except when applying wake turbulence separation criteria.

DISCRETE BEACON CODE–
(See DISCRETE CODE.)

DISCRETE CODE– As used in the Air Traffic Control Radar Beacon System (ATCRBS), any one of the 4096 selectable Mode 3/A aircraft transponder codes except those ending in zero zero; e.g., discrete codes: 0010, 1201, 2317, 7777; nondiscrete codes: 0100, 1200, 7700. Nondiscrete codes are normally reserved for radar facilities that are not equipped with discrete decoding capability and for other purposes such as emergencies (7700), VFR aircraft (1200), etc.

(See RADAR.)
(Refer to AIM.)

DISCRETE FREQUENCY− A separate radio frequency for use in direct pilot-controller communications in air traffic control which reduces frequency congestion by controlling the number of aircraft operating on a particular frequency at one time. Discrete frequencies are normally designated for each control sector in en route/terminal ATC facilities. Discrete frequencies are listed in the Chart Supplement U.S. and the DoD FLIP IFR En Route Supplement.

(See CONTROL SECTOR.)

DISPLACED THRESHOLD− A threshold that is located at a point on the runway other than the designated beginning of the runway.

(See THRESHOLD.)
(Refer to AIM.)

DISTANCE MEASURING EQUIPMENT (DME)− Equipment (airborne and ground) used to measure, in nautical miles, the slant range distance of an aircraft from the DME navigational aid.

(See TACAN.)
(See VORTAC.)

DISTRESS− A condition of being threatened by serious and/or imminent danger and of requiring immediate assistance.

DIVE BRAKES−

(See SPEED BRAKES.)

DIVERSE VECTOR AREA− In a radar environment, that area in which a prescribed departure route is not required as the only suitable route to avoid obstacles. The area in which random radar vectors below the MVA/MIA, established in accordance with the TERPS criteria for diverse departures, obstacles and terrain avoidance, may be issued to departing aircraft.

DIVERSION (DVRSN)− Flights that are required to land at other than their original destination for reasons beyond the control of the pilot/company, e.g. periods of significant weather.

DME−

(See DISTANCE MEASURING EQUIPMENT.)

DME FIX− A geographical position determined by reference to a navigational aid which provides distance and azimuth information. It is defined by a specific distance in nautical miles and a radial, azimuth, or course (i.e., localizer) in degrees magnetic from that aid.

(See DISTANCE MEASURING EQUIPMENT.)
(See FIX.)

DME SEPARATION− Spacing of aircraft in terms of distances (nautical miles) determined by reference to distance measuring equipment (DME).

(See DISTANCE MEASURING EQUIPMENT.)

DoD FLIP− Department of Defense Flight Information Publications used for flight planning, en route, and terminal operations. FLIP is produced by the National Geospatial−Intelligence Agency (NGA) for world-wide use. United States Government Flight Information Publications (en route charts and instrument approach procedure charts) are incorporated in DoD FLIP for use in the National Airspace System (NAS).

DOMESTIC AIRSPACE− Airspace which overlies the continental land mass of the United States plus Hawaii and U.S. possessions. Domestic airspace extends to 12 miles offshore.

DOMESTIC NOTICE− A special notice or notice containing graphics or plain language text pertaining to almost every aspect of aviation, such as military training areas, large scale sporting events, air show information, Special

Traffic Management Programs (STMPs), and airport−specific information. These notices are applicable to operations within the United States and can be found on the Domestic Notices website.

DOWNBURST− A strong downdraft which induces an outburst of damaging winds on or near the ground. Damaging winds, either straight or curved, are highly divergent. The sizes of downbursts vary from 1/2 mile or less to more than 10 miles. An intense downburst often causes widespread damage. Damaging winds, lasting 5 to 30 minutes, could reach speeds as high as 120 knots.

DOWNWIND LEG−
(See TRAFFIC PATTERN.)

DP−
(See INSTRUMENT DEPARTURE PROCEDURE.)

DRA−
(See DEBRIS RESPONSE AREA.)

DRAG CHUTE− A parachute device installed on certain aircraft which is deployed on landing roll to assist in deceleration of the aircraft.

DROP ZONE− Any pre-determined area upon which parachutists or objects land after making an intentional parachute jump or drop.
(Refer to 14 CFR §105.3, Definitions)

DSP−
(See DEPARTURE SEQUENCING PROGRAM.)

DTAS−
(See DIGITAL TERMINAL AUTOMATION SYSTEM.)

DUE REGARD− A phase of flight wherein an aircraft commander of a State-operated aircraft assumes responsibility to separate his/her aircraft from all other aircraft.
(See also FAA Order JO 7110.65, Para 1−2−1, WORD MEANINGS.)

DUTY RUNWAY−
(See RUNWAY IN USE/ACTIVE RUNWAY/DUTY RUNWAY.)

DVA−
(See DIVERSE VECTOR AREA.)

DVFR−
(See DEFENSE VISUAL FLIGHT RULES.)

DVFR FLIGHT PLAN− A flight plan filed for a VFR aircraft which intends to operate in airspace within which the ready identification, location, and control of aircraft are required in the interest of national security.

DVRSN−
(See DIVERSION.)

DYNAMIC− Continuous review, evaluation, and change to meet demands.

DYNAMIC RESTRICTIONS− Those restrictions imposed by the local facility on an “as needed” basis to manage unpredictable fluctuations in traffic demands.

E

EAS–
(See EN ROUTE AUTOMATION SYSTEM.)

EDCT–
(See EXPECT DEPARTURE CLEARANCE TIME.)

EDST–
(See EN ROUTE DECISION SUPPORT TOOL)

EFC–
(See EXPECT FURTHER CLEARANCE (TIME).)

ELT–
(See EMERGENCY LOCATOR TRANSMITTER.)

EMBEDDED ROUTE TEXT– An EDST notification that an ADR/ADAR/AAR has been applied to the flight plan. Within the route field, sub–fields consisting of an adapted route or an embedded change in the route are color–coded in cyan with cyan brackets around the sub–field.
(See EN ROUTE DECISION SUPPORT TOOL.)

EMERGENCY– A distress or an urgency condition.

EMERGENCY AUTOLAND SYSTEM– This system, if activated, will determine an optimal airport, plot a course, broadcast the aircraft's intentions, fly to the airport, land, and (depending on the model) shut down the engines. Though the system will broadcast the aircraft's intentions, the controller should assume that transmissions to the aircraft will not be acknowledged.

EMERGENCY DESCENT MODE– This automated system senses conditions conducive to hypoxia (cabin depressurization). If an aircraft is equipped and the system is activated, it is designed to turn the aircraft up to 90 degrees, then descend to a lower altitude and level off, giving the pilot(s) time to recover.

EMERGENCY LOCATOR TRANSMITTER (ELT)– A radio transmitter attached to the aircraft structure which operates from its own power source on 121.5 MHz and 243.0 MHz. It aids in locating downed aircraft by radiating a downward sweeping audio tone, 2-4 times per second. It is designed to function without human action after an accident.
(Refer to 14 CFR Part 91.)
(Refer to AIM.)

E-MSAW–
(See EN ROUTE MINIMUM SAFE ALTITUDE WARNING.)

ENHANCED FLIGHT VISION SYSTEM (EFVS)– An EFVS is an installed aircraft system which uses an electronic means to provide a display of the forward external scene topography (the natural or man–made features of a place or region especially in a way to show their relative positions and elevation) through the use of imaging sensors, including but not limited to forward–looking infrared, millimeter wave radiometry, millimeter wave radar, or low–light level image intensification. An EFVS includes the display element, sensors, computers and power supplies, indications, and controls. An operator's authorization to conduct an EFVS operation may have provisions which allow pilots to conduct IAPs when the reported weather is below minimums prescribed on the IAP to be flown.

ENHANCED SPECIAL REPORTING SERVICE (eSRS)– An automated service used to enhance search and rescue operations that provides flight service specialists in Alaska direct information from the aircraft's registered tracking device.

EN ROUTE AIR TRAFFIC CONTROL SERVICES– Air traffic control service provided aircraft on IFR flight plans, generally by centers, when these aircraft are operating between departure and destination terminal areas.

When equipment, capabilities, and controller workload permit, certain advisory/assistance services may be provided to VFR aircraft.

(See AIR ROUTE TRAFFIC CONTROL CENTER.)
(Refer to AIM.)

EN ROUTE AUTOMATION SYSTEM (EAS)– The complex integrated environment consisting of situation display systems, surveillance systems and flight data processing, remote devices, decision support tools, and the related communications equipment that form the heart of the automated IFR air traffic control system. It interfaces with automated terminal systems and is used in the control of en route IFR aircraft.

(Refer to AIM.)

EN ROUTE CHARTS–
(See AERONAUTICAL CHART.)

EN ROUTE DECISION SUPPORT TOOL (EDST)– An automated tool provided at each Radar Associate position in selected En Route facilities. This tool utilizes flight and radar data to determine present and future trajectories for all active and proposal aircraft and provides enhanced automated flight data management.

EN ROUTE DESCENT– Descent from the en route cruising altitude which takes place along the route of flight.

EN ROUTE HIGH ALTITUDE CHARTS–
(See AERONAUTICAL CHART.)

EN ROUTE LOW ALTITUDE CHARTS–
(See AERONAUTICAL CHART.)

EN ROUTE MINIMUM SAFE ALTITUDE WARNING (E–MSAW)– A function of the EAS that aids the controller by providing an alert when a tracked aircraft is below or predicted by the computer to go below a predetermined minimum IFR altitude (MIA).

EN ROUTE TRANSITION–
(See SEGMENTS OF A SID/STAR.)

EN ROUTE TRANSITION WAYPOINT
(See SEGMENTS OF A SID/STAR.)

eSRS–
(See ENHANCED SPECIAL REPORTING SERVICE.)

EST–
(See ESTIMATED.)

ESTABLISHED– To be stable or fixed at an altitude or on a course, route, route segment, heading, instrument approach or departure procedure, etc.

ESTABLISHED ON RNP (EoR) CONCEPT– A system of authorized instrument approaches, ATC procedures, surveillance, and communication requirements that allow aircraft operations to be safely conducted with approved reduced separation criteria once aircraft are established on a PBN segment of a published instrument flight procedure.

ESTIMATED (EST)–When used in NOTAMs "EST" is a contraction that is used by the issuing authority only when the condition is expected to return to service prior to the expiration time. Using "EST" lets the user know that this NOTAM has the possibility of returning to service earlier than the expiration time. Any NOTAM which includes an "EST" will be auto–expired at the designated expiration time.

ESTIMATED ELAPSED TIME [ICAO]– The estimated time required to proceed from one significant point to another.

(See ICAO Term TOTAL ESTIMATED ELAPSED TIME.)

ESTIMATED OFF-BLOCK TIME [ICAO]– The estimated time at which the aircraft will commence movement associated with departure.

ESTIMATED POSITION ERROR (EPE)–
(See Required Navigation Performance)

ESTIMATED TIME OF ARRIVAL– The time the flight is estimated to arrive at the gate (scheduled operators) or the actual runway on times for nonscheduled operators.

ESTIMATED TIME EN ROUTE– The estimated flying time from departure point to destination (lift-off to touchdown).

ETA–
(See ESTIMATED TIME OF ARRIVAL.)

ETE–
(See ESTIMATED TIME EN ROUTE.)

EXECUTE MISSED APPROACH– Instructions issued to a pilot making an instrument approach which means continue inbound to the missed approach point and execute the missed approach procedure as described on the Instrument Approach Procedure Chart or as previously assigned by ATC. The pilot may climb immediately to the altitude specified in the missed approach procedure upon making a missed approach. No turns should be initiated prior to reaching the missed approach point. When conducting an ASR or PAR approach, execute the assigned missed approach procedure immediately upon receiving instructions to "execute missed approach."
(Refer to AIM.)

EXPECT (ALTITUDE) AT (TIME) or (FIX)– Used under certain conditions to provide a pilot with an altitude to be used in the event of two-way communications failure. It also provides altitude information to assist the pilot in planning.
(Refer to AIM.)

EXPECT DEPARTURE CLEARANCE TIME (EDCT)– The runway release time assigned to an aircraft in a traffic management program and shown on the flight progress strip as an EDCT.
(See GROUND DELAY PROGRAM.)

EXPECT FURTHER CLEARANCE (TIME)– The time a pilot can expect to receive clearance beyond a clearance limit.

EXPECT FURTHER CLEARANCE VIA (AIRWAYS, ROUTES OR FIXES)– Used to inform a pilot of the routing he/she can expect if any part of the route beyond a short range clearance limit differs from that filed.

EXPEDITE– Used by ATC when prompt compliance is required to avoid the development of an imminent situation. Expedite climb/descent normally indicates to a pilot that the approximate best rate of climb/descent should be used without requiring an exceptional change in aircraft handling characteristics.

F

FAA-RECOGNIZED IDENTIFICATION AREA (FRIA)– A defined geographic area where persons can operate UAS without remote identification, provided they maintain visual line of sight.

FAF–
(See FINAL APPROACH FIX.)

FALLEN HERO– Remains of fallen members of the United States military are often returned home by aircraft. These flights may be identified with the phrase "FALLEN HERO" added to the remarks section of the flight plan, or they may be transmitted via air/ground communications. If able, these flights will receive priority handling.

FAST FILE– An FSS system whereby a pilot files a flight plan via telephone that is recorded and later transcribed for transmission to the appropriate air traffic facility. (Alaska only.)

FAWP– Final Approach Waypoint

FEATHERED PROPELLER– A propeller whose blades have been rotated so that the leading and trailing edges are nearly parallel with the aircraft flight path to stop or minimize drag and engine rotation. Normally used to indicate shutdown of a reciprocating or turboprop engine due to malfunction.

FEDERAL AIRWAYS–
(See LOW ALTITUDE AIRWAY STRUCTURE.)

FEEDER FIX– The fix depicted on Instrument Approach Procedure Charts which establishes the starting point of the feeder route.

FEEDER ROUTE– A route depicted on instrument approach procedure charts to designate routes for aircraft to proceed from the en route structure to the initial approach fix (IAF).
(See INSTRUMENT APPROACH PROCEDURE.)

FERRY FLIGHT– A flight for the purpose of:

a. Returning an aircraft to base.

b. Delivering an aircraft from one location to another.

c. Moving an aircraft to and from a maintenance base. Ferry flights, under certain conditions, may be conducted under terms of a special flight permit.

FIELD ELEVATION–
(See AIRPORT ELEVATION.)

FILED– Normally used in conjunction with flight plans, meaning a flight plan has been submitted to ATC.

FILED EN ROUTE DELAY– Any of the following preplanned delays at points/areas along the route of flight which require special flight plan filing and handling techniques.

a. Terminal Area Delay. A delay within a terminal area for touch-and-go, low approach, or other terminal area activity.

b. Special Use Airspace Delay. A delay within a Military Operations Area, Restricted Area, Warning Area, or ATC Assigned Airspace.

c. Aerial Refueling Delay. A delay within an Aerial Refueling Track or Anchor.

FILED FLIGHT PLAN– The flight plan as filed with an ATS unit by the pilot or his/her designated representative without any subsequent changes or clearances.

FINAL– Commonly used to mean that an aircraft is on the final approach course or is aligned with a landing area.
(See FINAL APPROACH COURSE.)
(See FINAL APPROACH-IFR.)
(See SEGMENTS OF AN INSTRUMENT APPROACH PROCEDURE.)

FINAL APPROACH [ICAO]– That part of an instrument approach procedure which commences at the specified final approach fix or point, or where such a fix or point is not specified.

a. At the end of the last procedure turn, base turn or inbound turn of a racetrack procedure, if specified; or

b. At the point of interception of the last track specified in the approach procedure; and ends at a point in the vicinity of an aerodrome from which:

1. A landing can be made; or

2. A missed approach procedure is initiated.

FINAL APPROACH COURSE– A bearing/radial/track of an instrument approach leading to a runway or an extended runway centerline all without regard to distance.

FINAL APPROACH FIX– The fix from which the final approach (IFR) to an airport is executed and which identifies the beginning of the final approach segment. It is designated on Government charts by the Maltese Cross symbol for nonprecision approaches and the lightning bolt symbol, designating the PFAF, for precision approaches; or when ATC directs a lower-than-published glideslope/path or vertical path intercept altitude, it is the resultant actual point of the glideslope/path or vertical path intercept.
(See FINAL APPROACH POINT.)
(See GLIDESLOPE INTERCEPT ALTITUDE.)
(See SEGMENTS OF AN INSTRUMENT APPROACH PROCEDURE.)

FINAL APPROACH-IFR– The flight path of an aircraft which is inbound to an airport on a final instrument approach course, beginning at the final approach fix or point and extending to the airport or the point where a circle-to-land maneuver or a missed approach is executed.
(See FINAL APPROACH COURSE.)
(See FINAL APPROACH FIX.)
(See FINAL APPROACH POINT.)
(See SEGMENTS OF AN INSTRUMENT APPROACH PROCEDURE.)
(See ICAO term FINAL APPROACH.)

FINAL APPROACH POINT– The point, applicable only to a nonprecision approach with no depicted FAF (such as an on airport VOR), where the aircraft is established inbound on the final approach course from the procedure turn and where the final approach descent may be commenced. The FAP serves as the FAF and identifies the beginning of the final approach segment.
(See FINAL APPROACH FIX.)
(See SEGMENTS OF AN INSTRUMENT APPROACH PROCEDURE.)

FINAL APPROACH SEGMENT–
(See SEGMENTS OF AN INSTRUMENT APPROACH PROCEDURE.)

FINAL APPROACH SEGMENT [ICAO]– That segment of an instrument approach procedure in which alignment and descent for landing are accomplished.

FINAL CONTROLLER– The controller providing information and final approach guidance during PAR and ASR approaches utilizing radar equipment.
(See RADAR APPROACH.)

FINAL GUARD SERVICE– A value added service provided in conjunction with LAA/RAA only during periods of significant and fast changing weather conditions that may affect landing and takeoff operations.

FINAL MONITOR AID– A high resolution color display that is equipped with the controller alert system hardware/software used to monitor the no transgression zone (NTZ) during simultaneous parallel approach operations. The display includes alert algorithms providing the target predictors, a color change alert when a target penetrates or is predicted to penetrate the no transgression zone (NTZ), synthesized voice alerts, and digital mapping.
(See RADAR APPROACH.)

FINAL MONITOR CONTROLLER– Air Traffic Control Specialist assigned to radar monitor the flight path of aircraft during simultaneous parallel (approach courses spaced less than 9000 feet/9200 feet above 5000 feet) and simultaneous close parallel approach operations. Each runway is assigned a final monitor controller during simultaneous parallel and simultaneous close parallel ILS approaches.

FIR–
(See FLIGHT INFORMATION REGION.)

FIRST PERSON VIEW– UAS operation in which imagery is transmitted to the UAS pilot by an onboard UA camera.

FIRST TIER CENTER– An ARTCC immediately adjacent to the impacted center.

FIS–B–
(See FLIGHT INFORMATION SERVICE–BROADCAST.)

FIX– A geographical position determined by visual reference to the surface, by reference to one or more radio NAVAIDs, by celestial plotting, or by another navigational device.

FIX BALANCING– A process whereby aircraft are evenly distributed over several available arrival fixes reducing delays and controller workload.

FLAG– A warning device incorporated in certain airborne navigation and flight instruments indicating that:

a. Instruments are inoperative or otherwise not operating satisfactorily, or

b. Signal strength or quality of the received signal falls below acceptable values.

FLAG ALARM–
(See FLAG.)

FLAMEOUT– An emergency condition caused by a loss of engine power.

FLAMEOUT PATTERN– An approach normally conducted by a single-engine military aircraft experiencing loss or anticipating loss of engine power or control. The standard overhead approach starts at a relatively high altitude over a runway ("high key") followed by a continuous 180 degree turn to a high, wide position ("low key") followed by a continuous 180 degree turn final. The standard straight-in pattern starts at a point that results in a straight-in approach with a high rate of descent to the runway. Flameout approaches terminate in the type approach requested by the pilot (normally fullstop).

FLIGHT CHECK– A call sign prefix used by FAA aircraft engaged in flight inspection/certification of navigational aids and flight procedures. The word "recorded" may be added as a suffix; e.g., "Flight Check 320 recorded" to indicate that an automated flight inspection is in progress in terminal areas.
(See FLIGHT INSPECTION.)
(Refer to AIM.)

FLIGHT DATA [FSS]– The primary task of the FSS flight data position is information management. Flight data services include the development, translation, processing, and coordination of aeronautical, meteorological, and aviation information.

FLIGHT FOLLOWING–
(See TRAFFIC ADVISORIES.)

FLIGHT INFORMATION REGION– An airspace of defined dimensions within which Flight Information Service and Alerting Service are provided.

a. Flight Information Service. A service provided for the purpose of giving advice and information useful for the safe and efficient conduct of flights.

b. Alerting Service. A service provided to notify appropriate organizations regarding aircraft in need of search and rescue aid and to assist such organizations as required.

FLIGHT INFORMATION SERVICE– A service provided for the purpose of giving advice and information useful for the safe and efficient conduct of flights.

FLIGHT INFORMATION SERVICE–BROADCAST (FIS–B)– A ground broadcast service provided through the ADS–B Broadcast Services network over the UAT data link that operates on 978 MHz. The FIS–B system provides pilots and flight crews of properly equipped aircraft with a cockpit display of certain aviation weather and aeronautical information.

FLIGHT INSPECTION– Inflight investigation and evaluation of a navigational aid to determine whether it meets established tolerances.

(See FLIGHT CHECK.)
(See NAVIGATIONAL AID.)

FLIGHT LEVEL– A level of constant atmospheric pressure related to a reference datum of 29.92 inches of mercury. Each is stated in three digits that represent hundreds of feet. For example, flight level (FL) 250 represents a barometric altimeter indication of 25,000 feet; FL 255, an indication of 25,500 feet.

(See ICAO term FLIGHT LEVEL.)

FLIGHT LEVEL [ICAO]– A surface of constant atmospheric pressure which is related to a specific pressure datum, 1013.2 hPa (1013.2 mb), and is separated from other such surfaces by specific pressure intervals.

Note 1: A pressure type altimeter calibrated in accordance with the standard atmosphere:

a. When set to a QNH altimeter setting, will indicate altitude;
b. When set to a QFE altimeter setting, will indicate height above the QFE reference datum; and
c. When set to a pressure of 1013.2 hPa (1013.2 mb), may be used to indicate flight levels.

Note 2: The terms 'height' and 'altitude,' used in Note 1 above, indicate altimetric rather than geometric heights and altitudes.

FLIGHT LINE– A term used to describe the precise movement of a civil photogrammetric aircraft along a predetermined course(s) at a predetermined altitude during the actual photographic run.

FLIGHT MANAGEMENT SYSTEMS– A computer system that uses a large data base to allow routes to be preprogrammed and fed into the system by means of a data loader. The system is constantly updated with respect to position accuracy by reference to conventional navigation aids. The sophisticated program and its associated data base ensures that the most appropriate aids are automatically selected during the information update cycle.

FLIGHT PATH– A line, course, or track along which an aircraft is flying or intended to be flown.

(See COURSE.)
(See TRACK.)

FLIGHT PLAN– Specified information relating to the intended flight of an aircraft that is filed electronically, orally, or in writing with an FSS, third–party vendor, or an ATC facility.

(See FAST FILE.)
(See FILED.)
(Refer to AIM.)

FLIGHT PLAN AREA (FPA)– The geographical area assigned to a flight service station (FSS) for the purpose of establishing primary responsibility for services that may include search and rescue for VFR aircraft, issuance of NOTAMs, pilot briefings, inflight services, broadcast services, emergency services, flight data processing, international operations, and aviation weather services. Large consolidated FSS facilities may combine FPAs into larger areas of responsibility (AOR).

(See FLIGHT SERVICE STATION.)
(See TIE-IN FACILITY.)

FLIGHT RECORDER– A general term applied to any instrument or device that records information about the performance of an aircraft in flight or about conditions encountered in flight. Flight recorders may make records of airspeed, outside air temperature, vertical acceleration, engine RPM, manifold pressure, and other pertinent variables for a given flight.

(See ICAO term FLIGHT RECORDER.)

FLIGHT RECORDER [ICAO]− Any type of recorder installed in the aircraft for the purpose of complementing accident/incident investigation.

Note: See Annex 6 Part I, for specifications relating to flight recorders.

FLIGHT SERVICE STATION (FSS)− An air traffic facility which provides pilot briefings, flight plan processing, en route flight advisories, search and rescue services, and assistance to lost aircraft and aircraft in emergency situations. FSS also relay ATC clearances, process Notices to Air Missions, and broadcast aviation weather and aeronautical information. In Alaska, FSS provide Airport Advisory Services.

(See FLIGHT PLAN AREA.)
(See TIE-IN FACILITY.)

FLIGHT STANDARDS DISTRICT OFFICE− An FAA field office serving an assigned geographical area and staffed with Flight Standards personnel who serve the aviation industry and the general public on matters relating to the certification and operation of air carrier and general aviation aircraft. Activities include general surveillance of operational safety, certification of airmen and aircraft, accident prevention, investigation, enforcement, etc.

FLIGHT TERMINATION− The intentional and deliberate process of terminating the flight of a UA in the event of an unrecoverable lost link, loss of_control, or other failure that compromises the safety of flight.

FLIGHT TEST− A flight for the purpose of:

a. Investigating the operation/flight characteristics of an aircraft or aircraft component.

b. Evaluating an applicant for a pilot certificate or rating.

FLIGHT VISIBILITY−

(See VISIBILITY.)

FLIP−

(See DoD FLIP.)

FLY-BY WAYPOINT− A fly-by waypoint requires the use of turn anticipation to avoid overshoot of the next flight segment.

FLY HEADING (DEGREES)− Informs the pilot of the heading he/she should fly. The pilot may have to turn to, or continue on, a specific compass direction in order to comply with the instructions. The pilot is expected to turn in the shorter direction to the heading unless otherwise instructed by ATC.

FLY-OVER WAYPOINT− A fly-over waypoint precludes any turn until the waypoint is overflown and is followed by an intercept maneuver of the next flight segment.

FLY VISUAL TO AIRPORT−

(See PUBLISHED INSTRUMENT APPROACH PROCEDURE VISUAL SEGMENT.)

FLYAWAY− When the pilot is unable to effect control of the aircraft and, as a result, the UA is not operating in a predictable or planned manner.

FMA−

(See FINAL MONITOR AID.)

FMS−

(See FLIGHT MANAGEMENT SYSTEM.)

FORMATION FLIGHT− More than one aircraft which, by prior arrangement between the pilots, operate as a single aircraft with regard to navigation and position reporting. Separation between aircraft within the formation is the responsibility of the flight leader and the pilots of the other aircraft in the flight. This includes transition periods when aircraft within the formation are maneuvering to attain separation from each other to effect individual control and during join-up and breakaway.

a. A standard formation is one in which a proximity of no more than 1 mile laterally or longitudinally and within 100 feet vertically from the flight leader is maintained by each wingman.

b. Nonstandard formations are those operating under any of the following conditions:

1. When the flight leader has requested and ATC has approved other than standard formation dimensions.

2. When operating within an authorized altitude reservation (ALTRV) or under the provisions of a letter of agreement.

3. When the operations are conducted in airspace specifically designed for a special activity.

(See ALTITUDE RESERVATION.)

(Refer to 14 CFR Part 91.)

FRC–

(See REQUEST FULL ROUTE CLEARANCE.)

FREEZE/FROZEN– Terms used in referring to arrivals which have been assigned ACLTs and to the lists in which they are displayed.

FREEZE HORIZON– The time or point at which an aircraft's STA becomes fixed and no longer fluctuates with each radar update. This setting ensures a constant time for each aircraft, necessary for the metering controller to plan his/her delay technique. This setting can be either in distance from the meter fix or a prescribed flying time to the meter fix.

FREEZE SPEED PARAMETER– A speed adapted for each aircraft to determine fast and slow aircraft. Fast aircraft freeze on parameter FCLT and slow aircraft freeze on parameter MLDI.

FRIA–

(See FAA–RECOGNIZED IDENTIFICATION AREA.)

FRICTION MEASUREMENT– A measurement of the friction characteristics of the runway pavement surface using continuous self-watering friction measurement equipment in accordance with the specifications, procedures and schedules contained in AC 150/5320–12, Measurement, Construction, and Maintenance of Skid Resistant Airport Pavement Surfaces.

FSDO–

(See FLIGHT STANDARDS DISTRICT OFFICE.)

FSPD–

(See FREEZE SPEED PARAMETER.)

FSS–

(See FLIGHT SERVICE STATION.)

FUEL DUMPING– Airborne release of usable fuel. This does not include the dropping of fuel tanks.

(See JETTISONING OF EXTERNAL STORES.)

FUEL REMAINING– A phrase used by either pilots or controllers when relating to the fuel remaining on board until actual fuel exhaustion. When transmitting such information in response to either a controller question or pilot initiated cautionary advisory to air traffic control, pilots will state the APPROXIMATE NUMBER OF MINUTES the flight can continue with the fuel remaining. All reserve fuel SHOULD BE INCLUDED in the time stated, as should an allowance for established fuel gauge system error.

FUEL SIPHONING– Unintentional release of fuel caused by overflow, puncture, loose cap, etc.

FUEL VENTING–

(See FUEL SIPHONING.)

FUSED TARGET-

(See DIGITAL TARGET)

FUSION [STARS]- the combination of all available surveillance sources (airport surveillance radar [ASR], air route surveillance radar [ARSR], ADS-B, etc.) into the display of a single tracked target for air traffic control separation services. FUSION is the equivalent of the current single-sensor radar display. FUSION performance is characteristic of a single-sensor radar display system. Terminal areas use mono-pulse secondary surveillance radar (ASR 9, Mode S or ASR 11, MSSR).

G

GATE HOLD PROCEDURES– Procedures at selected airports to hold aircraft at the gate or other ground location whenever departure delays exceed or are anticipated to exceed 15 minutes. The sequence for departure will be maintained in accordance with initial call–up unless modified by flow control restrictions. Pilots should monitor the ground control/clearance delivery frequency for engine start/taxi advisories or new proposed start/taxi time if the delay changes.

GCA–
(See GROUND CONTROLLED APPROACH.)

GDP–
(See GROUND DELAY PROGRAM.)

GENERAL AVIATION– That portion of civil aviation that does not include scheduled or unscheduled air carriers or commercial space operations.
(See ICAO term GENERAL AVIATION.)

GENERAL AVIATION [ICAO]– All civil aviation operations other than scheduled air services and nonscheduled air transport operations for remuneration or hire.

GEO MAP– The digitized map markings associated with the ASR-9 Radar System.

GLIDEPATH–
(See GLIDESLOPE.)

GLIDEPATH [ICAO]– A descent profile determined for vertical guidance during a final approach.

GLIDEPATH INTERCEPT ALTITUDE–
(See GLIDESLOPE INTERCEPT ALTITUDE.)

GLIDESLOPE– Provides vertical guidance for aircraft during approach and landing. The glideslope/glidepath is based on the following:

a. Electronic components emitting signals which provide vertical guidance by reference to airborne instruments during instrument approaches such as ILS; or,

b. Visual ground aids, such as VASI, which provide vertical guidance for a VFR approach or for the visual portion of an instrument approach and landing.

c. PAR. Used by ATC to inform an aircraft making a PAR approach of its vertical position (elevation) relative to the descent profile.
(See ICAO term GLIDEPATH.)

GLIDESLOPE INTERCEPT ALTITUDE– The published minimum altitude to intercept the glideslope in the intermediate segment of an instrument approach. Government charts use the lightning bolt symbol to identify this intercept point. This intersection is called the Precise Final Approach fix (PFAF). ATC directs a higher altitude, the resultant intercept becomes the PFAF.
(See FINAL APPROACH FIX.)
(See SEGMENTS OF AN INSTRUMENT APPROACH PROCEDURE.)

GLOBAL NAVIGATION SATELLITE SYSTEM (GNSS)– GNSS refers collectively to the worldwide positioning, navigation, and timing determination capability available from one or more satellite constellations. A GNSS constellation may be augmented by ground stations and/or geostationary satellites to improve integrity and position accuracy.
(See GROUND–BASED AUGMENTATION SYSTEM.)
(See SATELLITE–BASED AUGMENTATION SYSTEM.)

GLOBAL NAVIGATION SATELLITE SYSTEM MINIMUM EN ROUTE IFR ALTITUDE (GNSS MEA)– The minimum en route IFR altitude on a published ATS route or route segment which assures acceptable Global Navigation Satellite System reception and meets obstacle clearance requirements.
(Refer to 14 CFR Part 91.)
(Refer to 14 CFR Part 95.)

GLOBAL POSITIONING SYSTEM (GPS)– GPS refers to the worldwide positioning, navigation and timing determination capability available from the U.S. satellite constellation. The service provided by GPS for civil use is defined in the GPS Standard Positioning System Performance Standard. GPS is composed of space, control, and user elements.

GNSS [ICAO]–
(See GLOBAL NAVIGATION SATELLITE SYSTEM.)

GNSS MEA–
(See GLOBAL NAVIGATION SATELLITE SYSTEM MINIMUM EN ROUTE IFR ALTITUDE.)

GO AHEAD– Proceed with your message. Not to be used for any other purpose.

GO AROUND– Instructions for a pilot to abandon his/her approach to landing. Additional instructions may follow. Unless otherwise advised by ATC, a VFR aircraft or an aircraft conducting visual approach should overfly the runway while climbing to traffic pattern altitude and enter the traffic pattern via the crosswind leg. A pilot on an IFR flight plan making an instrument approach should execute the published missed approach procedure or proceed as instructed by ATC; e.g., "Go around" (additional instructions if required).
(See LOW APPROACH.)
(See MISSED APPROACH.)

GPD–
(See GRAPHIC PLAN DISPLAY.)

GPS–
(See GLOBAL POSITIONING SYSTEM.)

GRAPHICAL AIRMEN'S METEOROLOGICAL INFORMATION– A graphical depiction of weather that may be hazardous to aircraft, but are less severe than SIGMETs. G–AIRMETS are issued 3 hours apart for a period of up to 12 hours into the future for the lower 48 states and coastal waters. The weather hazards depicted can be:

a. Moderate turbulence

b. Low-level windshear

c. Strong surface winds greater than 30 knots

d. Moderate icing

e. Freezing level

f. Mountain obscuration

g. IFR

(See AIRMET.)
(See CONVECTIVE SIGMET.)
(See CWA.)
(See SAW.)
(See SIGMET.)
(Refer to AIM.)

GRAPHIC PLAN DISPLAY (GPD)– A view available with EDST that provides a graphic display of aircraft, traffic, and notification of predicted conflicts. Graphic routes for Current Plans and Trial Plans are displayed upon controller request.
(See EN ROUTE DECISION SUPPORT TOOL.)

GROSS NAVIGATION ERROR (GNE) – A lateral deviation of 10 NM or more from the aircraft's cleared route.

GROUND BASED AUGMENTATION SYSTEM (GBAS)– A ground based GNSS station which provides local differential corrections, integrity parameters and approach data via VHF data broadcast to GNSS users to meet real-time performance requirements for CAT I precision approaches. The aircraft applies the broadcast data to improve the accuracy and integrity of its GNSS signals and computes the deviations to the selected approach. A single ground station can serve multiple runway ends up to an approximate radius of 23 NM.

GROUND BASED AUGMENTATION SYSTEM (GBAS) LANDING SYSTEM (GLS)- A type of precision IAP based on local augmentation of GNSS data using a single GBAS station to transmit locally corrected GNSS data, integrity parameters and approach information. This improves the accuracy of aircraft GNSS receivers' signal in space, enabling the pilot to fly a precision approach with much greater flexibility, reliability and complexity. The GLS procedure is published on standard IAP charts, features the title GLS with the designated runway and minima as low as 200 feet DA. Future plans are expected to support Cat II and CAT III operations.

GROUND–BASED INTERVAL MANAGEMENT–SPACING (GIM–S), SPEED ADVISORY– A calculated speed that will allow aircraft to meet the TBFM schedule at en route and TRACON boundary meter fixes.

GROUND CLUTTER– A pattern produced on the radar scope by ground returns which may degrade other radar returns in the affected area. The effect of ground clutter is minimized by the use of moving target indicator (MTI) circuits in the radar equipment resulting in a radar presentation which displays only targets which are in motion.
(See CLUTTER.)

GROUND COMMUNICATION OUTLET (GCO)– An unstaffed, remotely controlled, ground/ground communications facility. Pilots at uncontrolled airports may contact ATC and FSS via VHF radio to a telephone connection. If the connection goes to ATC, the pilot can obtain an IFR clearance or close an IFR flight plan. If the connection goes to Flight Service, the pilot can open or close a VFR flight plan; obtain an updated weather briefing prior to takeoff; close an IFR flight plan; or, for Alaska or MEDEVAC only, obtain an IFR clearance. Pilots will use four "key clicks" on the VHF radio to contact the appropriate ATC facility or six "key clicks" to contact the FSS. The GCO system is intended to be used only on the ground.

GROUND CONTROLLED APPROACH– A radar approach system operated from the ground by air traffic control personnel transmitting instructions to the pilot by radio. The approach may be conducted with surveillance radar (ASR) only or with both surveillance and precision approach radar (PAR). Usage of the term "GCA" by pilots is discouraged except when referring to a GCA facility. Pilots should specifically request a "PAR" approach when a precision radar approach is desired or request an "ASR" or "surveillance" approach when a nonprecision radar approach is desired.
(See RADAR APPROACH.)

GROUND DELAY PROGRAM (GDP)– A traffic management process administered by the ATCSCC, when aircraft are held on the ground. The purpose of the program is to support the TM mission and limit airborne holding. It is a flexible program and may be implemented in various forms depending upon the needs of the AT system. Ground delay programs provide for equitable assignment of delays to all system users.

GROUND SPEED– The speed of an aircraft relative to the surface of the earth.

GROUND STOP (GS)– The GS is a process that requires aircraft that meet a specific criteria to remain on the ground. The criteria may be airport specific, airspace specific, or equipment specific; for example, all departures to San Francisco, or all departures entering Yorktown sector, or all Category I and II aircraft going to Charlotte. GSs normally occur with little or no warning.

GROUND VISIBILITY–
(See VISIBILITY.)

GS–
(See GROUND STOP.)

H

HAA–
(See HEIGHT ABOVE AIRPORT.)

HAL–
(See HEIGHT ABOVE LANDING.)

HANDOFF– An action taken to transfer the radar identification of an aircraft from one controller to another if the aircraft will enter the receiving controller's airspace and radio communications with the aircraft will be transferred.

HAT–
(See HEIGHT ABOVE TOUCHDOWN.)

HAVE NUMBERS– Used by pilots to inform ATC that they have received runway, wind, and altimeter information only.

HAZARDOUS MATERIALS (HAZMAT)– Hazardous materials as defined by 49 Code of Federal Regulations (CFR) §171.8.
(Refer to 49 CFR Part 171.8)
(Refer to AIM)

HAZARDOUS WEATHER INFORMATION–Summary of significant meteorological information (SIGMET/WS), convective significant meteorological information (convective SIGMET/WST), urgent pilot weather reports (urgent PIREP/UUA), center weather advisories (CWA), airmen's meteorological information (AIRMET/WA), graphical airmen's meteorological information (G–AIRMET) and any other weather such as isolated thunderstorms that are rapidly developing and increasing in intensity, or low ceilings and visibilities that are becoming widespread which is considered significant and are not included in a current hazardous weather advisory.

HAZMAT–
(See HAZARDOUS MATERIALS.)

HEAVY (AIRCRAFT)–
(See AIRCRAFT CLASSES.)

HEIGHT ABOVE AIRPORT (HAA)– The height of the Minimum Descent Altitude above the published airport elevation. This is published in conjunction with circling minimums.
(See MINIMUM DESCENT ALTITUDE.)

HEIGHT ABOVE LANDING (HAL)– The height above a designated helicopter landing area used for helicopter instrument approach procedures.
(Refer to 14 CFR Part 97.)

HEIGHT ABOVE TOUCHDOWN (HAT)– The height of the Decision Height or Minimum Descent Altitude above the highest runway elevation in the touchdown zone (first 3,000 feet of the runway). HAT is published on instrument approach charts in conjunction with all straight-in minimums.
(See DECISION HEIGHT.)
(See MINIMUM DESCENT ALTITUDE.)

HELICOPTER– A heavier-than-air aircraft supported in flight chiefly by the reactions of the air on one or more power-driven rotors on substantially vertical axes.

HELIPAD– A small, designated area, usually with a prepared surface, on a heliport, airport, landing/takeoff area, apron/ramp, or movement area used for takeoff, landing, or parking of helicopters.

HELIPORT– An area of land, water, or structure used or intended to be used for the landing and takeoff of helicopters and includes its buildings and facilities if any.

HELIPORT REFERENCE POINT (HRP)– The geographic center of a heliport.

HERTZ– The standard radio equivalent of frequency in cycles per second of an electromagnetic wave. Kilohertz (kHz) is a frequency of one thousand cycles per second. Megahertz (MHz) is a frequency of one million cycles per second.

HF–
(See HIGH FREQUENCY.)

HF COMMUNICATIONS–
(See HIGH FREQUENCY COMMUNICATIONS.)

HIGH FREQUENCY– The frequency band between 3 and 30 MHz.
(See HIGH FREQUENCY COMMUNICATIONS.)

HIGH FREQUENCY COMMUNICATIONS– High radio frequencies (HF) between 3 and 30 MHz used for air-to-ground voice communication in overseas operations.

HIGH SPEED EXIT–
(See HIGH SPEED TAXIWAY.)

HIGH SPEED TAXIWAY– A long radius taxiway designed and provided with lighting or marking to define the path of aircraft, traveling at high speed (up to 60 knots), from the runway center to a point on the center of a taxiway. Also referred to as long radius exit or turn-off taxiway. The high speed taxiway is designed to expedite aircraft turning off the runway after landing, thus reducing runway occupancy time.

HIGH SPEED TURNOFF–
(See HIGH SPEED TAXIWAY.)

HIGH UPDATE RATE SURVEILLANCE– A surveillance system that provides a sensor update rate of less than 4.8 seconds.

HOLD FOR RELEASE– Used by ATC to delay an aircraft for traffic management reasons; i.e., weather, traffic volume, etc. Hold for release instructions (including departure delay information) are used to inform a pilot or a controller (either directly or through an authorized relay) that an IFR departure clearance is not valid until a release time or additional instructions have been received.
(See ICAO term HOLDING POINT.)

HOLD–IN–LIEU OF PROCEDURE TURN– A hold–in–lieu of procedure turn shall be established over a final or intermediate fix when an approach can be made from a properly aligned holding pattern. The hold–in–lieu of procedure turn permits the pilot to align with the final or intermediate segment of the approach and/or descend in the holding pattern to an altitude that will permit a normal descent to the final approach fix altitude. The hold–in–lieu of procedure turn is a required maneuver (the same as a procedure turn) unless the aircraft is being radar vectored to the final approach course, when "NoPT" is shown on the approach chart, or when the pilot requests or the controller advises the pilot to make a "straight–in" approach.

HOLD PROCEDURE– A predetermined maneuver which keeps aircraft within a specified airspace while awaiting further clearance from air traffic control. Also used during ground operations to keep aircraft within a specified area or at a specified point while awaiting further clearance from air traffic control.
(See HOLDING FIX.)
(Refer to AIM.)

HOLDING FIX– A specified fix identifiable to a pilot by NAVAIDs or visual reference to the ground used as a reference point in establishing and maintaining the position of an aircraft while holding.
(See FIX.)
(See VISUAL HOLDING.)
(Refer to AIM.)

HOLDING POINT [ICAO]– A specified location, identified by visual or other means, in the vicinity of which the position of an aircraft in flight is maintained in accordance with air traffic control clearances.

HOLDING PROCEDURE–
(See HOLD PROCEDURE.)

HOLD-SHORT POINT– A point on the runway beyond which a landing aircraft with a LAHSO clearance is not authorized to proceed. This point may be located prior to an intersecting runway, taxiway, predetermined point, or approach/departure flight path.

HOLD-SHORT POSITION LIGHTS– Flashing in-pavement white lights located at specified hold-short points.

HOLD-SHORT POSITION MARKING– The painted runway marking located at the hold-short point on all LAHSO runways.

HOLD-SHORT POSITION SIGNS– Red and white holding position signs located alongside the hold-short point.

HOMING– Flight toward a NAVAID, without correcting for wind, by adjusting the aircraft heading to maintain a relative bearing of zero degrees.
(See BEARING.)
(See ICAO term HOMING.)

HOMING [ICAO]– The procedure of using the direction-finding equipment of one radio station with the emission of another radio station, where at least one of the stations is mobile, and whereby the mobile station proceeds continuously towards the other station.

HOT SPOT– A location on an airport movement area with a history of potential risk of collision or runway incursion, and where heightened attention by pilots/drivers is necessary.

HOVER CHECK– Used to describe when a helicopter/VTOL aircraft requires a stabilized hover to conduct a performance/power check prior to hover taxi, air taxi, or takeoff. Altitude of the hover will vary based on the purpose of the check.

HOVER TAXI– Used to describe a helicopter/VTOL aircraft movement conducted above the surface and in ground effect at airspeeds less than approximately 20 knots. The actual height may vary, and some helicopters may require hover taxi above 25 feet AGL to reduce ground effect turbulence or provide clearance for cargo slingloads.
(See AIR TAXI.)
(See HOVER CHECK.)
(Refer to AIM.)

HOW DO YOU HEAR ME?– A question relating to the quality of the transmission or to determine how well the transmission is being received.

HZ–
(See HERTZ.)

I

I SAY AGAIN– The message will be repeated.

IAF–
(See INITIAL APPROACH FIX.)

IAP–
(See INSTRUMENT APPROACH PROCEDURE.)

IAWP– Initial Approach Waypoint

ICAO–
(See ICAO Term INTERNATIONAL CIVIL AVIATION ORGANIZATION.)

ICAO 3LD–
(See ICAO Term ICAO Three–Letter Designator)

ICAO Three–Letter Designator (3LD)– An ICAO 3LD is an exclusive designator that, when used together with a flight number, becomes the aircraft call sign and provides distinct aircraft identification to air traffic control (ATC). ICAO approves 3LDs to enhance the safety and security of the air traffic system. An ICAO 3LD may be assigned to a company, agency, or organization and is used instead of the aircraft registration number for ATC operational and security purposes. An ICAO 3LD is also used for aircraft identification in the flight plan and associated messages and can be used for domestic and international flights. A telephony associated with an ICAO 3LD is used for radio communication.

ICING– The accumulation of airframe ice.

Types of icing are:

a. Rime Ice– Rough, milky, opaque ice formed by the instantaneous freezing of small supercooled water droplets.

b. Clear Ice– A glossy, clear, or translucent ice formed by the relatively slow freezing of large supercooled water droplets.

c. Mixed– A mixture of clear ice and rime ice.

Intensity of icing:

a. Trace– Ice becomes noticeable. The rate of accumulation is slightly greater than the rate of sublimation. A representative accretion rate for reference purposes is less than ¼ inch (6 mm) per hour on the outer wing. The pilot should consider exiting the icing conditions before they become worse.

b. Light– The rate of ice accumulation requires occasional cycling of manual deicing systems to minimize ice accretions on the airframe. A representative accretion rate for reference purposes is ¼ inch to 1 inch (0.6 to 2.5 cm) per hour on the unprotected part of the outer wing. The pilot should consider exiting the icing condition.

c. Moderate– The rate of ice accumulation requires frequent cycling of manual deicing systems to minimize ice accretions on the airframe. A representative accretion rate for reference purposes is 1 to 3 inches (2.5 to 7.5 cm) per hour on the unprotected part of the outer wing. The pilot should consider exiting the icing condition as soon as possible.

d. Severe– The rate of ice accumulation is such that ice protection systems fail to remove the accumulation of ice and ice accumulates in locations not normally prone to icing, such as areas aft of protected surfaces and any other areas identified by the manufacturer. A representative accretion rate for reference purposes is more than 3 inches (7.5 cm) per hour on the unprotected part of the outer wing. By regulation, immediate exit is required.

Note:
Severe icing is aircraft dependent, as are the other categories of icing intensity. Severe icing may occur at any ice accumulation rate when the icing rate or ice accumulations exceed the tolerance of the aircraft.

IDAC–
(See INTEGRATED DEPARTURE/ARRIVAL CAPABILITY.)

IDENT– A request for a pilot to activate the aircraft transponder identification feature. This will help the controller to confirm an aircraft identity or to identify an aircraft.
(Refer to AIM.)

IDENT FEATURE– The special feature in the Air Traffic Control Radar Beacon System (ATCRBS) equipment. It is used to immediately distinguish one displayed beacon target from other beacon targets.
(See IDENT.)

IDENTIFICATION [ICAO]– The situation which exists when the position indication of a particular aircraft is seen on a situation display and positively identified.

IF–
(See INTERMEDIATE FIX.)

IF NO TRANSMISSION RECEIVED FOR (TIME)– Used by ATC in radar approaches to prefix procedures which should be followed by the pilot in event of lost communications.
(See LOST COMMUNICATIONS.)

IFR–
(See INSTRUMENT FLIGHT RULES.)

IFR AIRCRAFT– An aircraft conducting flight in accordance with instrument flight rules.

IFR CONDITIONS– Weather conditions below the minimum for flight under visual flight rules.
(See INSTRUMENT METEOROLOGICAL CONDITIONS.)

IFR DEPARTURE PROCEDURE–
(See IFR TAKEOFF MINIMUMS AND DEPARTURE PROCEDURES.)
(Refer to AIM.)

IFR FLIGHT–
(See IFR AIRCRAFT.)

IFR LANDING MINIMUMS–
(See LANDING MINIMUMS.)

IFR MILITARY TRAINING ROUTES (IR)– Routes used by the Department of Defense and associated Reserve and Air Guard units for the purpose of conducting low-altitude navigation and tactical training in both IFR and VFR weather conditions below 10,000 feet MSL at airspeeds in excess of 250 knots IAS.

IFR TAKEOFF MINIMUMS AND DEPARTURE PROCEDURES– Title 14 Code of Federal Regulations Part 91, prescribes standard takeoff rules for certain civil users. At some airports, obstructions or other factors require the establishment of nonstandard takeoff minimums, departure procedures, or both to assist pilots in avoiding obstacles during climb to the minimum en route altitude. Those airports are listed in FAA/DoD Instrument Approach Procedures (IAPs) Charts under a section entitled "IFR Takeoff Minimums and Departure Procedures." The FAA/DoD IAP chart legend illustrates the symbol used to alert the pilot to nonstandard takeoff minimums and departure procedures. When departing IFR from such airports or from any airports where there are no departure procedures, DPs, or ATC facilities available, pilots should advise ATC of any departure limitations. Controllers may query a pilot to determine acceptable departure directions, turns, or headings after takeoff. Pilots should be familiar with the departure procedures and must assure that their aircraft can meet or exceed any specified climb gradients.

IF/IAWP– Intermediate Fix/Initial Approach Waypoint. The waypoint where the final approach course of a T approach meets the crossbar of the T. When designated (in conjunction with a TAA) this waypoint will be used as an IAWP when approaching the airport from certain directions, and as an IFWP when beginning the approach from another IAWP.

IFWP– Intermediate Fix Waypoint

ILS–
(See INSTRUMENT LANDING SYSTEM.)

ILS CATEGORIES– 1. Category I. An ILS approach procedure which provides for approach to a height above touchdown of not less than 200 feet and with runway visual range of not less than 1,800 feet.– 2. Special Authorization Category I. An ILS approach procedure which provides for approach to a height above touchdown of not less than 150 feet and with runway visual range of not less than 1,400 feet, HUD to DH. 3. Category II. An ILS approach procedure which provides for approach to a height above touchdown of not less than 100 feet and with runway visual range of not less than 1,200 feet (with autoland or HUD to touchdown and noted on authorization, RVR 1,000 feet).– 4. Special Authorization Category II with Reduced Lighting. An ILS approach procedure which provides for approach to a height above touchdown of not less than 100 feet and with runway visual range of not less than 1,200 feet with autoland or HUD to touchdown and noted on authorization (no touchdown zone and centerline lighting are required).– 5. Category III:

a. IIIA.–An ILS approach procedure which provides for approach without a decision height minimum and with runway visual range of not less than 700 feet.

b. IIIB.–An ILS approach procedure which provides for approach without a decision height minimum and with runway visual range of not less than 150 feet.

c. IIIC.–An ILS approach procedure which provides for approach without a decision height minimum and without runway visual range minimum.

IM–
(See INNER MARKER.)

IMC–
(See INSTRUMENT METEOROLOGICAL CONDITIONS.)

IMMEDIATELY– Used by ATC or pilots when such action compliance is required to avoid an imminent situation.

INCERFA (Uncertainty Phase) [ICAO]– A situation wherein uncertainty exists as to the safety of an aircraft and its occupants.

INCREASED SEPARATION REQUIRED (ISR)– Indicates the confidence level of the track requires 5 NM separation. 3 NM separation, 1 ½ NM separation, and target resolution cannot be used.

INCREASE SPEED TO (SPEED)–
(See SPEED ADJUSTMENT.)

INERTIAL NAVIGATION SYSTEM (INS)– An RNAV system which is a form of self-contained navigation.
(See Area Navigation/RNAV.)

INFLIGHT REFUELING–
(See AERIAL REFUELING.)

INFLIGHT SERVICES [FSS]– Services provided to or affecting aircraft inflight or otherwise operating on the airport surface. This includes services to airborne aircraft, such as the delivery of ATC clearances, advisories or requests, issuance of military flight advisory messages, NOTAM delivery, search and rescue communications searches, flight plan handling, transcribed or live broadcasts, weather observations, PIREPs, and pilot briefings.

INFLIGHT WEATHER ADVISORY–
(See WEATHER ADVISORY.)

INFORMATION REQUEST (INREQ)– A request originated by an FSS for information concerning an overdue VFR aircraft.

INITIAL APPROACH FIX (IAF)– The fixes depicted on instrument approach procedure charts that identify the beginning of the initial approach segment(s).
(See FIX.)
(See SEGMENTS OF AN INSTRUMENT APPROACH PROCEDURE.)

INITIAL APPROACH SEGMENT–
(See SEGMENTS OF AN INSTRUMENT APPROACH PROCEDURE.)

INITIAL APPROACH SEGMENT [ICAO]– That segment of an instrument approach procedure between the initial approach fix and the intermediate approach fix or, where applicable, the final approach fix or point.

INLAND NAVIGATION FACILITY– A navigation aid on a North American Route at which the common route and/or the noncommon route begins or ends.

INNER MARKER– A marker beacon used with an ILS (CAT II) precision approach located between the middle marker and the end of the ILS runway, transmitting a radiation pattern keyed at six dots per second and indicating to the pilot, both aurally and visually, that he/she is at the designated decision height (DH), normally 100 feet above the touchdown zone elevation, on the ILS CAT II approach. It also marks progress during a CAT III approach.
(See INSTRUMENT LANDING SYSTEM.)
(Refer to AIM.)

INNER MARKER BEACON–
(See INNER MARKER.)

INREQ–
(See INFORMATION REQUEST.)

INS–
(See INERTIAL NAVIGATION SYSTEM.)

INSTRUMENT APPROACH–
(See INSTRUMENT APPROACH PROCEDURE.)

INSTRUMENT APPROACH OPERATIONS [ICAO]– An approach and landing using instruments for navigation guidance based on an instrument approach procedure. There are two methods for executing instrument approach operations:

a. A two–dimensional (2D) instrument approach operation, using lateral navigation guidance only; and

b. A three–dimensional (3D) instrument approach operation, using both lateral and vertical navigation guidance.

Note: Lateral and vertical navigation guidance refers to the guidance provided either by:
a) a ground–based radio navigation aid; or
b) computer–generated navigation data from ground–based, space–based, self–contained navigation aids or a combination of these.

(See ICAO term INSTRUMENT APPROACH PROCEDURE.)

INSTRUMENT APPROACH PROCEDURE– A series of predetermined maneuvers for the orderly transfer of an aircraft under instrument flight conditions from the beginning of the initial approach to a landing or to a point from which a landing may be made visually. It is prescribed and approved for a specific airport by competent authority.
(See SEGMENTS OF AN INSTRUMENT APPROACH PROCEDURE.)
(Refer to 14 CFR Part 91.)
(Refer to AIM.)

a. U.S. civil standard instrument approach procedures are approved by the FAA as prescribed under 14 CFR Part 97 and are available for public use.

b. U.S. military standard instrument approach procedures are approved and published by the Department of Defense.

c. Special instrument approach procedures are approved by the FAA for individual operators but are not published in 14 CFR Part 97 for public use.
(See ICAO term INSTRUMENT APPROACH PROCEDURE.)

INSTRUMENT APPROACH PROCEDURE [ICAO]– A series of predetermined maneuvers by reference to flight instruments with specified protection from obstacles from the initial approach fix, or where applicable, from the beginning of a defined arrival route to a point from which a landing can be completed and thereafter, if a landing is not completed, to a position at which holding or en route obstacle clearance criteria apply.

(See ICAO term INSTRUMENT APPROACH OPERATIONS)

INSTRUMENT APPROACH PROCEDURE CHARTS–

(See AERONAUTICAL CHART.)

INSTRUMENT DEPARTURE PROCEDURE (DP)– A preplanned instrument flight rule (IFR) departure procedure published for pilot use, in graphic or textual format, that provides obstruction clearance from the terminal area to the appropriate en route structure. There are two types of DP, Obstacle Departure Procedure (ODP), printed either textually or graphically, and, Standard Instrument Departure (SID), which is always printed graphically.

(See IFR TAKEOFF MINIMUMS AND DEPARTURE PROCEDURES.)
(See OBSTACLE DEPARTURE PROCEDURES.)
(See STANDARD INSTRUMENT DEPARTURES.)
(Refer to AIM.)

INSTRUMENT DEPARTURE PROCEDURE (DP) CHARTS–

(See AERONAUTICAL CHART.)

INSTRUMENT FLIGHT RULES (IFR)– Rules governing the procedures for conducting instrument flight. Also a term used by pilots and controllers to indicate type of flight plan.

(See INSTRUMENT METEOROLOGICAL CONDITIONS.)
(See VISUAL FLIGHT RULES.)
(See VISUAL METEOROLOGICAL CONDITIONS.)
(See ICAO term INSTRUMENT FLIGHT RULES.)
(Refer to AIM.)

INSTRUMENT FLIGHT RULES [ICAO]– A set of rules governing the conduct of flight under instrument meteorological conditions.

INSTRUMENT LANDING SYSTEM (ILS)– A precision instrument approach system which normally consists of the following electronic components and visual aids:

a. Localizer.
(See LOCALIZER.)

b. Glideslope.
(See GLIDESLOPE.)

c. Outer Marker.
(See OUTER MARKER.)

d. Middle Marker.
(See MIDDLE MARKER.)

e. Approach Lights.
(See AIRPORT LIGHTING.)
(Refer to 14 CFR Part 91.)
(Refer to AIM.)

INSTRUMENT METEOROLOGICAL CONDITIONS (IMC)– Meteorological conditions expressed in terms of visibility, distance from cloud, and ceiling less than the minima specified for visual meteorological conditions.

(See INSTRUMENT FLIGHT RULES.)
(See VISUAL FLIGHT RULES.)
(See VISUAL METEOROLOGICAL CONDITIONS.)

INSTRUMENT RUNWAY– A runway equipped with electronic and visual navigation aids for which a precision or nonprecision approach procedure having straight-in landing minimums has been approved.

(See ICAO term INSTRUMENT RUNWAY.)

INSTRUMENT RUNWAY [ICAO]– One of the following types of runways intended for the operation of aircraft using instrument approach procedures:

a. Nonprecision Approach Runway– An instrument runway served by visual aids and a nonvisual aid providing at least directional guidance adequate for a straight-in approach.

b. Precision Approach Runway, Category I– An instrument runway served by ILS and visual aids intended for operations down to 60 m (200 feet) decision height and down to an RVR of the order of 800 m.

c. Precision Approach Runway, Category II– An instrument runway served by ILS and visual aids intended for operations down to 30 m (100 feet) decision height and down to an RVR of the order of 400 m.

d. Precision Approach Runway, Category III– An instrument runway served by ILS to and along the surface of the runway and:

1. Intended for operations down to an RVR of the order of 200 m (no decision height being applicable) using visual aids during the final phase of landing;

2. Intended for operations down to an RVR of the order of 50 m (no decision height being applicable) using visual aids for taxiing;

3. Intended for operations without reliance on visual reference for landing or taxiing.

Note 1: See Annex 10 Volume I, Part I, Chapter 3, for related ILS specifications.

Note 2: Visual aids need not necessarily be matched to the scale of nonvisual aids provided. The criterion for the selection of visual aids is the conditions in which operations are intended to be conducted.

INTEGRATED DEPARTURE/ARRIVAL CAPABILITY (IDAC)– A Tower/TRACON departure scheduling capability within TBFM that allows departures to be scheduled into either an arrival flow or an en route flow. IDAC provides a mechanism for electronic coordination of departure release times.

INTEGRITY– The ability of a system to provide timely warnings to users when the system should not be used for navigation.

INTERMEDIATE APPROACH SEGMENT–

(See SEGMENTS OF AN INSTRUMENT APPROACH PROCEDURE.)

INTERMEDIATE APPROACH SEGMENT [ICAO]– That segment of an instrument approach procedure between either the intermediate approach fix and the final approach fix or point, or between the end of a reversal, race track or dead reckoning track procedure and the final approach fix or point, as appropriate.

INTERMEDIATE FIX– The fix that identifies the beginning of the intermediate approach segment of an instrument approach procedure. The fix is not normally identified on the instrument approach chart as an intermediate fix (IF).

(See SEGMENTS OF AN INSTRUMENT APPROACH PROCEDURE.)

INTERMEDIATE LANDING– On the rare occasion that this option is requested, it should be approved. The departure center, however, must advise the ATCSCC so that the appropriate delay is carried over and assigned at the intermediate airport. An intermediate landing airport within the arrival center will not be accepted without coordination with and the approval of the ATCSCC.

INTERNATIONAL AIRPORT– Relating to international flight, it means:

a. An airport of entry which has been designated by the Secretary of Treasury or Commissioner of Customs as an international airport for customs service.

b. A landing rights airport at which specific permission to land must be obtained from customs authorities in advance of contemplated use.

c. Airports designated under the Convention on International Civil Aviation as an airport for use by international commercial air transport and/or international general aviation.

(See ICAO term INTERNATIONAL AIRPORT.)

(Refer to Chart Supplement U.S.)

INTERNATIONAL AIRPORT [ICAO]– Any airport designated by the Contracting State in whose territory it is situated as an airport of entry and departure for international air traffic, where the formalities incident to customs, immigration, public health, animal and plant quarantine and similar procedures are carried out.

INTERNATIONAL CIVIL AVIATION ORGANIZATION [ICAO]− A specialized agency of the United Nations whose objective is to develop the principles and techniques of international air navigation and to foster planning and development of international civil air transport.

INTERNATIONAL NOTICE− A notice containing flight prohibitions, potential hostile situations, or other international/foreign oceanic airspace matters. These notices can be found on the International Notices website.

INTERROGATOR− The ground-based surveillance radar beacon transmitter-receiver, which normally scans in synchronism with a primary radar, transmitting discrete radio signals which repetitiously request all transponders on the mode being used to reply. The replies received are mixed with the primary radar returns and displayed on the same plan position indicator (radar scope). Also, applied to the airborne element of the TACAN/DME system.

(See TRANSPONDER.)
(Refer to AIM.)

INTERSECTING RUNWAYS− Two or more runways which cross or meet within their lengths.

(See INTERSECTION.)

INTERSECTION−

a. A point defined by any combination of courses, radials, or bearings of two or more navigational aids.

b. Used to describe the point where two runways, a runway and a taxiway, or two taxiways cross or meet.

INTERSECTION DEPARTURE− A departure from any runway intersection except the end of the runway.

(See INTERSECTION.)

INTERSECTION TAKEOFF−

(See INTERSECTION DEPARTURE.)

IR−

(See IFR MILITARY TRAINING ROUTES.)

IRREGULAR SURFACE− A surface that is open for use but not per regulations.

ISR−

(See INCREASED SEPARATION REQUIRED.)

J

JAMMING− Denotes emissions that do not mimic Global Navigation Satellite System (GNSS) signals (e.g., GPS and WAAS), but rather interfere with the civil receiver's ability to acquire and track GNSS signals. Jamming can result in denial of GNSS navigation, positioning, timing and aircraft dependent functions.

JET BLAST− The rapid air movement produced by exhaust from jet engines.

JET ROUTE− A route designed to serve aircraft operations from 18,000 feet MSL up to and including flight level 450. The routes are referred to as "J" routes with numbering to identify the designated route; e.g., J105.

(See Class A AIRSPACE.)
(Refer to 14 CFR Part 71.)

JET STREAM− A migrating stream of high-speed winds present at high altitudes.

JETTISONING OF EXTERNAL STORES− Airborne release of external stores; e.g., tiptanks, ordnance.

(See FUEL DUMPING.)
(Refer to 14 CFR Part 91.)

JOINT USE RESTRICTED AREA−

(See RESTRICTED AREA.)

JUMP ZONE− The airspace directly associated with a Drop Zone. Vertical and horizontal limits may be locally defined.

K

KNOWN TRAFFIC− With respect to ATC clearances, means aircraft whose altitude, position, and intentions are known to ATC.

L

LAA–
(See LOCAL AIRPORT ADVISORY.)

LAANC–
(See LOW ALTITUDE AUTHORIZATION AND NOTIFICATION CAPABILITY.)

LAHSO– An acronym for "Land and Hold Short Operation." These operations include landing and holding short of an intersecting runway, a taxiway, a predetermined point, or an approach/departure flightpath.

LAHSO-DRY– Land and hold short operations on runways that are dry.

LAHSO-WET– Land and hold short operations on runways that are wet (but not contaminated).

LAND AND HOLD SHORT OPERATIONS– Operations which include simultaneous takeoffs and landings and/or simultaneous landings when a landing aircraft is able and is instructed by the controller to hold-short of the intersecting runway/taxiway or designated hold-short point. Pilots are expected to promptly inform the controller if the hold short clearance cannot be accepted.
(See PARALLEL RUNWAYS.)
(Refer to AIM.)

LAND–BASED AIR DEFENSE IDENTIFICATION ZONE (ADIZ)– An ADIZ over U.S. metropolitan areas, which is activated and deactivated as needed, with dimensions, activation dates, and other relevant information disseminated via NOTAM.
(See AIR DEFENSE IDENTIFICATION ZONE.)

LANDING AREA– Any locality either on land, water, or structures, including airports/heliports and intermediate landing fields, which is used, or intended to be used, for the landing and takeoff of aircraft whether or not facilities are provided for the shelter, servicing, or for receiving or discharging passengers or cargo.
(See ICAO term LANDING AREA.)

LANDING AREA [ICAO]– That part of a movement area intended for the landing or take-off of aircraft.

LANDING DIRECTION INDICATOR– A device which visually indicates the direction in which landings and takeoffs should be made.
(See TETRAHEDRON.)
(Refer to AIM.)

LANDING DISTANCE AVAILABLE (LDA)– The runway length declared available and suitable for a landing airplane.
(See ICAO term LANDING DISTANCE AVAILABLE.)

LANDING DISTANCE AVAILABLE [ICAO]– The length of runway which is declared available and suitable for the ground run of an aeroplane landing.

LANDING MINIMUMS– The minimum visibility prescribed for landing a civil aircraft while using an instrument approach procedure. The minimum applies with other limitations set forth in 14 CFR Part 91 with respect to the Minimum Descent Altitude (MDA) or Decision Height (DH) prescribed in the instrument approach procedures as follows:

a. Straight-in landing minimums. A statement of MDA and visibility, or DH and visibility, required for a straight-in landing on a specified runway, or

b. Circling minimums. A statement of MDA and visibility required for the circle-to-land maneuver.

Note: Descent below the MDA or DH must meet the conditions stated in 14 CFR Section 91.175.
(See CIRCLE-TO-LAND MANEUVER.)
(See DECISION HEIGHT.)
(See INSTRUMENT APPROACH PROCEDURE.)
(See MINIMUM DESCENT ALTITUDE.)
(See STRAIGHT-IN LANDING.)
(See VISIBILITY.)
(Refer to 14 CFR Part 91.)

LANDING ROLL− The distance from the point of touchdown to the point where the aircraft can be brought to a stop or exit the runway.

LANDING SEQUENCE− The order in which aircraft are positioned for landing.
(See APPROACH SEQUENCE.)

LAST ASSIGNED ALTITUDE− The last altitude/flight level assigned by ATC and acknowledged by the pilot.
(See MAINTAIN.)
(Refer to 14 CFR Part 91.)

LATERAL NAVIGATION (LNAV)− A function of area navigation (RNAV) equipment which calculates, displays, and provides lateral guidance to a profile or path.

LATERAL SEPARATION− The lateral spacing of aircraft at the same altitude by requiring operation on different routes or in different geographical locations.
(See SEPARATION.)

LDA−
(See LOCALIZER TYPE DIRECTIONAL AID.)
(See LANDING DISTANCE AVAILABLE.)
(See ICAO Term LANDING DISTANCE AVAILABLE.)

LF−
(See LOW FREQUENCY.)

LIGHTED AIRPORT− An airport where runway and obstruction lighting is available.
(See AIRPORT LIGHTING.)
(Refer to AIM.)

LIGHT GUN− A handheld directional light signaling device which emits a brilliant narrow beam of white, green, or red light as selected by the tower controller. The color and type of light transmitted can be used to approve or disapprove anticipated pilot actions where radio communication is not available. The light gun is used for controlling traffic operating in the vicinity of the airport and on the airport movement area.
(Refer to AIM.)

LIGHT-SPORT AIRCRAFT (LSA)− An FAA-registered aircraft, other than a helicopter or powered-lift, that meets certain weight and performance. Principally it is a single−engine aircraft with a maximum of two seats and weighing no more than 1,430 pounds if intended for operation on water, or 1,320 pounds if not. It must be of simple design (fixed landing gear (except if intended for operations on water or a glider), piston powered, nonpressurized, with a fixed or ground adjustable propeller). Performance is also limited to a maximum airspeed in level flight of not more than 120 knots calibrated airspeed (CAS), have a maximum never-exceed speed of not more than 120 knots CAS for a glider, and have a maximum stalling speed, without the use of lift-enhancing devices of not more than 45 knots CAS. It may be certificated as either Experimental LSA or as a Special LSA aircraft. A minimum of a sport pilot certificate is required to operate light-sport aircraft.
(Refer to 14 CFR Part 1, §1.1.)

LINE UP AND WAIT (LUAW)− Used by ATC to inform a pilot to taxi onto the departure runway to line up and wait. It is not authorization for takeoff. It is used when takeoff clearance cannot immediately be issued because of traffic or other reasons.
(See CLEARED FOR TAKEOFF.)

LOCAL AIRPORT ADVISORY (LAA)− A service available only in Alaska and provided by facilities that are located on the landing airport, have a discrete ground−to−air communication frequency or the tower frequency when the tower is closed, automated weather reporting with voice broadcasting, and a continuous ASOS/AWOS data display, other continuous direct reading instruments, or manual observations available to the specialist.

(See AIRPORT ADVISORY AREA.)

LOCAL TRAFFIC− Aircraft operating in the traffic pattern or within sight of the tower, or aircraft known to be departing or arriving from flight in local practice areas, or aircraft executing practice instrument approaches at the airport.

(See TRAFFIC PATTERN.)

LOCALIZER− The component of an ILS which provides course guidance to the runway.

(See INSTRUMENT LANDING SYSTEM.)
(See ICAO term LOCALIZER COURSE.)
(Refer to AIM.)

LOCALIZER COURSE [ICAO]− The locus of points, in any given horizontal plane, at which the DDM (difference in depth of modulation) is zero.

LOCALIZER OFFSET− An angular offset of the localizer aligned within 3° of the runway alignment.

LOCALIZER TYPE DIRECTIONAL AID (LDA)− A localizer with an angular offset that exceeds 3° of the runway alignment, used for nonprecision instrument approaches with utility and accuracy comparable to a localizer, but which are not part of a complete ILS.

(Refer to AIM.)

LOCALIZER TYPE DIRECTIONAL AID (LDA) PRECISION RUNWAY MONITOR (PRM) APPROACH− An approach, which includes a glideslope, used in conjunction with an ILS PRM, RNAV PRM or GLS PRM approach to an adjacent runway to conduct Simultaneous Offset Instrument Approaches (SOIA) to parallel runways whose centerlines are separated by less than 3,000 feet and at least 750 feet. NTZ monitoring is required to conduct these approaches.

(See SIMULTANEOUS OFFSET INSTRUMENT APPROACH (SOIA).)
(Refer to AIM)

LOCALIZER USABLE DISTANCE− The maximum distance from the localizer transmitter at a specified altitude, as verified by flight inspection, at which reliable course information is continuously received.

(Refer to AIM.)

LOCATOR [ICAO]− An LM/MF NDB used as an aid to final approach.

Note: A locator usually has an average radius of rated coverage of between 18.5 and 46.3 km (10 and 25 NM).

LONG RANGE NAVIGATION−

(See LORAN.)

LONGITUDINAL SEPARATION− The longitudinal spacing of aircraft at the same altitude by a minimum distance expressed in units of time or miles.

(See SEPARATION.)
(Refer to AIM.)

LORAN− An electronic navigational system by which hyperbolic lines of position are determined by measuring the difference in the time of reception of synchronized pulse signals from two fixed transmitters. Loran A operates in the 1750-1950 kHz frequency band. Loran C and D operate in the 100-110 kHz frequency band. In 2010, the U.S. Coast Guard terminated all U.S. LORAN-C transmissions.

(Refer to AIM.)

LOST COMMUNICATIONS− Loss of the ability to communicate by radio. Aircraft are sometimes referred to as NORDO (No Radio). Standard pilot procedures are specified in 14 CFR Part 91. Radar controllers issue procedures for pilots to follow in the event of lost communications during a radar approach when weather reports indicate that an aircraft will likely encounter IFR weather conditions during the approach.

(Refer to 14 CFR Part 91.)
(Refer to AIM.)

LOST LINK (LL)– An interruption or loss of the control link, or when the pilot is unable to effect control of the aircraft and, as a result, the UA will perform a predictable or planned maneuver. Loss of command and control link between the Control Station and the aircraft. There are two types of links:

a. An uplink which transmits command instructions to the aircraft, and

b. A downlink which transmits the status of the aircraft and provides situational awareness to the pilot.

LOST LINK PROCEDURE– Preprogrammed or predetermined mitigations to ensure the continued safe operation of the UA in the event of a lost link (LL). In the event positive link cannot be established, flight termination must be implemented.

LOW ALTITUDE AIRWAY STRUCTURE– The network of airways serving aircraft operations up to but not including 18,000 feet MSL.

(See AIRWAY.)
(Refer to AIM.)

LOW ALTITUDE ALERT, CHECK YOUR ALTITUDE IMMEDIATELY–

(See SAFETY ALERT.)

LOW ALTITUDE AUTHORIZATION AND NOTIFICATION CAPABILITY (LAANC)– FAA and industry collaboration which automates the process of obtaining a required authorization for operations in controlled airspace.

LOW APPROACH– An approach over an airport or runway following an instrument approach or a VFR approach including the go-around maneuver where the pilot intentionally does not make contact with the runway.

(Refer to AIM.)

LOW FREQUENCY (LF)– The frequency band between 30 and 300 kHz.

(Refer to AIM.)

LOCALIZER PERFORMANCE WITH VERTICAL GUIDANCE (LPV)– A type of approach with vertical guidance (APV) based on WAAS, published on RNAV (GPS) approach charts. This procedure takes advantage of the precise lateral guidance available from WAAS. The minima is published as a decision altitude (DA).

LUAW–

(See LINE UP AND WAIT.)

M

MAA–
(See MAXIMUM AUTHORIZED ALTITUDE.)

MACH NUMBER– The ratio of true airspeed to the speed of sound; e.g., MACH .82, MACH 1.6.
(See AIRSPEED.)

MACH TECHNIQUE [ICAO]– Describes a control technique used by air traffic control whereby turbojet aircraft operating successively along suitable routes are cleared to maintain appropriate MACH numbers for a relevant portion of the en route phase of flight. The principal objective is to achieve improved utilization of the airspace and to ensure that separation between successive aircraft does not decrease below the established minima.

MAHWP– Missed Approach Holding Waypoint

MAINTAIN–

a. Concerning altitude/flight level, the term means to remain at the altitude/flight level specified. The phrase "climb and" or "descend and" normally precedes "maintain" and the altitude assignment; e.g., "descend and maintain 5,000."

b. Concerning other ATC instructions, the term is used in its literal sense; e.g., maintain VFR.

MAINTENANCE PLANNING FRICTION LEVEL– The friction level specified in AC 150/5320-12, Measurement, Construction, and Maintenance of Skid Resistant Airport Pavement Surfaces, which represents the friction value below which the runway pavement surface remains acceptable for any category or class of aircraft operations but which is beginning to show signs of deterioration. This value will vary depending on the particular friction measurement equipment used.

MAKE SHORT APPROACH– Used by ATC to inform a pilot to alter his/her traffic pattern so as to make a short final approach.
(See TRAFFIC PATTERN.)

MAN PORTABLE AIR DEFENSE SYSTEMS (MANPADS)– MANPADS are lightweight, shoulder–launched, missile systems used to bring down aircraft and create mass casualties. The potential for MANPADS use against airborne aircraft is real and requires familiarity with the subject. Terrorists choose MANPADS because the weapons are low cost, highly mobile, require minimal set–up time, and are easy to use and maintain. Although the weapons have limited range, and their accuracy is affected by poor visibility and adverse weather, they can be fired from anywhere on land or from boats where there is unrestricted visibility to the target.

MANDATORY ALTITUDE– An altitude depicted on an instrument Approach Procedure Chart requiring the aircraft to maintain altitude at the depicted value.

MANPADS–
(See MAN PORTABLE AIR DEFENSE SYSTEMS.)

MAP–
(See MISSED APPROACH POINT.)

MARKER BEACON– An electronic navigation facility transmitting a 75 MHz vertical fan or boneshaped radiation pattern. Marker beacons are identified by their modulation frequency and keying code, and when received by compatible airborne equipment, indicate to the pilot, both aurally and visually, that he/she is passing over the facility.
(See INNER MARKER.)
(See MIDDLE MARKER.)
(See OUTER MARKER.)
(Refer to AIM.)

MARSA–
(See MILITARY AUTHORITY ASSUMES RESPONSIBILITY FOR SEPARATION OF AIRCRAFT.)

MAWP– Missed Approach Waypoint

MAXIMUM AUTHORIZED ALTITUDE– A published altitude representing the maximum usable altitude or flight level for an airspace structure or route segment. It is the highest altitude on a Federal airway, jet route, area navigation low or high route, or other direct route for which an MEA is designated in 14 CFR Part 95 at which adequate reception of navigation aid signals is assured.

MAXIMUM GROSS OPERATING WEIGHT (MGOW)– The maximum gross weight of an aircraft, including fuel and any external objects, at any point during the flight.

MAYDAY– The international radiotelephony distress signal. When repeated three times, it indicates imminent and grave danger and that immediate assistance is requested.
(See PAN-PAN.)
(Refer to AIM.)

MCA–
(See MINIMUM CROSSING ALTITUDE.)

MDA–
(See MINIMUM DESCENT ALTITUDE.)

MEA–
(See MINIMUM EN ROUTE IFR ALTITUDE.)

MEARTS–
(See MICRO-EN ROUTE AUTOMATED RADAR TRACKING SYSTEM.)

METEOROLOGICAL IMPACT STATEMENT– An unscheduled planning forecast describing conditions expected to begin within 4 to 12 hours which may impact the flow of air traffic in a specific center's (ARTCC) area.

METER FIX ARC– A semicircle, equidistant from a meter fix, usually in low altitude relatively close to the meter fix, used to help TBFM/ERAM calculate a meter time, and determine appropriate sector meter list assignments for aircraft not on an established arrival route or assigned a meter fix.

METER REFERENCE ELEMENT (MRE)– A constraint point through which traffic flows are managed. An MRE can be the runway threshold, a meter fix, or a meter arc.

METER REFERENCE POINT LIST (MRP)– A list of TBFM delay information conveyed to the controller on the situation display via the Meter Reference Point View, commonly known as the "Meter List."

METERING–A method of time–regulating traffic flows in the en route and terminal environments.

METERING AIRPORTS– Airports adapted for metering and for which optimum flight paths are defined. A maximum of 15 airports may be adapted.

METERING FIX– A fix along an established route from over which aircraft will be metered prior to entering terminal airspace. Normally, this fix should be established at a distance from the airport which will facilitate a profile descent 10,000 feet above airport elevation (AAE) or above.

MGOW–
(See MAXIMUM GROSS OPERATING WEIGHT.)

MHA–
(See MINIMUM HOLDING ALTITUDE.)

MIA–
(See MINIMUM IFR ALTITUDES.)

MICROBURST– A small downburst with outbursts of damaging winds extending 2.5 miles or less. In spite of its small horizontal scale, an intense microburst could induce wind speeds as high as 150 knots
(Refer to AIM.)

MICRO-EN ROUTE AUTOMATED RADAR TRACKING SYSTEM (MEARTS)– An automated radar and radar beacon tracking system capable of employing both short-range (ASR) and long-range (ARSR) radars. This microcomputer driven system provides improved tracking, continuous data recording, and use of full digital radar displays.

MID RVR–
(See VISIBILITY.)

MIDDLE COMPASS LOCATOR–
(See COMPASS LOCATOR.)

MIDDLE MARKER– A marker beacon that defines a point along the glideslope of an ILS normally located at or near the point of decision height (ILS Category I). It is keyed to transmit alternate dots and dashes, with the alternate dots and dashes keyed at the rate of 95 dot/dash combinations per minute on a 1300 Hz tone, which is received aurally and visually by compatible airborne equipment.
(See INSTRUMENT LANDING SYSTEM.)
(See MARKER BEACON.)
(Refer to AIM.)

MILES-IN-TRAIL– A specified distance between aircraft, normally, in the same stratum associated with the same destination or route of flight.

MILITARY AUTHORITY ASSUMES RESPONSIBILITY FOR SEPARATION OF AIRCRAFT (MARSA)– A condition whereby the military services involved assume responsibility for separation between participating military aircraft in the ATC system. It is used only for required IFR operations which are specified in letters of agreement or other appropriate FAA or military documents.

MILITARY LANDING ZONE– A landing strip used exclusively by the military for training. A military landing zone does not carry a runway designation.

MILITARY OPERATIONS AREA–
(See SPECIAL USE AIRSPACE.)

MILITARY TRAINING ROUTES– Airspace of defined vertical and lateral dimensions established for the conduct of military flight training at airspeeds in excess of 250 knots IAS.
(See IFR MILITARY TRAINING ROUTES.)
(See VFR MILITARY TRAINING ROUTES.)

MINIMA–
(See MINIMUMS.)

MINIMUM CROSSING ALTITUDE (MCA)– The lowest altitude at certain fixes at which an aircraft must cross when proceeding in the direction of a higher minimum en route IFR altitude (MEA).
(See MINIMUM EN ROUTE IFR ALTITUDE.)

MINIMUM DESCENT ALTITUDE (MDA)– The lowest altitude, expressed in feet above mean sea level, to which descent is authorized on final approach or during circle-to-land maneuvering in execution of a standard instrument approach procedure where no electronic glideslope is provided.
(See NONPRECISION APPROACH PROCEDURE.)

MINIMUM EN ROUTE IFR ALTITUDE (MEA)– The lowest published altitude between radio fixes which assures acceptable navigational signal coverage and meets obstacle clearance requirements between those fixes. The MEA prescribed for a Federal airway or segment thereof, area navigation low or high route, or other direct route applies to the entire width of the airway, segment, or route between the radio fixes defining the airway, segment, or route.

(Refer to 14 CFR Part 91.)
(Refer to 14 CFR Part 95.)
(Refer to AIM.)

MINIMUM FRICTION LEVEL− The friction level specified in AC 150/5320-12, Measurement, Construction, and Maintenance of Skid Resistant Airport Pavement Surfaces, that represents the minimum recommended wet pavement surface friction value for any turbojet aircraft engaged in LAHSO. This value will vary with the particular friction measurement equipment used.

MINIMUM FUEL− Indicates that an aircraft's fuel supply has reached a state where, upon reaching the destination, it can accept little or no delay. This is not an emergency situation but merely indicates an emergency situation is possible should any undue delay occur.

(Refer to AIM.)

MINIMUM HOLDING ALTITUDE− The lowest altitude prescribed for a holding pattern which assures navigational signal coverage, communications, and meets obstacle clearance requirements.

MINIMUM IFR ALTITUDES (MIA)− Minimum altitudes for IFR operations as prescribed in 14 CFR Part 91. These altitudes are published on aeronautical charts and prescribed in 14 CFR Part 95 for airways and routes, and in 14 CFR Part 97 for standard instrument approach procedures. If no applicable minimum altitude is prescribed in 14 CFR Part 95 or 14 CFR Part 97, the following minimum IFR altitude applies:

a. In designated mountainous areas, 2,000 feet above the highest obstacle within a horizontal distance of 4 nautical miles from the course to be flown; or

b. Other than mountainous areas, 1,000 feet above the highest obstacle within a horizontal distance of 4 nautical miles from the course to be flown; or

c. As otherwise authorized by the Administrator or assigned by ATC.

(See MINIMUM CROSSING ALTITUDE.)
(See MINIMUM EN ROUTE IFR ALTITUDE.)
(See MINIMUM OBSTRUCTION CLEARANCE ALTITUDE.)
(See MINIMUM SAFE ALTITUDE.)
(See MINIMUM VECTORING ALTITUDE.)
(Refer to 14 CFR Part 91.)

MINIMUM OBSTRUCTION CLEARANCE ALTITUDE (MOCA)− The lowest published altitude in effect between radio fixes on VOR airways, off-airway routes, or route segments which meets obstacle clearance requirements for the entire route segment and which assures acceptable navigational signal coverage only within 25 statute (22 nautical) miles of a VOR.

(Refer to 14 CFR Part 91.)
(Refer to 14 CFR Part 95.)

MINIMUM RECEPTION ALTITUDE (MRA)− The lowest altitude at which an intersection can be determined.

(Refer to 14 CFR Part 95.)

MINIMUM SAFE ALTITUDE (MSA)−

a. The Minimum Safe Altitude (MSA) specified in 14 CFR Part 91 for various aircraft operations.

b. Altitudes depicted on approach charts or departure procedure (DP) graphic charts which provide at least 1,000 feet of obstacle clearance for emergency use. These altitudes will be identified as Minimum Safe Altitudes or Emergency Safe Altitudes and are established as follows:

1. Minimum Safe Altitude (MSA). Altitudes depicted on approach charts or on a DP graphic chart which provide at least 1,000 feet of obstacle clearance within a 25−mile radius of the navigation facility, waypoint, or airport reference point upon which the MSA is predicated. MSAs are for emergency use only and do not necessarily assure acceptable navigational signal coverage.

(See ICAO term Minimum Sector Altitude.)

2. Emergency Safe Altitude (ESA). Altitudes depicted on approach charts which provide at least 1,000 feet of obstacle clearance in nonmountainous areas and 2,000 feet of obstacle clearance in designated mountainous areas within a 100-mile radius of the navigation facility or waypoint used as the ESA center. These altitudes are normally used only in military procedures and are identified on published procedures as "Emergency Safe Altitudes."

MINIMUM SAFE ALTITUDE WARNING (MSAW)− A function of the EAS and STARS computer that aids the controller by alerting him/her when a tracked Mode C equipped aircraft is below or is predicted by the computer to go below a predetermined minimum safe altitude.
(Refer to AIM.)

MINIMUM SECTOR ALTITUDE [ICAO]− The lowest altitude which may be used under emergency conditions which will provide a minimum clearance of 300 m (1,000 feet) above all obstacles located in an area contained within a sector of a circle of 46 km (25 NM) radius centered on a radio aid to navigation.

MINIMUMS− Weather condition requirements established for a particular operation or type of operation; e.g., IFR takeoff or landing, alternate airport for IFR flight plans, VFR flight, etc.
(See IFR CONDITIONS.)
(See IFR TAKEOFF MINIMUMS AND DEPARTURE PROCEDURES.)
(See LANDING MINIMUMS.)
(See VFR CONDITIONS.)
(Refer to 14 CFR Part 91.)
(Refer to AIM.)

MINIMUM VECTORING ALTITUDE (MVA)− The lowest MSL altitude at which an IFR aircraft will be vectored by a radar controller, except as otherwise authorized for radar approaches, departures, and missed approaches. The altitude meets IFR obstacle clearance criteria. It may be lower than the published MEA along an airway or J-route segment. It may be utilized for radar vectoring only upon the controller's determination that an adequate radar return is being received from the aircraft being controlled. Charts depicting minimum vectoring altitudes are normally available only to the controllers and not to pilots.
(Refer to AIM.)

MINUTES-IN-TRAIL− A specified interval between aircraft expressed in time. This method would more likely be utilized regardless of altitude.

MIS−
(See METEOROLOGICAL IMPACT STATEMENT.)

MISSED APPROACH−

a. A maneuver conducted by a pilot when an instrument approach cannot be completed to a landing. The route of flight and altitude are shown on instrument approach procedure charts. A pilot executing a missed approach prior to the Missed Approach Point (MAP) must continue along the final approach to the MAP.

b. A term used by the pilot to inform ATC that he/she is executing the missed approach.

c. At locations where ATC radar service is provided, the pilot should conform to radar vectors when provided by ATC in lieu of the published missed approach procedure.
(See MISSED APPROACH POINT.)
(Refer to AIM.)

MISSED APPROACH POINT (MAP)− A point prescribed in each instrument approach procedure at which a missed approach procedure shall be executed if the required visual reference does not exist.
(See MISSED APPROACH.)
(See SEGMENTS OF AN INSTRUMENT APPROACH PROCEDURE.)

MISSED APPROACH PROCEDURE [ICAO]− The procedure to be followed if the approach cannot be continued.

MISSED APPROACH SEGMENT−
(See SEGMENTS OF AN INSTRUMENT APPROACH PROCEDURE.)

MM−
(See MIDDLE MARKER.)

MOA−
(See MILITARY OPERATIONS AREA.)

MOCA−
(See MINIMUM OBSTRUCTION CLEARANCE ALTITUDE.)

MODE− The letter or number assigned to a specific pulse spacing of radio signals transmitted or received by ground interrogator or airborne transponder components of the Air Traffic Control Radar Beacon System (ATCRBS). Mode A (military Mode 3) and Mode C (altitude reporting) are used in air traffic control.
(See INTERROGATOR.)
(See RADAR.)
(See TRANSPONDER.)
(See ICAO term MODE.)
(Refer to AIM.)

MODE (SSR MODE) [ICAO]− The letter or number assigned to a specific pulse spacing of the interrogation signals transmitted by an interrogator. There are 4 modes, A, B, C and D specified in Annex 10, corresponding to four different interrogation pulse spacings.

MODE C INTRUDER ALERT− A function of certain air traffic control automated systems designed to alert radar controllers to existing or pending situations between a tracked target (known IFR or VFR aircraft) and an untracked target (unknown IFR or VFR aircraft) that requires immediate attention/action.
(See CONFLICT ALERT.)

MODEL AIRCRAFT− An unmanned aircraft that is: (1) capable of sustained flight in the atmosphere; (2) flown within visual line of sight of the person operating the aircraft; and (3) flown for hobby or recreational purposes.

MONITOR− (When used with communication transfer) listen on a specific frequency and stand by for instructions. Under normal circumstances do not establish communications.

MONITOR ALERT (MA)− A function of the TFMS that provides traffic management personnel with a tool for predicting potential capacity problems in individual operational sectors. The MA is an indication that traffic management personnel need to analyze a particular sector for actual activity and to determine the required action(s), if any, needed to control the demand.

MONITOR ALERT PARAMETER (MAP)− The number designated for use in monitor alert processing by the TFMS. The MAP is designated for each operational sector for increments of 15 minutes.

MOSAIC/MULTI−SENSOR MODE− Accepts positional data from multiple approved surveillance sources. Targets are displayed from a single source according to the hierarchy of the sources assigned in a given geographic area.

MOUNTAIN WAVE− Mountain waves occur when air is being blown over a mountain range or even the ridge of a sharp bluff area. As the air hits the upwind side of the range, it starts to climb, thus creating what is generally a smooth updraft which turns into a turbulent downdraft as the air passes the crest of the ridge. Mountain waves can cause significant fluctuations in airspeed and altitude with or without associated turbulence.
(Refer to AIM.)

MOVEMENT AREA− The runways, taxiways, and other areas of an airport/heliport which are utilized for taxiing/hover taxiing, air taxiing, takeoff, and landing of aircraft, exclusive of loading ramps and parking areas. At those airports/heliports with a tower, specific approval for entry onto the movement area must be obtained from ATC.
(See ICAO term MOVEMENT AREA.)

MOVEMENT AREA [ICAO]– That part of an aerodrome to be used for the takeoff, landing and taxiing of aircraft, consisting of the maneuvering area and the apron(s).

MOVING AIRSPACE RESERVATION– The term used in oceanic ATC for airspace that encompasses oceanic activities and advances with the mission progress; i.e., the reservation moves with the aircraft or flight.

(See MOVING ALTITUDE RESERVATION.)

MOVING ALTITUDE RESERVATION– An altitude reservation which encompasses en route activities and advances with the mission progress; i.e., the reservation moves with the aircraft or flight.

MOVING TARGET INDICATOR– An electronic device which will permit radar scope presentation only from targets which are in motion. A partial remedy for ground clutter.

MRA–

(See MINIMUM RECEPTION ALTITUDE.)

MRE–

(See METER REFERENCE ELEMENT.)

MRP

(See METER REFERENCE POINT LIST.)

MSA–

(See MINIMUM SAFE ALTITUDE.)

MSAW–

(See MINIMUM SAFE ALTITUDE WARNING.)

MTI–

(See MOVING TARGET INDICATOR.)

MTR–

(See MILITARY TRAINING ROUTES.)

MULTICOM– A mobile service not open to public correspondence used to provide communications essential to conduct the activities being performed by or directed from private aircraft.

MULTIPLE RUNWAYS– The utilization of a dedicated arrival runway(s) for departures and a dedicated departure runway(s) for arrivals when feasible to reduce delays and enhance capacity.

MVA–

(See MINIMUM VECTORING ALTITUDE.)

N

NAS–
(See NATIONAL AIRSPACE SYSTEM.)

NAT HLA–
(See NORTH ATLANTIC HIGH LEVEL AIRSPACE.)

NATIONAL AIRSPACE SYSTEM– The common network of U.S. airspace; air navigation facilities, equipment and services, airports or landing areas; aeronautical charts, information and services; rules, regulations and procedures, technical information, and manpower and material. Included are system components shared jointly with the military.

NATIONAL BEACON CODE ALLOCATION PLAN AIRSPACE (NBCAP)– Airspace over United States territory located within the North American continent between Canada and Mexico, including adjacent territorial waters outward to about boundaries of oceanic control areas (CTA)/Flight Information Regions (FIR).
(See FLIGHT INFORMATION REGION.)

NATIONAL FLIGHT DATA DIGEST (NFDD)– A daily (except weekends and Federal holidays) publication of flight information appropriate to aeronautical charts, aeronautical publications, Notices to Air Missions, or other media serving the purpose of providing operational flight data essential to safe and efficient aircraft operations.

NATIONAL SEARCH AND RESCUE PLAN– An interagency agreement which provides for the effective utilization of all available facilities in all types of search and rescue missions.

NATIONAL SECURITY AREA (NSA)–
(See SPECIAL USE AIRSPACE.)

NAVAID–
(See NAVIGATIONAL AID.)

NAVAID CLASSES– VOR, VORTAC, and TACAN aids are classed according to their operational use. The three classes of NAVAIDs are:

a. T– Terminal.

b. L– Low altitude.

c. H– High altitude.

Note: The normal service range for T, L, and H class aids is found in the AIM. Certain operational requirements make it necessary to use some of these aids at greater service ranges than specified. Extended range is made possible through flight inspection determinations. Some aids also have lesser service range due to location, terrain, frequency protection, etc. Restrictions to service range are listed in the Chart Supplement.

NAVIGABLE AIRSPACE– Airspace at and above the minimum flight altitudes prescribed in the CFRs including airspace needed for safe takeoff and landing.
(Refer to 14 CFR Part 91.)

NAVIGATION REFERENCE SYSTEM (NRS)– The NRS is a system of waypoints developed for use within the United States for flight planning and navigation without reference to ground based navigational aids. The NRS waypoints are located in a grid pattern along defined latitude and longitude lines. The initial use of the NRS will be in the high altitude environment. The NRS waypoints are intended for use by aircraft capable of point–to–point navigation.

NAVIGATION SPECIFICATION [ICAO]– A set of aircraft and flight crew requirements needed to support performance–based navigation operations within a defined airspace. There are two kinds of navigation specifications:

a. RNP specification. A navigation specification based on area navigation that includes the requirement for performance monitoring and alerting, designated by the prefix RNP; e.g., RNP 4, RNP APCH.

b. RNAV specification. A navigation specification based on area navigation that does not include the requirement for performance monitoring and alerting, designated by the prefix RNAV; e.g., RNAV 5, RNAV 1.

Note: The Performance–based Navigation Manual (Doc 9613), Volume II contains detailed guidance on navigation specifications.

NAVIGATIONAL AID– Any visual or electronic device airborne or on the surface which provides point-to-point guidance information or position data to aircraft in flight.
(See AIR NAVIGATION FACILITY.)

NAVSPEC-
(See NAVIGATION SPECIFICATION [ICAO].)

NBCAP AIRSPACE–
(See NATIONAL BEACON CODE ALLOCATION PLAN AIRSPACE.)

NDB–
(See NONDIRECTIONAL BEACON.)

NEGATIVE– "No," or "permission not granted," or "that is not correct."

NEGATIVE CONTACT– Used by pilots to inform ATC that:

a. Previously issued traffic is not in sight. It may be followed by the pilot's request for the controller to provide assistance in avoiding the traffic.

b. They were unable to contact ATC on a particular frequency.

NFDD–
(See NATIONAL FLIGHT DATA DIGEST.)

NIGHT– The time between the end of evening civil twilight and the beginning of morning civil twilight, as published in the Air Almanac, converted to local time.
(See ICAO term NIGHT.)

NIGHT [ICAO]– The hours between the end of evening civil twilight and the beginning of morning civil twilight or such other period between sunset and sunrise as may be specified by the appropriate authority.

Note: Civil twilight ends in the evening when the center of the sun's disk is 6 degrees below the horizon and begins in the morning when the center of the sun's disk is 6 degrees below the horizon.

NO GYRO APPROACH– A radar approach/vector provided in case of a malfunctioning gyro-compass or directional gyro. Instead of providing the pilot with headings to be flown, the controller observes the radar track and issues control instructions "turn right/left" or "stop turn" as appropriate.
(Refer to AIM.)

NO GYRO VECTOR–
(See NO GYRO APPROACH.)

NO TRANSGRESSION ZONE (NTZ)– The NTZ is a 2,000 foot wide zone, located equidistant between parallel runway or SOIA final approach courses, in which flight is normally not allowed.

NONAPPROACH CONTROL TOWER– Author-izes aircraft to land or takeoff at the airport controlled by the tower or to transit the Class D airspace. The primary function of a nonapproach control tower is the sequencing of aircraft in the traffic pattern and on the landing area. Nonapproach control towers also separate aircraft operating under instrument flight rules clearances from approach controls and centers. They provide ground control services to aircraft, vehicles, personnel, and equipment on the airport movement area.

NONCOMMON ROUTE/PORTION– That segment of a North American Route between the inland navigation facility and a designated North American terminal.

NON−COOPERATIVE SURVEILLANCE− Any surveillance system, such as primary radar, that is not dependent upon the presence of any equipment on the aircraft or vehicle to be tracked.

(See COOPERATIVE SURVEILLANCE.)
(See RADAR.)

NONDIRECTIONAL BEACON− An L/MF or UHF radio beacon transmitting nondirectional signals whereby the pilot of an aircraft equipped with direction finding equipment can determine his/her bearing to or from the radio beacon and "home" on or track to or from the station. When the radio beacon is installed in conjunction with the Instrument Landing System marker, it is normally called a Compass Locator.

(See AUTOMATIC DIRECTION FINDER.)
(See COMPASS LOCATOR.)

NONMOVEMENT AREAS− Taxiways and apron (ramp) areas not under the control of air traffic.

NONPRECISION APPROACH−

(See NONPRECISION APPROACH PROCEDURE.)

NONPRECISION APPROACH PROCEDURE− A standard instrument approach procedure in which no electronic glideslope is provided; e.g., VOR, TACAN, NDB, LOC, ASR, LDA, or SDF approaches.

NONRADAR− Precedes other terms and generally means without the use of radar, such as:

a. Nonradar Approach. Used to describe instrument approaches for which course guidance on final approach is not provided by ground-based precision or surveillance radar. Radar vectors to the final approach course may or may not be provided by ATC. Examples of nonradar approaches are VOR, NDB, TACAN, ILS, RNAV, and GLS approaches.

(See FINAL APPROACH COURSE.)
(See FINAL APPROACH-IFR.)
(See INSTRUMENT APPROACH PROCEDURE.)
(See RADAR APPROACH.)

b. Nonradar Approach Control. An ATC facility providing approach control service without the use of radar.

(See APPROACH CONTROL FACILITY.)
(See APPROACH CONTROL SERVICE.)

c. Nonradar Arrival. An aircraft arriving at an airport without radar service or at an airport served by a radar facility and radar contact has not been established or has been terminated due to a lack of radar service to the airport.

(See RADAR ARRIVAL.)
(See RADAR SERVICE.)

d. Nonradar Route. A flight path or route over which the pilot is performing his/her own navigation. The pilot may be receiving radar separation, radar monitoring, or other ATC services while on a nonradar route.

(See RADAR ROUTE.)

e. Nonradar Separation. The spacing of aircraft in accordance with established minima without the use of radar; e.g., vertical, lateral, or longitudinal separation.

(See RADAR SEPARATION.)

NON−RESTRICTIVE ROUTING (NRR)− Portions of a proposed route of flight where a user can flight plan the most advantageous flight path with no requirement to make reference to ground−based NAVAIDs.

NOPAC−

(See NORTH PACIFIC.)

NORDO (No Radio)− Aircraft that cannot or do not communicate by radio when radio communication is required are referred to as "NORDO."

(See LOST COMMUNICATIONS.)

NORMAL OPERATING ZONE (NOZ)− The NOZ is the operating zone within which aircraft flight remains during normal independent simultaneous parallel ILS approaches.

NORTH AMERICAN ROUTE– A numerically coded route preplanned over existing airway and route systems to and from specific coastal fixes serving the North Atlantic. North American Routes consist of the following:

a. Common Route/Portion. That segment of a North American Route between the inland navigation facility and the coastal fix.

b. Noncommon Route/Portion. That segment of a North American Route between the inland navigation facility and a designated North American terminal.

c. Inland Navigation Facility. A navigation aid on a North American Route at which the common route and/or the noncommon route begins or ends.

d. Coastal Fix. A navigation aid or intersection where an aircraft transitions between the domestic route structure and the oceanic route structure.

NORTH AMERICAN ROUTE PROGRAM (NRP)– The NRP is a set of rules and procedures which are designed to increase the flexibility of user flight planning within published guidelines.

NORTH ATLANTIC HIGH LEVEL AIRSPACE (NAT HLA)– That volume of airspace (as defined in ICAO Document 7030) between FL 285 and FL 420 within the Oceanic Control Areas of Bodo Oceanic, Gander Oceanic, New York Oceanic East, Reykjavik, Santa Maria, and Shanwick, excluding the Shannon and Brest Ocean Transition Areas. ICAO Doc 007 *North Atlantic Operations and Airspace Manual* provides detailed information on related aircraft and operational requirements.

NORTH PACIFIC– An organized route system between the Alaskan west coast and Japan.

NOT STANDARD– Varying from what is expected or published. For use in NOTAMs only.

NOT STD-
(See NOT STANDARD.)

NOTAM–
(See NOTICE TO AIR MISSIONS.)

NOTAM [ICAO]– A notice containing information concerning the establishment, condition or change in any aeronautical facility, service, procedure or hazard, the timely knowledge of which is essential to personnel concerned with flight operations.

a. I Distribution– Distribution by means of telecommunication.

b. II Distribution– Distribution by means other than telecommunications.

NOTICE TO AIR MISSIONS (NOTAM)– A notice containing information (not known sufficiently in advance to publicize by other means) concerning the establishment, condition, or change in any component (facility, service, or procedure of, or hazard in the National Airspace System) the timely knowledge of which is essential to personnel concerned with flight operations.

a. NOTAM (D)– A NOTAM given (in addition to local dissemination) distant dissemination beyond the area of responsibility of the Flight Service Station. These NOTAMs will be stored and available until canceled.

b. FDC NOTAM– A NOTAM regulatory in nature, transmitted by USNOF and given system wide dissemination.
(See ICAO term NOTAM.)

NRR–
(See NON–RESTRICTIVE ROUTING.)

NRS–
(See NAVIGATION REFERENCE SYSTEM.)

NUMEROUS TARGETS VICINITY (LOCATION)– A traffic advisory issued by ATC to advise pilots that targets on the radar scope are too numerous to issue individually.
(See TRAFFIC ADVISORIES.)

O

OBSTACLE− An existing object, object of natural growth, or terrain at a fixed geographical location or which may be expected at a fixed location within a prescribed area with reference to which vertical clearance is or must be provided during flight operation.

OBSTACLE DEPARTURE PROCEDURE (ODP)− A preplanned instrument flight rule (IFR) departure procedure printed for pilot use in textual or graphic form to provide obstruction clearance via the least onerous route from the terminal area to the appropriate en route structure. ODPs are recommended for obstruction clearance and may be flown without ATC clearance unless an alternate departure procedure (SID or radar vector) has been specifically assigned by ATC.

(See IFR TAKEOFF MINIMUMS AND DEPARTURE PROCEDURES.)
(See STANDARD INSTRUMENT DEPARTURES.)
(Refer to AIM.)

OBSTACLE FREE ZONE− The OFZ is a three−dimensional volume of airspace which protects the transition of aircraft to and from the runway. The OFZ clearing standard precludes taxiing and parked airplanes and object penetrations, except for frangible NAVAID locations that are fixed by function. Additionally, vehicles, equipment, and personnel may be authorized by air traffic control to enter the area using the provisions of FAA Order JO 7110.65, paragraph 3−1−5, Vehicles/Equipment/Personnel Near/On Runways. The runway OFZ and when applicable, the inner-approach OFZ, and the inner-transitional OFZ, comprise the OFZ.

a. Runway OFZ. The runway OFZ is a defined volume of airspace centered above the runway. The runway OFZ is the airspace above a surface whose elevation at any point is the same as the elevation of the nearest point on the runway centerline. The runway OFZ extends 200 feet beyond each end of the runway. The width is as follows:

1. For runways serving large airplanes, the greater of:

(a) 400 feet, or

(b) 180 feet, plus the wingspan of the most demanding airplane, plus 20 feet per 1,000 feet of airport elevation.

2. For runways serving only small airplanes:

(a) 300 feet for precision instrument runways.

(b) 250 feet for other runways serving small airplanes with approach speeds of 50 knots, or more.

(c) 120 feet for other runways serving small airplanes with approach speeds of less than 50 knots.

b. Inner-approach OFZ. The inner-approach OFZ is a defined volume of airspace centered on the approach area. The inner-approach OFZ applies only to runways with an approach lighting system. The inner-approach OFZ begins 200 feet from the runway threshold at the same elevation as the runway threshold and extends 200 feet beyond the last light unit in the approach lighting system. The width of the inner-approach OFZ is the same as the runway OFZ and rises at a slope of 50 (horizontal) to 1 (vertical) from the beginning.

c. Inner-transitional OFZ. The inner transitional surface OFZ is a defined volume of airspace along the sides of the runway and inner-approach OFZ and applies only to precision instrument runways. The inner-transitional surface OFZ slopes 3 (horizontal) to 1 (vertical) out from the edges of the runway OFZ and inner-approach OFZ to a height of 150 feet above the established airport elevation.

(Refer to AC 150/5300-13, Chapter 3.)
(Refer to FAA Order JO 7110.65, Para 3−1−5, Vehicles/Equipment/Personnel Near/On Runways.)

OBSTRUCTION− Any object/obstacle exceeding the obstruction standards specified by 14 CFR Part 77, Subpart C.

OBSTRUCTION LIGHT− A light or one of a group of lights, usually red or white, frequently mounted on a surface structure or natural terrain to warn pilots of the presence of an obstruction.

OCEANIC AIRSPACE– Airspace over the oceans of the world, considered international airspace, where oceanic separation and procedures per the International Civil Aviation Organization are applied. Responsibility for the provisions of air traffic control service in this airspace is delegated to various countries, based generally upon geographic proximity and the availability of the required resources.

OCEANIC ERROR REPORT– A report filed when ATC observes an Oceanic Error as defined by FAA Order JO 7210.632, Air Traffic Organization Occurrence Reporting.

OCEANIC PUBLISHED ROUTE– A route established in international airspace and charted or described in flight information publications, such as Route Charts, DoD En route Charts, Chart Supplements, NOTAMs, and Track Messages.

OCEANIC TRANSITION ROUTE– An ATS route established for the purpose of transitioning aircraft to/from an organized track system.

ODP–
(See OBSTACLE DEPARTURE PROCEDURE.)

OFF COURSE– A term used to describe a situation where an aircraft has reported a position fix or is observed on radar at a point not on the ATC-approved route of flight.

OFF-ROUTE OBSTRUCTION CLEARANCE ALTITUDE (OROCA)– A published altitude which provides terrain and obstruction clearance with a 1,000 foot buffer in non–mountainous areas and a 2,000 foot buffer in designated mountainous areas within the United States, and a 3,000 foot buffer outside the US ADIZ. These altitudes are not assessed for NAVAID signal coverage, air traffic control surveillance, or communications coverage, and are published for general situational awareness, flight planning, and in–flight contingency use.

OFF-ROUTE VECTOR– A vector by ATC which takes an aircraft off a previously assigned route. Altitudes assigned by ATC during such vectors provide required obstacle clearance.

OFFSET PARALLEL RUNWAYS– Staggered runways having centerlines which are parallel.

OFFSHORE/CONTROL AIRSPACE AREA– That portion of airspace between the U.S. 12 NM limit and the oceanic CTA/FIR boundary within which air traffic control is exercised. These areas are established to provide air traffic control services. Offshore/Control Airspace Areas may be classified as either Class A airspace or Class E airspace.

OFT–
(See OUTER FIX TIME.)

OM–
(See OUTER MARKER.)

ON COURSE–

a. Used to indicate that an aircraft is established on the route centerline.

b. Used by ATC to advise a pilot making a radar approach that his/her aircraft is lined up on the final approach course.
(See ON-COURSE INDICATION.)

ON-COURSE INDICATION– An indication on an instrument, which provides the pilot a visual means of determining that the aircraft is located on the centerline of a given navigational track, or an indication on a radar scope that an aircraft is on a given track.

ONE-MINUTE WEATHER– The most recent one minute updated weather broadcast received by a pilot from an uncontrolled airport ASOS/AWOS.

ONER–
(See OCEANIC NAVIGATIONAL ERROR REPORT.)

OOP–
(See OPERATIONS OVER PEOPLE.)

OPEN LOOP CLEARANCE− Provides a lateral vector solution that does not include a return to route point.

OPERATIONAL−
(See DUE REGARD.)

OPERATIONS OVER PEOPLE (OOP)− Operations of small unmanned aircraft over people.
(Refer to 14 CFR Part 107)

OPERATIONS SPECIFICATIONS [ICAO]− The authorizations, conditions and limitations associated with the air operator certificate and subject to the conditions in the operations manual.

OPERATOR (UAS)− The owner and/or remote pilot of a UAS.

OPPOSITE DIRECTION AIRCRAFT− Aircraft are operating in opposite directions when:

a. They are following the same track in reciprocal directions; or

b. Their tracks are parallel and the aircraft are flying in reciprocal directions; or

c. Their tracks intersect at an angle of more than 135°.

OPTION APPROACH− An approach requested and conducted by a pilot which will result in either a touch-and-go, missed approach, low approach, stop-and-go, or full stop landing. Pilots should advise ATC if they decide to remain on the runway, of any delay in their stop and go, delay clearing the runway, or are unable to comply with the instruction(s).
(See CLEARED FOR THE OPTION.)
(Refer to AIM.)

ORGANIZED TRACK SYSTEM− A series of ATS routes which are fixed and charted; i.e., CEP, NOPAC, or flexible and described by NOTAM; i.e., NAT TRACK MESSAGE.

OTR−
(See OCEANIC TRANSITION ROUTE.)

OTS−
(See ORGANIZED TRACK SYSTEM.)

OUT− The conversation is ended and no response is expected.

OUT OF SERVICE/UNSERVICEABLE (U/S)− When a piece of equipment, a NAVAID, a facility or a service is not operational, certified (if required) and immediately "available" for Air Traffic or public use.

OUTER AREA (associated with Class C airspace)− Non−regulatory airspace surrounding designated Class C airspace airports wherein ATC provides radar vectoring and sequencing on a full-time basis for all IFR and participating VFR aircraft. The service provided in the outer area is called Class C service which includes: IFR/IFR−IFR separation; IFR/VFR−traffic advisories and conflict resolution; and VFR/VFR−traffic advisories and, as appropriate, safety alerts. The normal radius will be 20 nautical miles with some variations based on site-specific requirements. The outer area extends outward from the primary Class C airspace airport and extends from the lower limits of radar/radio coverage up to the ceiling of the approach control's delegated airspace excluding the Class C charted area and other airspace as appropriate.
(See CONFLICT RESOLUTION.)
(See CONTROLLED AIRSPACE.)

OUTER COMPASS LOCATOR−
(See COMPASS LOCATOR.)

OUTER FIX− A general term used within ATC to describe fixes in the terminal area, other than the final approach fix. Aircraft are normally cleared to these fixes by an Air Route Traffic Control Center or an Approach Control Facility. Aircraft are normally cleared from these fixes to the final approach fix or final approach course.

OR

OUTER FIX− An adapted fix along the converted route of flight, prior to the meter fix, for which crossing times are calculated and displayed in the metering position list.

OUTER FIX ARC− A semicircle, usually about a 50−70 mile radius from a meter fix, usually in high altitude, which is used by CTAS/ERAM to calculate outer fix times and determine appropriate sector meter list assignments for aircraft on an established arrival route that will traverse the arc.

OUTER FIX TIME− A calculated time to depart the outer fix in order to cross the vertex at the ACLT. The time reflects descent speed adjustments and any applicable delay time that must be absorbed prior to crossing the meter fix.

OUTER MARKER− A marker beacon at or near the glideslope intercept altitude of an ILS approach. It is keyed to transmit two dashes per second on a 400 Hz tone, which is received aurally and visually by compatible airborne equipment. The OM is normally located four to seven miles from the runway threshold on the extended centerline of the runway.

(See INSTRUMENT LANDING SYSTEM.)
(See MARKER BEACON.)
(Refer to AIM.)

OVER− My transmission is ended; I expect a response.

OVERHEAD MANEUVER− A series of predetermined maneuvers prescribed for aircraft (often in formation) for entry into the visual flight rules (VFR) traffic pattern and to proceed to a landing. An overhead maneuver is not an instrument flight rules (IFR) approach procedure. An aircraft executing an overhead maneuver is considered VFR and the IFR flight plan is canceled when the aircraft reaches the "initial point" on the initial approach portion of the maneuver. The pattern usually specifies the following:

a. The radio contact required of the pilot.

b. The speed to be maintained.

c. An initial approach 3 to 5 miles in length.

d. An elliptical pattern consisting of two 180 degree turns.

e. A break point at which the first 180 degree turn is started.

f. The direction of turns.

g. Altitude (at least 500 feet above the conventional pattern).

h. A "Roll-out" on final approach not less than 1/4 mile from the landing threshold and not less than 300 feet above the ground.

OVERLYING CENTER− The ARTCC facility that is responsible for arrival/departure operations at a specific terminal.

P

P TIME–
(See PROPOSED DEPARTURE TIME.)

P-ACP–
(See PREARRANGED COORDINATION PROCEDURES.)

PAN-PAN– The international radio-telephony urgency signal. When repeated three times, indicates uncertainty or alert followed by the nature of the urgency.
(See MAYDAY.)
(Refer to AIM.)

PAO–
(See PUBLIC AIRCRAFT OPERATION.)

PAR–
(See PRECISION APPROACH RADAR.)

PAR [ICAO]–
(See ICAO Term PRECISION APPROACH RADAR.)

PARALLEL ILS APPROACHES– Approaches to parallel runways by IFR aircraft which, when established inbound toward the airport on the adjacent final approach courses, are radar-separated by at least 2 miles.
(See FINAL APPROACH COURSE.)
(See SIMULTANEOUS ILS APPROACHES.)

PARALLEL OFFSET ROUTE– A parallel track to the left or right of the designated or established airway/route. Normally associated with Area Navigation (RNAV) operations.
(See AREA NAVIGATION.)

PARALLEL RUNWAYS– Two or more runways at the same airport whose centerlines are parallel. In addition to runway number, parallel runways are designated as L (left) and R (right) or, if three parallel runways exist, L (left), C (center), and R (right).

PBCT–
(See PROPOSED BOUNDARY CROSSING TIME.)

PBN–
(See ICAO Term PERFORMANCE–BASED NAVIGATION.)

PDC–
(See PRE–DEPARTURE CLEARANCE.)

PDRR–
(See PRE–DEPARTURE REROUTE.)

PERFORMANCE–BASED NAVIGATION (PBN) [ICAO]– Area navigation based on performance requirements for aircraft operating along an ATS route, on an instrument approach procedure or in a designated airspace.

Note: Performance requirements are expressed in navigation specifications (RNAV specification, RNP specification) in terms of accuracy, integrity, continuity, availability, and functionality needed for the proposed operation in the context of a particular airspace concept.

PERMANENT ECHO– Radar signals reflected from fixed objects on the earth's surface; e.g., buildings, towers, terrain. Permanent echoes are distinguished from "ground clutter" by being definable locations rather than large areas. Under certain conditions they may be used to check radar alignment.

PERTI−
(See PLAN, EXECUTE, REVIEW, TRAIN, IMPROVE.)

PGUI−
(See PLANVIEW GRAPHICAL USER INTERFACE.)

PHOTO RECONNAISSANCE− Military activity that requires locating individual photo targets and navigating to the targets at a preplanned angle and altitude. The activity normally requires a lateral route width of 16 NM and altitude range of 1,500 feet to 10,000 feet AGL.

PILOT BRIEFING− The gathering, translation, interpretation, and summarization of weather and aeronautical information into a form usable by the pilot or flight supervisory personnel to assist in flight planning and decision−making for the safe and efficient operation of aircraft. These briefings may include, but are not limited to, weather observations, forecasts, and aeronautical information (for example, NOTAMs, military activities, flow control information, and temporary flight restrictions [TFR]).
(Refer to AIM.)

PILOT IN COMMAND− The pilot responsible for the operation and safety of an aircraft during flight time.
(Refer to 14 CFR Part 91.)

PILOT WEATHER REPORT− A report of meteorological phenomena encountered by aircraft in flight.
(Refer to AIM.)

PILOT'S DISCRETION− When used in conjunction with altitude assignments, means that ATC has offered the pilot the option of starting climb or descent whenever he/she wishes and conducting the climb or descent at any rate he/she wishes. He/she may temporarily level off at any intermediate altitude. However, once he/she has vacated an altitude, he/she may not return to that altitude.

PIREP−
(See PILOT WEATHER REPORT.)

PITCH POINT− A fix/waypoint that serves as a transition point from a departure procedure or the low altitude ground−based navigation structure into the high altitude waypoint system.

PLAN, EXECUTE, REVIEW, TRAIN, IMPROVE (PERTI)− A process that delivers a one−day detailed plan for NAS operations, and a two−day outlook, which sets NAS performance goals for high impact constraints. PLAN: Increase lead time for identifying aviation system constraint planning and goals while utilizing historical NAS performance data and constraints to derive successful and/or improved advance planning strategies. EXECUTE: Set goals and a strategy. The Air Traffic Control System Command Center (ATCSCC), FAA field facilities, and aviation stakeholders execute the strategy and work to achieve the desired/planned outcomes. REVIEW: Utilize post event analysis and lessons learned to define and implement future strategies and operational triggers based on past performance and outcomes, both positive and negative. TRAIN: Develop training that includes rapid and continuous feedback to operational personnel and provides increased data and weather knowledge and tools for analytical usage and planning. IMPROVE: Implement better information sharing processes, technologies, and procedures that improve the skills and technology needed to implement operational insights and improvements.

PLANS DISPLAY− A display available in EDST that provides detailed flight plan and predicted conflict information in textual format for requested Current Plans and all Trial Plans.
(See EN ROUTE DECISION SUPPORT TOOL)

PLANVIEW GRAPHICAL USER INTERFACE (PGUI)− A TBFM display that provides a spatial display of individual aircraft track information.

POFZ−
(See PRECISION OBSTACLE FREE ZONE.)

POINT OUT−
(See RADAR POINT OUT.)

POINT–TO–POINT (PTP)– A level of NRR service for aircraft that is based on traditional waypoints in their FMSs or RNAV equipage.

POLAR TRACK STRUCTURE– A system of organized routes between Iceland and Alaska which overlie Canadian MNPS Airspace.

POSITION REPORT– A report over a known location as transmitted by an aircraft to ATC.
(Refer to AIM.)

POSITION SYMBOL– A computer-generated indication shown on a radar display to indicate the mode of tracking.

POSITIVE CONTROL– The separation of all air traffic within designated airspace by air traffic control.

PRACTICE INSTRUMENT APPROACH– An instrument approach procedure conducted by a VFR or an IFR aircraft for the purpose of pilot training or proficiency demonstrations.

PRE–DEPARTURE CLEARANCE– An application with the Terminal Data Link System (TDLS) that provides clearance information to subscribers, through a service provider, in text to the cockpit or gate printer.

PRE–DEPARTURE REROUTE (PDRR)– A capability within the Traffic Flow Management System that enables ATC to quickly amend and execute revised departure clearances that mitigate en route constraints or balance en route traffic flows.

PREARRANGED COORDINATION– A standardized procedure which permits an air traffic controller to enter the airspace assigned to another air traffic controller without verbal coordination. The procedures are defined in a facility directive which ensures approved separation between aircraft.

PREARRANGED COORDINATION PROCEDURES– A facility's standardized procedure that describes the process by which one controller shall allow an aircraft to penetrate or transit another controller's airspace in a manner that assures approved separation without individual coordination for each aircraft.

PRECIPITATION– Any or all forms of water particles (rain, sleet, hail, or snow) that fall from the atmosphere and reach the surface.

PRECISION APPROACH–
(See PRECISION APPROACH PROCEDURE.)

PRECISION APPROACH PROCEDURE– A standard instrument approach procedure in which an electronic glideslope or other type of glidepath is provided; e.g., ILS, PAR, and GLS.
(See INSTRUMENT LANDING SYSTEM.)
(See PRECISION APPROACH RADAR.)

PRECISION APPROACH RADAR– Radar equipment in some ATC facilities operated by the FAA and/or the military services at joint-use civil/military locations and separate military installations to detect and display azimuth, elevation, and range of aircraft on the final approach course to a runway. This equipment may be used to monitor certain nonradar approaches, but is primarily used to conduct a precision instrument approach (PAR) wherein the controller issues guidance instructions to the pilot based on the aircraft's position in relation to the final approach course (azimuth), the glidepath (elevation), and the distance (range) from the touchdown point on the runway as displayed on the radar scope.
(See GLIDEPATH.)
(See PAR.)
(See ICAO term PRECISION APPROACH RADAR.)
(Refer to AIM.)

PRECISION APPROACH RADAR [ICAO]– Primary radar equipment used to determine the position of an aircraft during final approach, in terms of lateral and vertical deviations relative to a nominal approach path, and in range relative to touchdown.

PRECISION OBSTACLE FREE ZONE (POFZ)– An 800 foot wide by 200 foot long area centered on the runway centerline adjacent to the threshold designed to protect aircraft flying precision approaches from ground vehicles and other aircraft when ceiling is less than 250 feet or visibility is less than 3/4 statute mile (or runway visual range below 4,000 feet.)

PRECISION RUNWAY MONITOR (PRM) SYSTEM– Provides air traffic controllers monitoring the NTZ during simultaneous close parallel PRM approaches with precision, high update rate secondary surveillance data. The high update rate surveillance sensor component of the PRM system is only required for specific runway or approach course separation. The high resolution color monitoring display, Final Monitor Aid (FMA) of the PRM system, or other FMA with the same capability, presents NTZ surveillance track data to controllers along with detailed maps depicting approaches and no transgression zone and is required for all simultaneous close parallel PRM NTZ monitoring operations.

(Refer to AIM.)

PREDICTIVE WIND SHEAR ALERT SYSTEM (PWS)– A self–contained system used on board some aircraft to alert the flight crew to the presence of a potential wind shear. PWS systems typically monitor 3 miles ahead and 25 degrees left and right of the aircraft's heading at or below 1200' AGL. Departing flights may receive a wind shear alert after they start the takeoff roll and may elect to abort the takeoff. Aircraft on approach receiving an alert may elect to go around or perform a wind shear escape maneuver.

PREFERRED IFR ROUTES– Routes established between busier airports to increase system efficiency and capacity. They normally extend through one or more ARTCC areas and are designed to achieve balanced traffic flows among high density terminals. IFR clearances are issued on the basis of these routes except when severe weather avoidance procedures or other factors dictate otherwise. Preferred IFR Routes are listed in the Chart Supplement U.S., and are also available at https://www.fly.faa.gov/rmt/nfdc_preferred_routes_database.jsp. If a flight is planned to or from an area having such routes but the departure or arrival point is not listed in the Chart Supplement U.S., pilots may use that part of a Preferred IFR Route which is appropriate for the departure or arrival point that is listed. Preferred IFR Routes may be defined by DPs, SIDs, or STARs; NAVAIDs, Waypoints, etc.; high or low altitude airways; or any combinations thereof. Because they often share elements with adapted routes, pilots' use of preferred IFR routes can minimize flight plan route amendments.

(See ADAPTED ROUTES.)
(See CENTER'S AREA.)
(See INSTRUMENT APPROACH PROCEDURE.)
(See INSTRUMENT DEPARTURE PROCEDURE.)
(See STANDARD TERMINAL ARRIVAL.)
(Refer to CHART SUPPLEMENT U.S.)

PRE-FLIGHT PILOT BRIEFING–
(See PILOT BRIEFING.)

PREVAILING VISIBILITY–
(See VISIBILITY.)

PRIMARY RADAR TARGET– An analog or digital target, exclusive of a secondary radar target, presented on a radar display.

PRM–
(See AREA NAVIGATION (RNAV) GLOBAL POSITIONING SYSTEM (GPS) PRECISION RUNWAY MONITORING (PRM) APPROACH.)
(See PRM APPROACH.)
(See PRECISION RUNWAY MONITOR SYSTEM.)

PRM APPROACH– An instrument approach procedure titled ILS PRM, RNAV PRM, LDA PRM, or GLS PRM conducted to parallel runways separated by less than 4,300 feet and at least 3,000 feet where independent closely spaced approaches are permitted. Use of an enhanced display with alerting, a No Transgression Zone (NTZ), secondary monitor frequency, pilot PRM training, and publication of an Attention All Users Page are required for all PRM approaches. Depending on the runway spacing, the approach courses may be parallel or one approach course must be offset. PRM procedures are also used to conduct Simultaneous Offset Instrument

Approach (SOIA) operations. In SOIA, one straight–in ILS PRM, RNAV PRM, GLS PRM, and one offset LDA PRM, RNAV PRM or GLS PRM approach are utilized. PRM procedures are terminated and a visual segment begins at the offset approach missed approach point where the minimum distance between the approach courses is 3000 feet. Runway spacing can be as close as 750 feet.

(Refer to AIM.)

PROCEDURAL CONTROL [ICAO]– Term used to indicate that information derived from an ATS surveillance system is not required for the provision of air traffic control service.

PROCEDURAL SEPARATION [ICAO]– The separation used when providing procedural control.

PROCEDURE TURN– The maneuver prescribed when it is necessary to reverse direction to establish an aircraft on the intermediate approach segment or final approach course. The outbound course, direction of turn, distance within which the turn must be completed, and minimum altitude are specified in the procedure. However, unless otherwise restricted, the point at which the turn may be commenced and the type and rate of turn are left to the discretion of the pilot.

(See ICAO term PROCEDURE TURN.)

PROCEDURE TURN [ICAO]– A maneuver in which a turn is made away from a designated track followed by a turn in the opposite direction to permit the aircraft to intercept and proceed along the reciprocal of the designated track.

Note 1: Procedure turns are designated "left" or "right" according to the direction of the initial turn.

Note 2: Procedure turns may be designated as being made either in level flight or while descending, according to the circumstances of each individual approach procedure.

PROCEDURE TURN INBOUND– That point of a procedure turn maneuver where course reversal has been completed and an aircraft is established inbound on the intermediate approach segment or final approach course. A report of "procedure turn inbound" is normally used by ATC as a position report for separation purposes.

(See FINAL APPROACH COURSE.)
(See PROCEDURE TURN.)
(See SEGMENTS OF AN INSTRUMENT APPROACH PROCEDURE.)

PROFILE DESCENT– An uninterrupted descent (except where level flight is required for speed adjustment; e.g., 250 knots at 10,000 feet MSL) from cruising altitude/level to interception of a glideslope or to a minimum altitude specified for the initial or intermediate approach segment of a nonprecision instrument approach. The profile descent normally terminates at the approach gate or where the glideslope or other appropriate minimum altitude is intercepted.

PROGRESS REPORT–

(See POSITION REPORT.)

PROGRESSIVE TAXI– Precise taxi instructions given to a pilot unfamiliar with the airport or issued in stages as the aircraft proceeds along the taxi route.

PROHIBITED AREA–

(See SPECIAL USE AIRSPACE.)
(See ICAO term PROHIBITED AREA.)

PROHIBITED AREA [ICAO]– An airspace of defined dimensions, above the land areas or territorial waters of a State, within which the flight of aircraft is prohibited.

PROMINENT OBSTACLE– An obstacle that meets one or more of the following conditions:

a. An obstacle which stands out beyond the adjacent surface of surrounding terrain and immediately projects a noticeable hazard to aircraft in flight.

b. An obstacle, not characterized as low and close in, whose height is no less than 300 feet above the departure end of takeoff runway (DER) elevation, is within 10 NM from the DER, and that penetrates that airport/heliport's diverse departure obstacle clearance surface (OCS).

c. An obstacle beyond 10 NM from an airport/heliport that requires an obstacle departure procedure (ODP) to ensure obstacle avoidance.

(See OBSTACLE.)
(See OBSTRUCTION.)

PROPELLER (PROP) WASH (PROP BLAST)– The disturbed mass of air generated by the motion of a propeller.

PROPOSED BOUNDARY CROSSING TIME– Each center has a PBCT parameter for each internal airport. Proposed internal flight plans are transmitted to the adjacent center if the flight time along the proposed route from the departure airport to the center boundary is less than or equal to the value of PBCT or if airport adaptation specifies transmission regardless of PBCT.

PROPOSED DEPARTURE TIME– The time that the aircraft expects to become airborne.

PROTECTED AIRSPACE– The airspace on either side of an oceanic route/track that is equal to one-half the lateral separation minimum except where reduction of protected airspace has been authorized.

PROTECTED SEGMENT- The protected segment is a segment on the amended TFM route that is to be inhibited from automatic adapted route alteration by ERAM.

PT–

(See PROCEDURE TURN.)

PTP–

(See POINT–TO–POINT.)

PTS–

(See POLAR TRACK STRUCTURE.)

PUBLIC AIRCRAFT OPERATION (PAO)– A UAS operation meeting the qualifications and conditions required for the operation of a public aircraft.

(See AC–1.1)
(See AIM)

PUBLISHED INSTRUMENT APPROACH PROCEDURE VISUAL SEGMENT– A segment on an IAP chart annotated as "Fly Visual to Airport" or "Fly Visual." A dashed arrow will indicate the visual flight path on the profile and plan view with an associated note on the approximate heading and distance. The visual segment should be flown as a dead reckoning course while maintaining visual conditions.

PUBLISHED ROUTE– A route for which an IFR altitude has been established and published; e.g., Federal Airways, Jet Routes, Area Navigation Routes, Specified Direct Routes.

PWS–

(See PREDICTIVE WIND SHEAR ALERT SYSTEM.)

Q

Q ROUTE– 'Q' is the designator assigned to published RNAV routes used by the United States.

QFE– The atmospheric pressure at aerodrome elevation (or at runway threshold).

QNE– The barometric pressure used for the standard altimeter setting (29.92 inches Hg.).

QNH– The barometric pressure as reported by a particular station.

QUADRANT– A quarter part of a circle, centered on a NAVAID, oriented clockwise from magnetic north as follows: NE quadrant 000-089, SE quadrant 090-179, SW quadrant 180-269, NW quadrant 270-359.

QUEUING–
(See STAGING/QUEUING.)

QUICK LOOK– A feature of the EAS and STARS which provides the controller the capability to display full data blocks of tracked aircraft from other control positions.

R

RAD–
(See ROUTE AMENDMENT DIALOG.)

RADAR– A device that provides information on range, azimuth, and/or elevation of objects by measuring the time interval between transmission and reception of directional radio pulses and correlating the angular orientation of the radiated antenna beam or beams in azimuth and/or elevation.

a. Primary Radar– A radar system in which a minute portion of a radio pulse transmitted from a site is reflected by an object and then received back at that site for processing and display at an air traffic control facility.

b. Secondary Radar/Radar Beacon (ATCRBS)– A radar system in which the object to be detected is fitted with cooperative equipment in the form of a radio receiver/transmitter (transponder). Radar pulses transmitted from the searching transmitter/receiver (interrogator) site are received in the cooperative equipment and used to trigger a distinctive transmission from the transponder. This reply transmission, rather than a reflected signal, is then received back at the transmitter/receiver site for processing and display at an air traffic control facility.
(See COOPERATIVE SURVEILLANCE.)
(See INTERROGATOR.)
(See NON–COOPERATIVE SURVEILLANCE.)
(See TRANSPONDER.)
(See ICAO term RADAR.)
(Refer to AIM.)

RADAR [ICAO]– A radio detection device which provides information on range, azimuth and/or elevation of objects.

a. Primary Radar– Radar system which uses reflected radio signals.

b. Secondary Radar– Radar system wherein a radio signal transmitted from a radar station initiates the transmission of a radio signal from another station.

RADAR ADVISORY– The provision of advice and information based on radar observations.
(See ADVISORY SERVICE.)

RADAR ALTIMETER–
(See RADIO ALTIMETER.)

RADAR APPROACH– An instrument approach procedure which utilizes Precision Approach Radar (PAR) or Airport Surveillance Radar (ASR).
(See AIRPORT SURVEILLANCE RADAR.)
(See INSTRUMENT APPROACH PROCEDURE.)
(See PRECISION APPROACH RADAR.)
(See SURVEILLANCE APPROACH.)
(See ICAO term RADAR APPROACH.)
(Refer to AIM.)

RADAR APPROACH [ICAO]– An approach, executed by an aircraft, under the direction of a radar controller.

RADAR APPROACH CONTROL FACILITY– A terminal ATC facility that uses radar and nonradar capabilities to provide approach control services to aircraft arriving, departing, or transiting airspace controlled by the facility.
(See APPROACH CONTROL SERVICE.)

a. Provides radar ATC services to aircraft operating in the vicinity of one or more civil and/or military airports in a terminal area. The facility may provide services of a ground controlled approach (GCA); i.e., ASR and PAR approaches. A radar approach control facility may be operated by FAA, USAF, US Army, USN, USMC, or jointly by FAA and a military service. Specific facility nomenclatures are used for administrative purposes only and are related to the physical location of the facility and the operating service generally as follows:

1. Army Radar Approach Control (ARAC)
(US Army).

2. Radar Air Traffic Control Facility (RATCF) (USN/FAA and USMC/FAA).

3. Radar Approach Control (RAPCON)
(USAF/FAA, USN/FAA, and USMC/FAA).

4. Terminal Radar Approach Control (TRACON) (FAA).

5. Airport Traffic Control Tower (ATCT) (FAA). (Only those towers delegated approach control authority.)

RADAR ARRIVAL– An aircraft arriving at an airport served by a radar facility and in radar contact with the facility.
(See NONRADAR.)

RADAR BEACON–
(See RADAR.)

RADAR CLUTTER [ICAO]– The visual indication on a radar display of unwanted signals.

RADAR CONTACT–

a. Used by ATC to inform an aircraft that it is identified using an approved ATC surveillance source on an air traffic controller's display and that radar flight following will be provided until radar service is terminated. Radar service may also be provided within the limits of necessity and capability. When a pilot is informed of "radar contact," he/she automatically discontinues reporting over compulsory reporting points.
(See ATC SURVEILLANCE SOURCE.)
(See RADAR CONTACT LOST.)
(See RADAR FLIGHT FOLLOWING.)
(See RADAR SERVICE.)
(See RADAR SERVICE TERMINATED.)
(Refer to AIM.)

b. The term used to inform the controller that the aircraft is identified and approval is granted for the aircraft to enter the receiving controllers airspace.
(See ICAO term RADAR CONTACT.)

RADAR CONTACT [ICAO]– The situation which exists when the radar blip or radar position symbol of a particular aircraft is seen and identified on a radar display.

RADAR CONTACT LOST– Used by ATC to inform a pilot that the surveillance data used to determine the aircraft's position is no longer being received, or is no longer reliable and radar service is no longer being provided. The loss may be attributed to several factors including the aircraft merging with weather or ground clutter, the aircraft operating below radar line of sight coverage, the aircraft entering an area of poor radar return, failure of the aircraft's equipment, or failure of the surveillance equipment.
(See CLUTTER.)
(See RADAR CONTACT.)

RADAR ENVIRONMENT– An area in which radar service may be provided.
(See ADDITIONAL SERVICES.)
(See RADAR CONTACT.)
(See RADAR SERVICE.)
(See TRAFFIC ADVISORIES.)

RADAR FLIGHT FOLLOWING− The observation of the progress of radar−identified aircraft, whose primary navigation is being provided by the pilot, wherein the controller retains and correlates the aircraft identity with the appropriate target or target symbol displayed on the radar scope.

(See RADAR CONTACT.)
(See RADAR SERVICE.)
(Refer to AIM.)

RADAR IDENTIFICATION− The process of ascertaining that an observed radar target is the radar return from a particular aircraft.

(See RADAR CONTACT.)
(See RADAR SERVICE.)

RADAR IDENTIFIED AIRCRAFT− An aircraft, the position of which has been correlated with an observed target or symbol on the radar display.

(See RADAR CONTACT.)
(See RADAR CONTACT LOST.)

RADAR MONITORING−

(See RADAR SERVICE.)

RADAR NAVIGATIONAL GUIDANCE−

(See RADAR SERVICE.)

RADAR POINT OUT− An action taken by a controller to transfer the radar identification of an aircraft to another controller if the aircraft will or may enter the airspace or protected airspace of another controller and radio communications will not be transferred.

RADAR REQUIRED− A term displayed on charts and approach plates and included in FDC NOTAMs to alert pilots that segments of either an instrument approach procedure or a route are not navigable because of either the absence or unusability of a NAVAID. The pilot can expect to be provided radar navigational guidance while transiting segments labeled with this term.

(See RADAR ROUTE.)
(See RADAR SERVICE.)

RADAR ROUTE− A flight path or route over which an aircraft is vectored. Navigational guidance and altitude assignments are provided by ATC.

(See FLIGHT PATH.)
(See ROUTE.)

RADAR SEPARATION−

(See RADAR SERVICE.)

RADAR SERVICE− A term which encompasses one or more of the following services based on the use of radar which can be provided by a controller to a pilot of a radar identified aircraft.

a. Radar Monitoring− The radar flight-following of aircraft, whose primary navigation is being performed by the pilot, to observe and note deviations from its authorized flight path, airway, or route. When being applied specifically to radar monitoring of instrument approaches; i.e., with precision approach radar (PAR) or radar monitoring of simultaneous ILS,RNAV and GLS approaches, it includes advice and instructions whenever an aircraft nears or exceeds the prescribed PAR safety limit or simultaneous ILS RNAV and GLS no transgression zone.

(See ADDITIONAL SERVICES.)
(See TRAFFIC ADVISORIES.)

b. Radar Navigational Guidance− Vectoring aircraft to provide course guidance.

c. Radar Separation− Radar spacing of aircraft in accordance with established minima.

(See ICAO term RADAR SERVICE.)

RADAR SERVICE [ICAO]– Term used to indicate a service provided directly by means of radar.

a. Monitoring– The use of radar for the purpose of providing aircraft with information and advice relative to significant deviations from nominal flight path.

b. Separation– The separation used when aircraft position information is derived from radar sources.

RADAR SERVICE TERMINATED– Used by ATC to inform a pilot that he/she will no longer be provided any of the services that could be received while in radar contact. Radar service is automatically terminated, and the pilot is not advised in the following cases:

a. An aircraft cancels its IFR flight plan, except within Class B airspace, Class C airspace, a TRSA, or where Basic Radar service is provided.

b. An aircraft conducting an instrument, visual, or contact approach has landed or has been instructed to change to advisory frequency.

c. An arriving VFR aircraft, receiving radar service to a tower-controlled airport within Class B airspace, Class C airspace, a TRSA, or where sequencing service is provided, has landed; or to all other airports, is instructed to change to tower or advisory frequency.

d. An aircraft completes a radar approach.

RADAR SURVEILLANCE– The radar observation of a given geographical area for the purpose of performing some radar function.

RADAR TRAFFIC ADVISORIES– Advisories issued to alert pilots to known or observed radar traffic which may affect the intended route of flight of their aircraft.
(See TRAFFIC ADVISORIES.)

RADAR TRAFFIC INFORMATION SERVICE–
(See TRAFFIC ADVISORIES.)

RADAR VECTORING [ICAO]– Provision of navigational guidance to aircraft in the form of specific headings, based on the use of radar.

RADIAL– A magnetic bearing extending from a VOR/VORTAC/TACAN navigation facility.

RADIO–

a. A device used for communication.

b. Used to refer to a flight service station; e.g., "Seattle Radio" is used to call Seattle FSS.

RADIO ALTIMETER– Aircraft equipment which makes use of the reflection of radio waves from the ground to determine the height of the aircraft above the surface.

RADIO BEACON–
(See NONDIRECTIONAL BEACON.)

RADIO–CONTROLLED (RC)– The use of control signals transmitted radio to a remotely controlled device, as in radio–controlled model airplanes.

RADIO DETECTION AND RANGING–
(See RADAR.)

RADIO MAGNETIC INDICATOR– An aircraft navigational instrument coupled with a gyro compass or similar compass that indicates the direction of a selected NAVAID and indicates bearing with respect to the heading of the aircraft.

RAIS–
(See REMOTE AIRPORT INFORMATION SERVICE.)

RAMP–
(See APRON.)

RANDOM ALTITUDE− An altitude inappropriate for direction of flight and/or not in accordance with FAA Order JO 7110.65, paragraph 4−5−1, VERTICAL SEPARATION MINIMA.

RANDOM ROUTE− Any route not established or charted/published or not otherwise available to all users.

RC
(See RADIO−CONTROLLED.)

RC−
(See ROAD RECONNAISSANCE.)

RCAG−
(See REMOTE COMMUNICATIONS AIR/GROUND FACILITY.)

RCC−
(See RESCUE COORDINATION CENTER.)

RCO−
(See REMOTE COMMUNICATIONS OUTLET.)

RCR−
(See RUNWAY CONDITION READING.)

READ BACK− Repeat my message back to me.

RECEIVER AUTONOMOUS INTEGRITY MONITORING (RAIM)− A technique whereby a civil GNSS receiver/processor determines the integrity of the GNSS navigation signals without reference to sensors or non-DoD integrity systems other than the receiver itself. This determination is achieved by a consistency check among redundant pseudorange measurements.

RECEIVING CONTROLLER− A controller/facility receiving control of an aircraft from another controller/facility.

RECEIVING FACILITY−
(See RECEIVING CONTROLLER.)

RECONFORMANCE− The automated process of bringing an aircraft's Current Plan Trajectory into conformance with its track.

RECREATIONAL FLYER− Pilot of a UAS who is operating under 49 USC §44809, Exception for Limited Recreational Operations of Unmanned Aircraft.

REDUCE SPEED TO (SPEED)−
(See SPEED ADJUSTMENT.)

REDUCED VERTICAL SEPARATION MINIMUM (RVSM) AIRSPACE− RVSM airspace is defined as any airspace between FL 290 and FL 410 inclusive, where eligible aircraft are separated vertically by 1,000 feet. Authorization guidance for operations in this airspace is provided in Advisory Circular AC 91−85.

REFINED HAZARD AREA (RHA)− Used by ATC. Airspace that is defined and distributed after a failure of a launch or reentry operation to provide a more concise depiction of the hazard location than a Contingency Hazard Area.
(See AIRCRAFT HAZARD AREA.)
(See CONTINGENCY HAZARD AREA.)
(See TRANSITIONAL HAZARD AREA.)

REIL−
(See RUNWAY END IDENTIFIER LIGHTS.)

RELEASE TIME− A departure time restriction issued to a pilot by ATC (either directly or through an authorized relay) when necessary to separate a departing aircraft from other traffic.
(See ICAO term RELEASE TIME.)

RELEASE TIME [ICAO]– Time prior to which an aircraft should be given further clearance or prior to which it should not proceed in case of radio failure.

REMOTE AIRPORT INFORMATION SERVICE (RAIS)– A temporary service provided by facilities, which are not located on the landing airport, but have communication capability and automated weather reporting available to the pilot at the landing airport.

REMOTE COMMUNICATIONS AIR/GROUND FACILITY– An unmanned VHF/UHF transmitter/receiver facility which is used to expand ARTCC air/ground communications coverage and to facilitate direct contact between pilots and controllers. RCAG facilities are sometimes not equipped with emergency frequencies 121.5 MHz and 243.0 MHz.

(Refer to AIM.)

REMOTE COMMUNICATIONS OUTLET (RCO)– An unmanned communications facility remotely controlled by air traffic personnel. RCOs serve FSSs. Remote Transmitter/Receivers (RTR) serve terminal ATC facilities. An RCO or RTR may be UHF or VHF and will extend the communication range of the air traffic facility. There are several classes of RCOs and RTRs. The class is determined by the number of transmitters or receivers. Classes A through G are used primarily for air/ground purposes. RCO and RTR class O facilities are nonprotected outlets subject to undetected and prolonged outages. RCO (O's) and RTR (O's) were established for the express purpose of providing ground-to-ground communications between air traffic control specialists and pilots located at a satellite airport for delivering en route clearances, issuing departure authorizations, and acknowledging instrument flight rules cancellations or departure/landing times. As a secondary function, they may be used for advisory purposes whenever the aircraft is below the coverage of the primary air/ground frequency.

REMOTE IDENTIFICATION (RID)– A system for electronic identification and secure oversight of UAS.

(See 4 CFR Part 89)

(See AIM)

REMOTE PILOT– Pilot of a UAS who is not operating as a recreational flyer under 49 USC §44809, the Exception for Limited Recreational Operations of Unmanned Aircraft.

REMOTE PILOT IN COMMAND (RPIC)– The RPIC is directly responsible for and is the final authority as to the operation of the unmanned aircraft system.

REMOTE TRANSMITTER/RECEIVER (RTR)–

(See REMOTE COMMUNICATIONS OUTLET.)

REPORT– Used to instruct pilots to advise ATC of specified information; e.g., "Report passing Hamilton VOR."

REPORTING POINT– A geographical location in relation to which the position of an aircraft is reported.

(See COMPULSORY REPORTING POINTS.)

(See ICAO term REPORTING POINT.)

(Refer to AIM.)

REPORTING POINT [ICAO]– A specified geographical location in relation to which the position of an aircraft can be reported.

REQUEST FULL ROUTE CLEARANCE– Used by pilots to request that the entire route of flight be read verbatim in an ATC clearance. Such request should be made to preclude receiving an ATC clearance based on the original filed flight plan when a filed IFR flight plan has been revised by the pilot, company, or operations prior to departure.

REQUIRED NAVIGATION PERFORMANCE (RNP)– A statement of the navigational performance necessary for operation within a defined airspace. The following terms are commonly associated with RNP:

a. Required Navigation Performance Level or Type (RNP-X). A value, in nautical miles (NM), from the intended horizontal position within which an aircraft would be at least 95-percent of the total flying time.

b. Advanced – Required Navigation Performance (A–RNP). A navigation specification based on RNP that requires advanced functions such as scalable RNP, radius–to–fix (RF) legs, and tactical parallel offsets. This sophisticated Navigation Specification (NavSpec) is designated by the abbreviation "A–RNP".

c. Required Navigation Performance (RNP) Airspace. A generic term designating airspace, route(s), leg(s), operation(s), or procedure(s) where minimum required navigational performance (RNP) have been established.

d. Actual Navigation Performance (ANP). A measure of the current estimated navigational performance. Also referred to as Estimated Position Error (EPE).

e. Estimated Position Error (EPE). A measure of the current estimated navigational performance. Also referred to as Actual Navigation Performance (ANP).

f. Lateral Navigation (LNAV). A function of area navigation (RNAV) equipment which calculates, displays, and provides lateral guidance to a profile or path.

g. Vertical Navigation (VNAV). A function of area navigation (RNAV) equipment which calculates, displays, and provides vertical guidance to a profile or path.

REROUTE IMPACT ASSESSMENT (RRIA)– A capability within the Traffic Flow Management System that is used to define and evaluate a potential reroute prior to implementation, with or without miles–in–trail (MIT) restrictions. RRIA functions estimate the impact on demand (e.g., sector loads) and performance (e.g., flight delay). Using RRIA, traffic management personnel can determine whether the reroute will sufficiently reduce demand in the Flow Constraint Area and not create excessive "spill over" demand in the adjacent airspace on a specific route segment or point of interest (POI).

RESCUE COORDINATION CENTER (RCC)– A search and rescue (SAR) facility equipped and manned to coordinate and control SAR operations in an area designated by the SAR plan. The U.S. Coast Guard and the U.S. Air Force have responsibility for the operation of RCCs.

(See ICAO term RESCUE CO-ORDINATION CENTRE.)

RESCUE CO-ORDINATION CENTRE [ICAO]– A unit responsible for promoting efficient organization of search and rescue service and for coordinating the conduct of search and rescue operations within a search and rescue region.

RESOLUTION ADVISORY– A display indication given to the pilot by the Traffic alert and Collision Avoidance System (TCAS II) recommending a maneuver to increase vertical separation relative to an intruding aircraft. Positive, negative, and vertical speed limit (VSL) advisories constitute the resolution advisories. A resolution advisory is also classified as corrective or preventive.

RESTRICTED AREA–

(See SPECIAL USE AIRSPACE.)
(See ICAO term RESTRICTED AREA.)

RESTRICTED AREA [ICAO]– An airspace of defined dimensions, above the land areas or territorial waters of a State, within which the flight of aircraft is restricted in accordance with certain specified conditions.

RESUME NORMAL SPEED– Used by ATC to advise a pilot to resume an aircraft's normal operating speed. It is issued to terminate a speed adjustment where no published speed restrictions apply. It does not delete speed restrictions in published procedures of upcoming segments of flight. This does not relieve the pilot of those speed restrictions that are applicable to 14 CFR Section 91.117.

RESUME OWN NAVIGATION– Used by ATC to advise a pilot to resume his/her own navigational responsibility. It is issued after completion of a radar vector or when radar contact is lost while the aircraft is being radar vectored.

(See RADAR CONTACT LOST.)
(See RADAR SERVICE TERMINATED.)

RESUME PUBLISHED SPEED– Used by ATC to advise a pilot to resume published speed restrictions that are applicable to a SID, STAR, or other instrument procedure. It is issued to terminate a speed adjustment where speed restrictions are published on a charted procedure.

RHA–
(See REFINED HAZARD AREA.)

RID–
(See REMOTE IDENTIFICATION.)

RMI–
(See RADIO MAGNETIC INDICATOR.)

RNAV–
(See AREA NAVIGATION (RNAV).)

RNAV APPROACH– An instrument approach procedure which relies on aircraft area navigation equipment for navigational guidance.
(See AREA NAVIGATION (RNAV).)
(See INSTRUMENT APPROACH PROCEDURE.)

RNAV VISUAL FLIGHT PROCEDURE (RVFP)– An RVFP is a special visual flight procedure flown on an IFR flight plan. It is flown in visual conditions and clear of clouds must be maintained. An RVFP is flown using an approved RNAV system to maintain published lateral and vertical paths to runways without an instrument approach procedure. It requires an ATC clearance and may begin at other points along the path of the charted procedure when approved by ATC. An RVFP is not published in the Federal Register for public use and the operator is required to have a specific Operations Specification approval. Required ceiling and visibility minima are published on the procedure chart. An RVFP does not have a missed approach procedure and is not evaluated for obstacle protection.

ROAD RECONNAISSANCE (RC)– Military activity requiring navigation along roads, railroads, and rivers. Reconnaissance route/route segments are seldom along a straight line and normally require a lateral route width of 10 NM to 30 NM and an altitude range of 500 feet to 10,000 feet AGL.

ROGER– I have received all of your last transmission. It should not be used to answer a question requiring a yes or a no answer.
(See AFFIRMATIVE.)
(See NEGATIVE.)

ROLLOUT RVR–
(See VISIBILITY.)

ROTOR WASH– A phenomenon resulting from the vertical down wash of air generated by the main rotor(s) of a helicopter.

ROUND–ROBIN FLIGHT PLAN– A single flight plan filed from the departure airport to an intermediary destination(s) and then returning to the original departure airport.

ROUTE– A defined path, consisting of one or more courses in a horizontal plane, which aircraft traverse over the surface of the earth.
(See AIRWAY.)
(See JET ROUTE.)
(See PUBLISHED ROUTE.)
(See UNPUBLISHED ROUTE.)

ROUTE ACTION NOTIFICATION– EDST notification that an ADR/ADAR/AAR has been applied to the flight plan.
(See ATC PREFERRED ROUTE NOTIFICATION.)
(See EN ROUTE DECISION SUPPORT TOOL.)

ROUTE AMENDMENT DIALOG (RAD)– A capability within the Traffic Flow Management System that allows traffic management personnel to submit or edit a route amendment for one or more flights.

ROUTE SEGMENT– As used in Air Traffic Control, a part of a route that can be defined by two navigational fixes, two NAVAIDs, or a fix and a NAVAID.
(See FIX.)
(See ROUTE.)
(See ICAO term ROUTE SEGMENT.)

ROUTE SEGMENT [ICAO]– A portion of a route to be flown, as defined by two consecutive significant points specified in a flight plan.

RPIC–
(See REMOTE PILOT IN COMMAND.)

RRIA–
(See REROUTE IMPACT ASSESSMENT.)

RSA–
(See RUNWAY SAFETY AREA.)

RTR–
(See REMOTE TRANSMITTER/RECEIVER.)

RUNWAY– A defined rectangular area on a land airport prepared for the landing and takeoff run of aircraft along its length. Runways are normally numbered in relation to their magnetic direction rounded off to the nearest 10 degrees; e.g., Runway 1, Runway 25.
(See PARALLEL RUNWAYS.)
(See ICAO term RUNWAY.)

RUNWAY [ICAO]– A defined rectangular area on a land aerodrome prepared for the landing and takeoff of aircraft.

RUNWAY CENTERLINE LIGHTING–
(See AIRPORT LIGHTING.)

RUNWAY CONDITION CODES (RwyCC)– Numerical readings, provided by airport operators, that indicate runway surface contamination (for example, slush, ice, rain, etc.). These values range from "1" (poor) to "6" (dry) and must be included on the ATIS when the reportable condition is less than 6 in any one or more of the three runway zones (touchdown, midpoint, rollout).

RUNWAY CONDITION READING– Numerical decelerometer readings relayed by air traffic controllers at USAF and certain civil bases for use by the pilot in determining runway braking action. These readings are routinely relayed only to USAF and Air National Guard Aircraft.
(See BRAKING ACTION.)

RUNWAY CONDITION REPORT (RwyCR)– A data collection worksheet used by airport operators that correlates the runway percentage of coverage along with the depth and type of contaminant for the purpose of creating a FICON NOTAM.
(See RUNWAY CONDITION CODES.)

RUNWAY END IDENTIFIER LIGHTS (REIL)–
(See AIRPORT LIGHTING.)

RUNWAY ENTRANCE LIGHTS (REL)–An array of red lights which include the first light at the hold line followed by a series of evenly spaced lights to the runway edge aligned with the taxiway centerline, and one additional light at the runway centerline in line with the last two lights before the runway edge.

RUNWAY GRADIENT– The average slope, measured in percent, between two ends or points on a runway. Runway gradient is depicted on Government aerodrome sketches when total runway gradient exceeds 0.3%.

RUNWAY HEADING– The magnetic direction that corresponds with the runway centerline extended, not the painted runway number. When cleared to "fly or maintain runway heading," pilots are expected to fly or maintain the heading that corresponds with the extended centerline of the departure runway. Drift correction shall not be applied; e.g., Runway 4, actual magnetic heading of the runway centerline 044, fly 044.

RUNWAY IN USE/ACTIVE RUNWAY/DUTY RUNWAY– Any runway or runways currently being used for takeoff or landing. When multiple runways are used, they are all considered active runways. In the metering sense, a selectable adapted item which specifies the landing runway configuration or direction of traffic flow. The adapted optimum flight plan from each transition fix to the vertex is determined by the runway configuration for arrival metering processing purposes.

RUNWAY LIGHTS–
(See AIRPORT LIGHTING.)

RUNWAY MARKINGS–
(See AIRPORT MARKING AIDS.)

RUNWAY OVERRUN– In military aviation exclusively, a stabilized or paved area beyond the end of a runway, of the same width as the runway plus shoulders, centered on the extended runway centerline.

RUNWAY PROFILE DESCENT– An instrument flight rules (IFR) air traffic control arrival procedure to a runway published for pilot use in graphic and/or textual form and may be associated with a STAR. Runway Profile Descents provide routing and may depict crossing altitudes, speed restrictions, and headings to be flown from the en route structure to the point where the pilot will receive clearance for and execute an instrument approach procedure. A Runway Profile Descent may apply to more than one runway if so stated on the chart.
(Refer to AIM.)

RUNWAY SAFETY AREA– A defined surface surrounding the runway prepared, or suitable, for reducing the risk of damage to airplanes in the event of an undershoot, overshoot, or excursion from the runway. The dimensions of the RSA vary and can be determined by using the criteria contained within AC 150/5300-13, Airport Design, Chapter 3. Figure 3-1 in AC 150/5300-13 depicts the RSA. The design standards dictate that the RSA shall be:

a. Cleared, graded, and have no potentially hazardous ruts, humps, depressions, or other surface variations;

b. Drained by grading or storm sewers to prevent water accumulation;

c. Capable, under dry conditions, of supporting snow removal equipment, aircraft rescue and firefighting equipment, and the occasional passage of aircraft without causing structural damage to the aircraft; and,

d. Free of objects, except for objects that need to be located in the runway safety area because of their function. These objects shall be constructed on low impact resistant supports (frangible mounted structures) to the lowest practical height with the frangible point no higher than 3 inches above grade.
(Refer to AC 150/5300-13, Airport Design, Chapter 3.)

RUNWAY STATUS LIGHTS (RWSL) SYSTEM– The RWSL is a system of runway and taxiway lighting to provide pilots increased situational awareness by illuminating runway entry lights (REL) when the runway is unsafe for entry or crossing, and take-off hold lights (THL) when the runway is unsafe for departure.

RUNWAY TRANSITION–
(See SEGMENTS OF A SID/STAR)

RUNWAY TRANSITION WAYPOINT–
(See SEGMENTS OF A SID/STAR.)

RUNWAY USE PROGRAM– A noise abatement runway selection plan designed to enhance noise abatement efforts with regard to airport communities for arriving and departing aircraft. These plans are developed into runway use programs and apply to all turbojet aircraft 12,500 pounds or heavier; turbojet aircraft less than 12,500 pounds are included only if the airport proprietor determines that the aircraft creates a noise problem. Runway use programs are coordinated with FAA offices, and safety criteria used in these programs are developed by the

Office of Flight Operations. Runway use programs are administered by the Air Traffic Service as "Formal" or "Informal" programs.

a. Formal Runway Use Program− An approved noise abatement program which is defined and acknowledged in a Letter of Understanding between Flight Operations, Air Traffic Service, the airport proprietor, and the users. Once established, participation in the program is mandatory for aircraft operators and pilots as provided for in 14 CFR Section 91.129.

b. Informal Runway Use Program− An approved noise abatement program which does not require a Letter of Understanding, and participation in the program is voluntary for aircraft operators/pilots.

RUNWAY VISUAL RANGE (RVR)−
(See VISIBILITY.)

RVFP−
(See RNAV VISUAL FLIGHT PROCEDURE.)

RwyCC−
(See RUNWAY CONDITION CODES.)

RwyCR−
(See RUNWAY CONDITION REPORT.)

S

SAA–
(See SENSE AND AVOID.)
(See SPECIAL ACTIVITY AIRSPACE.)

SAFETY ALERT– A safety alert issued by ATC to aircraft under their control if ATC is aware the aircraft is at an altitude which, in the controller's judgment, places the aircraft in unsafe proximity to terrain, obstructions, or other aircraft. The controller may discontinue the issuance of further alerts if the pilot advises he/she is taking action to correct the situation or has the other aircraft in sight.

a. Terrain/Obstruction Alert– A safety alert issued by ATC to aircraft under their control if ATC is aware the aircraft is at an altitude which, in the controller's judgment, places the aircraft in unsafe proximity to terrain/obstructions; e.g., "Low Altitude Alert, check your altitude immediately."

b. Aircraft Conflict Alert– A safety alert issued by ATC to aircraft under their control if ATC is aware of an aircraft that is not under their control at an altitude which, in the controller's judgment, places both aircraft in unsafe proximity to each other. With the alert, ATC will offer the pilot an alternate course of action when feasible; e.g., "Traffic Alert, advise you turn right heading zero niner zero or climb to eight thousand immediately."

Note: The issuance of a safety alert is contingent upon the capability of the controller to have an awareness of an unsafe condition. The course of action provided will be predicated on other traffic under ATC control. Once the alert is issued, it is solely the pilot's prerogative to determine what course of action, if any, he/she will take.

SAFETY LOGIC SYSTEM– A software enhancement to ASDE–3, ASDE–X, and ASSC, that predicts the path of aircraft landing and/or departing, and/or vehicular movements on runways. Visual and aural alarms are activated when the safety logic projects a potential collision. The Airport Movement Area Safety System (AMASS) is a safety logic system enhancement to the ASDE–3. The Safety Logic System for ASDE–X and ASSC is an integral part of the software program.

SAFETY LOGIC SYSTEM ALERTS–

a. ALERT–

1. An actual situation involving two real Safety Logic tracks (aircraft/aircraft, aircraft/vehicle, or aircraft/other tangible object) that the Safety Logic System has predicted will result in an imminent collision, based upon the Safety Logic parameters.

2. An actual situation involving a single Safety Logic track arriving to, or departing from, a closed runway.

3. An actual situation involving a single Safety Logic track arriving to a taxiway.

b. FALSE ALERT–

1. Alerts generated by one or more false surface radar or cooperative surveillance targets, that the ASDE system has interpreted as real tracks and placed into Safety Logic.

2. Alerts in which the Safety Logic System did not perform correctly, based upon the design specifications and Safety Logic parameters.

3. Alerts generated by surface radar targets caused by moderate or greater precipitation.

c. NUISANCE ALERT– An alert in which one or more of the following is true:

1. The alert is generated by a known situation that is not considered an unsafe operation, such as LAHSO or other approved operations.

2. The alert is generated by inaccurate cooperative surveillance data received by the Safety Logic System.

3. One or more of the aircraft involved in the alert is not intending to use a runway/taxiway (helicopter, pipeline patrol, non–Mode C overflight, etc.).

d. VALID NON–ALERT– A situation in which the Safety Logic System correctly determines that an alert is not required, based upon the design specifications and Safety Logic parameters.

e. INVALID NON–ALERT– A situation in which the Safety Logic System did not issue an alert when an alert was required, based upon the design specifications and Safety Logic parameters.

SAIL BACK– A maneuver during high wind conditions (usually with power off) where float plane movement is controlled by water rudders/opening and closing cabin doors.

SAME DIRECTION AIRCRAFT– Aircraft are operating in the same direction when:

a. They are following the same track in the same direction; or

b. Their tracks are parallel and the aircraft are flying in the same direction; or

c. Their tracks intersect at an angle of less than 45 degrees.

SAR–
(See SEARCH AND RESCUE.)

SATELLITE–BASED AUGMENTATION SYSTEM (SBAS) – A wide coverage augmentation system in which the user receives augmentation information from a satellite–based transmitter.
(See WIDE–AREA AUGMENTATION SYSTEM (WAAS.)

SAW–
(See AVIATION WATCH NOTIFICATION MESSAGE.)

SAY AGAIN– Used to request a repeat of the last transmission. Usually specifies transmission or portion thereof not understood or received; e.g., "Say again all after ABRAM VOR."

SAY ALTITUDE– Used by ATC to ascertain an aircraft's specific altitude/flight level. When the aircraft is climbing or descending, the pilot should state the indicated altitude rounded to the nearest 100 feet.

SAY HEADING– Used by ATC to request an aircraft heading. The pilot should state the actual heading of the aircraft.

SCHEDULED TIME OF ARRIVAL (STA)– A STA is the desired time that an aircraft should cross a certain point (landing or metering fix). It takes other traffic and airspace configuration into account. A STA time shows the results of the TBFM scheduler that has calculated an arrival time according to parameters such as optimized spacing, aircraft performance, and weather.

SDF–
(See SIMPLIFIED DIRECTIONAL FACILITY.)

SE SAR–
(See SURVEILLANCE ENHANCED SEARCH AND RESCUE.)

SEA LANE– A designated portion of water outlined by visual surface markers for and intended to be used by aircraft designed to operate on water.

SEARCH AND RESCUE– A service which seeks missing aircraft and assists those found to be in need of assistance. It is a cooperative effort using the facilities and services of available Federal, state and local agencies. The U.S. Coast Guard is responsible for coordination of search and rescue for the Maritime Region, and the U.S. Air Force is responsible for search and rescue for the Inland Region. Information pertinent to search and rescue should be passed through any air traffic facility or be transmitted directly to the Rescue Coordination Center by telephone.
(See FLIGHT SERVICE STATION.)
(See RESCUE COORDINATION CENTER.)
(Refer to AIM.)

SEARCH AND RESCUE FACILITY– A facility responsible for maintaining and operating a search and rescue (SAR) service to render aid to persons and property in distress. It is any SAR unit, station, NET, or other operational activity which can be usefully employed during an SAR Mission; e.g., a Civil Air Patrol Wing, or a Coast Guard Station.
(See SEARCH AND RESCUE.)

SECNOT–
(See SECURITY NOTICE.)

SECONDARY RADAR TARGET– A target derived from a transponder return presented on a radar display.

SECTIONAL AERONAUTICAL CHARTS–
(See AERONAUTICAL CHART.)

SECTOR LIST DROP INTERVAL– A parameter number of minutes after the meter fix time when arrival aircraft will be deleted from the arrival sector list.

SECURITY NOTICE (SECNOT) – A SECNOT is a request originated by the Air Traffic Security Coordinator (ATSC) for an extensive communications search for aircraft involved, or suspected of being involved, in a security violation, or are considered a security risk. A SECNOT will include the aircraft identification, search area, and expiration time. The search area, as defined by the ATSC, could be a single airport, multiple airports, a radius of an airport or fix, or a route of flight. Once the expiration time has been reached, the SECNOT is considered to be canceled.

SECURITY SERVICES AIRSPACE – Areas established through the regulatory process or by NOTAM, issued by the Administrator under title 14, CFR, sections 99.7, 91.141, and 91.139, which specify that ATC security services are required; i.e., ADIZ or temporary flight rules areas.

SEE AND AVOID– When weather conditions permit, pilots operating IFR or VFR are required to observe and maneuver to avoid other aircraft. Right-of-way rules are contained in 14 CFR Part 91.

SEGMENTED CIRCLE– A system of visual indicators designed to provide traffic pattern information at airports without operating control towers.
(Refer to AIM.)

SEGMENTS OF A SID/STAR–

a. En Route Transition– The segment(s) of a SID/STAR that connect to/from en route flight. Not all SIDs/STARs will contain an en route transition.

b. En Route Transition Waypoint– The NAVAID/fix/waypoint that defines the beginning of the SID/STAR en route transition.

c. Common Route– The segment(s) of a SID/STAR procedure that provides a single route serving an airport/runway or multiple airports/runways. The common route may consist of a single point. Not all conventional SIDs will contain a common route.

d. Runway Transition– The segment(s) of a SID/STAR between the common route/point and the runway(s). Not all SIDs/STARs will contain a runway transition.

e. Runway Transition Waypoint (RTW)– On a STAR, the NAVAID/fix/waypoint that defines the end of the common route or en route transition and the beginning of a runway transition (In the arrival route description found on the STAR chart, the last fix of the common route and the first fix of the runway transition(s)).

SEGMENTS OF AN INSTRUMENT APPROACH PROCEDURE– An instrument approach procedure may have as many as four separate segments depending on how the approach procedure is structured.

a. Initial Approach– The segment between the initial approach fix and the intermediate fix or the point where the aircraft is established on the intermediate course or final approach course.
(See ICAO term INITIAL APPROACH SEGMENT.)

b. Intermediate Approach– The segment between the intermediate fix or point and the final approach fix.
(See ICAO term INTERMEDIATE APPROACH SEGMENT.)

c. Final Approach– The segment between the final approach fix or point and the runway, airport, or missed approach point.
(See ICAO term FINAL APPROACH SEGMENT.)

d. Missed Approach– The segment between the missed approach point or the point of arrival at decision height and the missed approach fix at the prescribed altitude.
(Refer to 14 CFR Part 97.)
(See ICAO term MISSED APPROACH PROCEDURE.)

SELF–BRIEFING– A self–briefing is a review, using automated tools, of all meteorological and aeronautical information that may influence the pilot in planning, altering, or canceling a proposed route of flight.

SENSE AND AVOID (SAA) – The capability of an unmanned aircraft to detect (sense) and avoid collisions with other aircraft and all obstacles, whether airborne or on the ground while operating in the NAS.

SEPARATION– In air traffic control, the spacing of aircraft to achieve their safe and orderly movement in flight and while landing and taking off.
(See SEPARATION MINIMA.)
(See ICAO term SEPARATION.)

SEPARATION [ICAO]– Spacing between aircraft, levels or tracks.

SEPARATION MINIMA– The minimum longitudinal, lateral, or vertical distances by which aircraft are spaced through the application of air traffic control procedures.
(See SEPARATION.)

SERVICE– A generic term that designates functions or assistance available from or rendered by air traffic control. For example, Class C service would denote the ATC services provided within a Class C airspace area.

SEVERE WEATHER AVOIDANCE PLAN (SWAP)– An approved plan to minimize the affect of severe weather on traffic flows in impacted terminal and/or ARTCC areas. A SWAP is normally implemented to provide the least disruption to the ATC system when flight through portions of airspace is difficult or impossible due to severe weather.

SEVERE WEATHER FORECAST ALERTS– Preliminary messages issued in order to alert users that a Severe Weather Watch Bulletin (WW) is being issued. These messages define areas of possible severe thunderstorms or tornado activity. The messages are unscheduled and issued as required by the Storm Prediction Center (SPC) at Norman, Oklahoma.
(See AIRMET.)
(See CONVECTIVE SIGMET.)
(See CWA.)
(See GRAPHICAL AIRMEN'S METEOROLOGICAL INFORMATION.)
(See SIGMET.)

SFA–
(See SINGLE FREQUENCY APPROACH.)

SFO–
(See SIMULATED FLAMEOUT.)

SGI
(See SPECIAL GOVERNMENT INTEREST.)

SHF–
(See SUPER HIGH FREQUENCY.)

SHORT RANGE CLEARANCE– A clearance issued to a departing IFR flight which authorizes IFR flight to a specific fix short of the destination while air traffic control facilities are coordinating and obtaining the complete clearance.

SHORT TAKEOFF AND LANDING AIRCRAFT (STOL)– An aircraft which, at some weight within its approved operating weight, is capable of operating from a runway in compliance with the applicable STOL characteristics, airworthiness, operations, noise, and pollution standards.
(See VERTICAL TAKEOFF AND LANDING AIRCRAFT.)

SIAP–
(See STANDARD INSTRUMENT APPROACH PROCEDURE.)

SID–
(See STANDARD INSTRUMENT DEPARTURE.)

SIDESTEP MANEUVER– A visual maneuver accomplished by a pilot at the completion of an instrument approach to permit a straight-in landing on a parallel runway not more than 1,200 feet to either side of the runway to which the instrument approach was conducted.

(Refer to AIM.)

SIGMET– A weather advisory issued concerning weather significant to the safety of all aircraft. SIGMET advisories cover severe and extreme turbulence, severe icing, and widespread dust or sandstorms that reduce visibility to less than 3 miles.

(See AIRMET.)
(See CONVECTIVE SIGMET.)
(See CWA.)
(See GRAPHICAL AIRMEN'S METEOROLOGICAL INFORMATION.)
(See ICAO term SIGMET INFORMATION.)
(See SAW.)
(Refer to AIM.)

SIGMET INFORMATION [ICAO]– Information issued by a meteorological watch office concerning the occurrence or expected occurrence of specified en-route weather phenomena which may affect the safety of aircraft operations.

SIGNIFICANT METEOROLOGICAL INFORMATION–

(See SIGMET.)

SIGNIFICANT POINT– A point, whether a named intersection, a NAVAID, a fix derived from a NAVAID(s), or geographical coordinate expressed in degrees of latitude and longitude, which is established for the purpose of providing separation, as a reporting point, or to delineate a route of flight.

SIMPLIFIED DIRECTIONAL FACILITY (SDF)– A NAVAID used for nonprecision instrument approaches. The final approach course is similar to that of an ILS localizer except that the SDF course may be offset from the runway, generally not more than 3 degrees, and the course may be wider than the localizer, resulting in a lower degree of accuracy.

(Refer to AIM.)

SIMULATED FLAMEOUT– A practice approach by a jet aircraft (normally military) at idle thrust to a runway. The approach may start at a runway (high key) and may continue on a relatively high and wide downwind leg with a continuous turn to final. It terminates in landing or low approach. The purpose of this approach is to simulate a flameout.

(See FLAMEOUT.)

SIMULTANEOUS CLOSE PARALLEL APPROACHES– A simultaneous, independent approach operation permitting ILS/RNAV/GLS approaches to airports having parallel runways separated by at least 3,000 feet and less than 4,300–feet between centerlines. Aircraft are permitted to pass each other during these simultaneous operations. Integral parts of a total system are radar, NTZ monitoring with enhanced FMA color displays that include aural and visual alerts and predictive aircraft position software, communications override, ATC procedures, an Attention All Users Page (AAUP), PRM in the approach name, and appropriate ground based and airborne equipment. High update rate surveillance sensor required for certain runway or approach course separations.

SIMULTANEOUS (CONVERGING) DEPENDENT APPROACHES- An approach operation permitting ILS/RNAV/GLS approaches to runways or missed approach courses that intersect where required minimum spacing between the aircraft on each final approach course is required.

SIMULTANEOUS (CONVERGING) INDEPENDENT APPROACHES- An approach operation permitting ILS/RNAV/GLS approaches to non-parallel runways where approach procedure design maintains the required aircraft spacing throughout the approach and missed approach and hence the operations may be conducted independently.

SIMULTANEOUS ILS APPROACHES– An approach system permitting simultaneous ILS approaches to airports having parallel runways separated by at least 4,300 feet between centerlines. Integral parts of a total system are ILS, radar, communications, ATC procedures, and appropriate airborne equipment.
(See PARALLEL RUNWAYS.)
(Refer to AIM.)

SIMULTANEOUS OFFSET INSTRUMENT APPROACH (SOIA)– An instrument landing system comprised of an ILS PRM, RNAV PRM or GLS PRM approach to one runway and an offset LDA PRM with glideslope or an RNAV PRM or GLS PRM approach utilizing vertical guidance to another where parallel runway spaced less than 3,000 feet and at least 750 feet apart. The approach courses converge by 2.5 to 3 degrees. Simultaneous close parallel PRM approach procedures apply up to the point where the approach course separation becomes 3,000 feet, at the offset MAP. From the offset MAP to the runway threshold, visual separation by the aircraft conducting the offset approach is utilized.
(Refer to AIM)

SIMULTANEOUS (PARALLEL) DEPENDENT APPROACHES- An approach operation permitting ILS/RNAV/GLS approaches to adjacent parallel runways where prescribed diagonal spacing must be maintained. Aircraft are not permitted to pass each other during simultaneous dependent operations. Integral parts of a total system ATC procedures, and appropriate airborne and ground based equipment.

SINGLE DIRECTION ROUTES– Preferred IFR Routes which are sometimes depicted on high altitude en route charts and which are normally flown in one direction only.
(See PREFERRED IFR ROUTES.)
(Refer to CHART SUPPLEMENT U.S.)

SINGLE FREQUENCY APPROACH– A service provided under a letter of agreement to military single-piloted turbojet aircraft which permits use of a single UHF frequency during approach for landing. Pilots will not normally be required to change frequency from the beginning of the approach to touchdown except that pilots conducting an en route descent are required to change frequency when control is transferred from the air route traffic control center to the terminal facility. The abbreviation "SFA" in the DoD FLIP IFR Supplement under "Communications" indicates this service is available at an aerodrome.

SINGLE-PILOTED AIRCRAFT– A military turbojet aircraft possessing one set of flight controls, tandem cockpits, or two sets of flight controls but operated by one pilot is considered single-piloted by ATC when determining the appropriate air traffic service to be applied.
(See SINGLE FREQUENCY APPROACH.)

SKYSPOTTER– A pilot who has received specialized training in observing and reporting inflight weather phenomena.

SLASH– A radar beacon reply displayed as an elongated target.

SLDI–
(See SECTOR LIST DROP INTERVAL.)

SLOW TAXI– To taxi a float plane at low power or low RPM.

SMALL UNMANNED AIRCRAFT SYSTEM (sUAS)– An unmanned aircraft weighing less than 55 pounds on takeoff, including everything that is on board or otherwise attached to the aircraft.

SMAR–
(See SPECIAL MILITARY ACTIVITY ROUTE.)

SN–
(See SYSTEM STRATEGIC NAVIGATION.)

SPACE–BASED ADS–B (SBA)– A constellation of satellites that receives ADS–B Out broadcasts and relays that information to the appropriate surveillance facility. The currently deployed SBA system is only capable of receiving broadcasts from 1090ES–equipped aircraft, and not from those equipped with only a universal access transceiver (UAT). Also, aircraft with a top–of–fuselage–mounted transponder antenna (required for TCAS II installations) will be better received by SBA, especially at latitudes below 45 degrees.

(See AUTOMATIC DEPENDENT SURVEILLANCE–BROADCAST.)
(See AUTOMATIC DEPENDENT SURVEILLANCE–BROADCAST OUT.)

SPACE LAUNCH AND REENTRY AREA– Locations where commercial space launch and/or reentry operations occur. For pilot awareness, a rocket–shaped symbol is used to depict space launch and reentry areas on sectional aeronautical charts.

SPEAK SLOWER– Used in verbal communications as a request to reduce speech rate.

SPECIAL ACTIVITY AIRSPACE (SAA)– Airspace with defined dimensions within the National Airspace System wherein limitations may be imposed upon operations for national defense, homeland security, public interest, or public safety. Special activity airspace includes but is not limited to the following; Air Traffic Control Assigned Airspace (ATCAA), Altitude Reservations (ALTRV), Military Training Routes (MTR), Air Refueling Tracks and Anchors, Temporary Flight Restrictions (TFR), Special Security Instructions (SSI), etc. Special Use Airspace (SUA) is a subset of Special Activity Airspace.

(See SPECIAL USE AIRSPACE.)

SPECIAL AIR TRAFFIC RULES (SATR)– Rules that govern procedures for conducting flights in certain areas listed in 14 CFR Part 93. The term "SATR" is used in the United States to describe the rules for operations in specific areas designated in the Code of Federal Regulations.

(Refer to 14 CFR Part 93.)

SPECIAL EMERGENCY– A condition of air piracy or other hostile act by a person(s) aboard an aircraft which threatens the safety of the aircraft or its passengers.

SPECIAL FLIGHT RULES AREA (SFRA)– An area in the NAS, described in 14 CFR Part 93, wherein the flight of aircraft is subject to special traffic rules, unless otherwise authorized by air traffic control. Not all areas listed in 14 CFR Part 93 are designated SFRA, but special air traffic rules apply to all areas described in 14 CFR Part 93.

SPECIAL GOVERNMENT INTEREST (SGI)– A near real-time airspace authorization for Part 91 or Part 107 UAS, which supports activities that answer significant and urgent governmental interests. These include: national defense, homeland security, law enforcement, and emergency operations objectives.

SPECIAL INSTRUMENT APPROACH PROCEDURE–

(See INSTRUMENT APPROACH PROCEDURE.)

SPECIAL MILITARY ACTIVITY ROUTE (SMAR)– A route, which may also be charted on the VFR Sectional Chart, that shows the extent of the airspace allocated to an associated IFR Military Training Route within which the Department of Defense conducts periodic operations involving Unmanned Aircraft Systems (UAS).

SPECIAL USE AIRSPACE– Airspace of defined dimensions identified by an area on the surface of the earth wherein activities must be confined because of their nature and/or wherein limitations may be imposed upon aircraft operations that are not a part of those activities. Types of special use airspace are:

a. Alert Area– Airspace which may contain a high volume of pilot training activities or an unusual type of aerial activity, neither of which is hazardous to aircraft. Alert Areas are depicted on aeronautical charts for the information of nonparticipating pilots. All activities within an Alert Area are conducted in accordance with Federal Aviation Regulations, and pilots of participating aircraft as well as pilots transiting the area are equally responsible for collision avoidance.

b. Controlled Firing Area– Airspace wherein activities are conducted under conditions so controlled as to eliminate hazards to nonparticipating aircraft and to ensure the safety of persons and property on the ground.

c. Military Operations Area (MOA)– Permanent and temporary MOAs are airspace established outside of Class A airspace area to separate or segregate certain nonhazardous military activities from IFR traffic and to identify for VFR traffic where these activities are conducted. Permanent MOAs are depicted on Sectional Aeronautical, VFR Terminal Area, and applicable En Route Low Altitude Charts.

Note: Temporary MOAs are not charted.

(Refer to AIM.)

d. National Security Area (NSA)– Airspace of defined vertical and lateral dimensions established at locations where there is a requirement for increased security of ground facilities. Pilots are requested to voluntarily avoid flying through the depicted NSA. When a greater level of security is required, flight through an NSA may be temporarily prohibited by establishing a TFR under the provisions of 14 CFR Section 99.7. Such prohibitions will be issued by FAA Headquarters and disseminated via the U.S. NOTAM System.

(Refer to AIM)

e. Prohibited Area– Airspace designated under 14 CFR Part 73 within which no person may operate an aircraft without the permission of the using agency.

(Refer to AIM.)

(Refer to En Route Charts.)

f. Restricted Area– Permanent and temporary restricted areas are airspace designated under 14 CFR Part 73, within which the flight of aircraft, while not wholly prohibited, is subject to restriction. Most restricted areas are designated joint use and IFR/VFR operations in the area may be authorized by the controlling ATC facility when it is not being utilized by the using agency. Permanent restricted areas are depicted on Sectional Aeronautical, VFR Terminal Area, and applicable En Route charts. Where joint use is authorized, the name of the ATC controlling facility is also shown.

Note: Temporary restricted areas are not charted.

(Refer to 14 CFR Part 73.)

(Refer to AIM.)

g. Warning Area– A warning area is airspace of defined dimensions extending from 3 nautical miles outward from the coast of the United States, that contains activity that may be hazardous to nonparticipating aircraft. The purpose of such warning area is to warn nonparticipating pilots of the potential danger. A warning area may be located over domestic or international waters or both.

SPECIAL VFR CONDITIONS– Meteorological conditions that are less than those required for basic VFR flight in Class B, C, D, or E surface areas and in which some aircraft are permitted flight under visual flight rules.

(See SPECIAL VFR OPERATIONS.)

(Refer to 14 CFR Part 91.)

SPECIAL VFR FLIGHT [ICAO]– A VFR flight cleared by air traffic control to operate within Class B, C, D, and E surface areas in meteorological conditions below VMC.

SPECIAL VFR OPERATIONS– Aircraft operating in accordance with clearances within Class B, C, D, and E surface areas in weather conditions less than the basic VFR weather minima. Such operations must be requested by the pilot and approved by ATC.

(See SPECIAL VFR CONDITIONS.)

(See ICAO term SPECIAL VFR FLIGHT.)

SPECIALIST–PROVIDED SERVICES–
Services delivered directly by a flight service specialist via ground/ground communication, air/ground communication, in–person, or technology (for example, speech–to–text, email, or short message service).

SPEED–

(See AIRSPEED.)

(See GROUND SPEED.)

SPEED ADJUSTMENT– An ATC procedure used to request pilots to adjust aircraft speed to a specific value for the purpose of providing desired spacing. Pilots are expected to maintain a speed of plus or minus 10 knots or 0.02 Mach number of the specified speed. Examples of speed adjustments are:

a. "Increase/reduce speed to Mach point (number)."

b. "Increase/reduce speed to (speed in knots)" or "Increase/reduce speed (number of knots) knots."

SPEED ADVISORY– Speed advisories that are generated within Time–Based Flow Management to assist controllers to meet the Scheduled Time of Arrival (STA) at the meter fix/meter arc. See also Ground–Based Interval Management–Spacing (GIM–S) Speed Advisory.

SPEED BRAKES– Moveable aerodynamic devices on aircraft that reduce airspeed during descent and landing.

SPEED SEGMENTS– Portions of the arrival route between the transition point and the vertex along the optimum flight path for which speeds and altitudes are specified. There is one set of arrival speed segments adapted from each transition point to each vertex. Each set may contain up to six segments.

SPOOFING– Denotes emissions of GNSS–like signals that may be acquired and tracked in combination with or instead of the intended signals by civil receivers. The onset of spoofing effects can be instantaneous or delayed, and effects can persist after the spoofing has ended. Spoofing can result in false and potentially confusing, or hazardously misleading, position, navigation, and/or date/time information in addition to loss of GNSS use.

SQUAWK (Mode, Code, Function)– Used by ATC to instruct a pilot to activate the aircraft transponder and ADS–B Out with altitude reporting enabled, or (military) to activate only specific modes, codes, or functions. Examples: "Squawk five seven zero seven;" "Squawk three/alpha, two one zero five."
(See TRANSPONDER.)

STA–
(See SCHEDULED TIME OF ARRIVAL.)

STAGING/QUEUING– The placement, integration, and segregation of departure aircraft in designated movement areas of an airport by departure fix, EDCT, and/or restriction.

STAND BY– Means the controller or pilot must pause for a few seconds, usually to attend to other duties of a higher priority. Also means to wait as in "stand by for clearance." The caller should reestablish contact if a delay is lengthy. "Stand by" is not an approval or denial.

STANDARD INSTRUMENT APPROACH PROCEDURE (SIAP)–
(See INSTRUMENT APPROACH PROCEDURE.)

STANDARD INSTRUMENT DEPARTURE (SID)– A preplanned instrument flight rule (IFR) air traffic control (ATC) departure procedure printed for pilot/controller use in graphic form to provide obstacle clearance and a transition from the terminal area to the appropriate en route structure. SIDs are primarily designed for system enhancement to expedite traffic flow and to reduce pilot/controller workload. ATC clearance must always be received prior to flying a SID.
(See IFR TAKEOFF MINIMUMS AND DEPARTURE PROCEDURES.)
(See OBSTACLE DEPARTURE PROCEDURE.)
(Refer to AIM.)

STANDARD RATE TURN– A turn of three degrees per second.

STANDARD TERMINAL ARRIVAL (STAR)– A preplanned instrument flight rule (IFR) air traffic control arrival procedure published for pilot use in graphic and/or textual form. STARs provide transition from the en route structure to an outer fix or an instrument approach fix/arrival waypoint in the terminal area.

STANDARD TERMINAL ARRIVAL CHARTS–
(See AERONAUTICAL CHART.)

STANDARD TERMINAL AUTOMATION REPLACEMENT SYSTEM (STARS)–
(See DTAS.)

STAR–
(See STANDARD TERMINAL ARRIVAL.)

STATE AIRCRAFT− Aircraft used in military, customs and police service, in the exclusive service of any government or of any political subdivision thereof, including the government of any state, territory, or possession of the United States or the District of Columbia, but not including any government-owned aircraft engaged in carrying persons or property for commercial purposes.

STATIC RESTRICTIONS− Those restrictions that are usually not subject to change, fixed, in place, and/or published.

STATIONARY AIRSPACE RESERVATION− The term used in oceanic ATC for airspace that encompasses activities in a fixed volume of airspace to be occupied for a specified time period. Stationary Airspace Reservations may include activities such as special tests of weapons systems or equipment; certain U.S. Navy carrier, fleet, and anti−submarine operations; rocket, missile, and drone operations; and certain aerial refueling or similar operations.

(See STATIONARY ALTITUDE RESERVATION.)

STATIONARY ALTITUDE RESERVATION (STATIONARY ALTRV)− An altitude reservation which encompasses activities in a fixed volume of airspace to be occupied for a specified time period. Stationary ALTRVs may include activities such as special tests of weapons systems or equipment; certain U.S. Navy carrier, fleet, and anti−submarine operations; rocket, missile, and drone operations; and certain aerial refueling or similar operations.

STEP TAXI− To taxi a float plane at full power or high RPM.

STEP TURN− A maneuver used to put a float plane in a planing configuration prior to entering an active sea lane for takeoff. The STEP TURN maneuver should only be used upon pilot request.

STEPDOWN FIX− A fix permitting additional descent within a segment of an instrument approach procedure by identifying a point at which a controlling obstacle has been safely overflown.

STEREO ROUTE− A routinely used route of flight established by users and ARTCCs identified by a coded name; e.g., ALPHA 2. These routes minimize flight plan handling and communications.

STNR ALT RESERVATION− An abbreviation for Stationary Altitude Reservation commonly used in NOTAMs.

(See STATIONARY ALTITUDE RESERVATION.)

STOL AIRCRAFT−

(See SHORT TAKEOFF AND LANDING AIRCRAFT.)

STOP ALTITUDE SQUAWK− Used by ATC to instruct a pilot to turn off the automatic altitude reporting feature of the aircraft transponder and ADS−B Out. It is issued when a verbally reported altitude varies by 300 feet or more from the automatic altitude report.

(See ALTITUDE READOUT.)
(See TRANSPONDER.)

STOP AND GO− A procedure wherein an aircraft will land, make a complete stop on the runway, and then commence a takeoff from that point.

(See LOW APPROACH.)
(See OPTION APPROACH.)

STOP BURST−

(See STOP STREAM.)

STOP BUZZER−

(See STOP STREAM.)

STOP SQUAWK (Mode or Code)− Used by ATC to instruct a pilot to stop transponder and ADS−B transmissions, or to turn off only specified functions of the aircraft transponder (military).

(See STOP ALTITUDE SQUAWK.)
(See TRANSPONDER.)

STOP STREAM– Used by ATC to request a pilot to suspend electronic attack activity.
(See JAMMING.)

STOPOVER FLIGHT PLAN– A flight plan format which permits in a single submission the filing of a sequence of flight plans through interim full-stop destinations to a final destination.

STOPWAY– An area beyond the takeoff runway no less wide than the runway and centered upon the extended centerline of the runway, able to support the airplane during an aborted takeoff, without causing structural damage to the airplane, and designated by the airport authorities for use in decelerating the airplane during an aborted takeoff.

STRAIGHT-IN APPROACH IFR– An instrument approach wherein final approach is begun without first having executed a procedure turn, not necessarily completed with a straight-in landing or made to straight-in landing minimums.
(See LANDING MINIMUMS.)
(See STRAIGHT-IN APPROACH VFR.)
(See STRAIGHT-IN LANDING.)

STRAIGHT-IN APPROACH VFR– Entry into the traffic pattern by interception of the extended runway centerline (final approach course) without executing any other portion of the traffic pattern.
(See TRAFFIC PATTERN.)

STRAIGHT-IN LANDING– A landing made on a runway aligned within 30° of the final approach course following completion of an instrument approach.
(See STRAIGHT-IN APPROACH IFR.)

STRAIGHT-IN LANDING MINIMUMS–
(See LANDING MINIMUMS.)

STRAIGHT-IN MINIMUMS–
(See STRAIGHT-IN LANDING MINIMUMS.)

STRATEGIC PLANNING– Planning whereby solutions are sought to resolve potential conflicts.

sUAS–
(See SMALL UNMANNED AIRCRAFT SYSTEM.)

SUBSTITUTE ROUTE– A route assigned to pilots when any part of an airway or route is unusable because of NAVAID status. These routes consist of:

a. Substitute routes which are shown on U.S. Government charts.

b. Routes defined by ATC as specific NAVAID radials or courses.

c. Routes defined by ATC as direct to or between NAVAIDs.

SUNSET AND SUNRISE– The mean solar times of sunset and sunrise as published in the Nautical Almanac, converted to local standard time for the locality concerned. Within Alaska, the end of evening civil twilight and the beginning of morning civil twilight, as defined for each locality.

SUPPLEMENTAL WEATHER SERVICE LOCATION– Airport facilities staffed with contract personnel who take weather observations and provide current local weather to pilots via telephone or radio. (All other services are provided by the parent FSS.)

SUPPS– Refers to ICAO Document 7030 Regional Supplementary Procedures. SUPPS contain procedures for each ICAO Region which are unique to that Region and are not covered in the worldwide provisions identified in the ICAO Air Navigation Plan. Procedures contained in Chapter 8 are based in part on those published in SUPPS.

SURFACE AREA– The airspace contained by the lateral boundary of the Class B, C, D, or E airspace designated for an airport that begins at the surface and extends upward.

SURFACE METERING PROGRAM– A capability within Terminal Flight Data Manager that provides the user with the ability to tactically manage surface traffic flows through adjusting desired minimum and maximum departure queue lengths to balance surface demand with capacity. When a demand/capacity imbalance for a surface resource is predicted, a metering procedure is recommended.

SURFACE VIEWER– A capability within the Traffic Flow Management System that provides situational awareness for a user–selected airport. The Surface Viewer displays a top–down view of an airport depicting runways, taxiways, gate areas, ramps, and buildings. The display also includes icons representing aircraft and vehicles currently on the surface, with identifying information. In addition, the display includes current airport configuration information such as departure/arrival runways and airport departure/arrival rates.

SURPIC– A description of surface vessels in the area of a Search and Rescue incident including their predicted positions and their characteristics.

(Refer to FAA Order JO 7110.65, Para 10–6–4, INFLIGHT CONTINGENCIES.)

SURVEILLANCE APPROACH– An instrument approach wherein the air traffic controller issues instructions, for pilot compliance, based on aircraft position in relation to the final approach course (azimuth), and the distance (range) from the end of the runway as displayed on the controller's radar scope. The controller will provide recommended altitudes on final approach if requested by the pilot.

(Refer to AIM.)

SURVEILLANCE ENHANCED SEARCH AND RESCUE (SE SAR)– An automated service used to enhance search and rescue operations that provides federal contract flight service specialists direct information from the aircraft's registered tracking device.

SUSPICIOUS UAS– Suspicious UAS operations may include operating without authorization, loitering in the vicinity of sensitive locations, (e.g., national security, law enforcement facilities, and critical infrastructure), or disrupting normal air traffic operations resulting in runway changes, ground stops, pilot evasive action, etc. The report of a UAS operation alone does not constitute suspicious activity. Development of a comprehensive list of suspicious activities is not possible due to the vast number of situations that could be considered suspicious. ATC must exercise sound judgment when identifying situations that could constitute or indicate a suspicious activity.

SWAP–

(See SEVERE WEATHER AVOIDANCE PLAN.)

SWSL–

(See SUPPLEMENTAL WEATHER SERVICE LOCATION.)

SYSTEM STRATEGIC NAVIGATION– Military activity accomplished by navigating along a preplanned route using internal aircraft systems to maintain a desired track. This activity normally requires a lateral route width of 10 NM and altitude range of 1,000 feet to 6,000 feet AGL with some route segments that permit terrain following.

T

TACAN–
(See TACTICAL AIR NAVIGATION.)

TACAN-ONLY AIRCRAFT– An aircraft, normally military, possessing TACAN with DME but no VOR navigational system capability. Clearances must specify TACAN or VORTAC fixes and approaches.

TACTICAL AIR NAVIGATION (TACAN)– An ultra-high frequency electronic rho-theta air navigation aid which provides suitably equipped aircraft a continuous indication of bearing and distance to the TACAN station.
(See VORTAC.)
(Refer to AIM.)

TAILWIND– Any wind more than 90 degrees to the longitudinal axis of the runway. The magnetic direction of the runway shall be used as the basis for determining the longitudinal axis.

TAKEOFF AREA–
(See LANDING AREA.)

TAKEOFF DISTANCE AVAILABLE (TODA)– The takeoff run available plus the length of any remaining runway or clearway beyond the far end of the takeoff run available.
(See ICAO term TAKEOFF DISTANCE AVAILABLE.)

TAKEOFF DISTANCE AVAILABLE [ICAO]– The length of the takeoff run available plus the length of the clearway, if provided.

TAKEOFF HOLD LIGHTS (THL)– The THL system is composed of in-pavement lighting in a double, longitudinal row of lights aligned either side of the runway centerline. The lights are focused toward the arrival end of the runway at the "line up and wait" point, and they extend for 1,500 feet in front of the holding aircraft. Illuminated red lights indicate to an aircraft in position for takeoff or rolling that it is unsafe to takeoff because the runway is occupied or about to be occupied by an aircraft or vehicle.

TAKEOFF ROLL – The process whereby an aircraft is aligned with the runway centerline and the aircraft is moving with the intent to take off. For helicopters, this pertains to the act of becoming airborne after departing a takeoff area.

TAKEOFF RUN AVAILABLE (TORA) – The runway length declared available and suitable for the ground run of an airplane taking off.
(See ICAO term TAKEOFF RUN AVAILABLE.)

TAKEOFF RUN AVAILABLE [ICAO]– The length of runway declared available and suitable for the ground run of an aeroplane take-off.

TARGET– The indication shown on a display resulting from a primary radar return, a radar beacon reply, or an ADS–B report. The specific target symbol presented to ATC may vary based on the surveillance source and automation platform.
(See ASSOCIATED.)
(See DIGITAL TARGET.)
(See DIGITIZED RADAR TARGET.)
(See FUSED TARGET.)
(See PRIMARY RADAR TARGET.)
(See RADAR.)
(See SECONDARY RADAR TARGET.)
(See ICAO term TARGET.)
(See UNASSOCIATED.)

TARGET [ICAO]– In radar:

a. Generally, any discrete object which reflects or retransmits energy back to the radar equipment.

b. Specifically, an object of radar search or surveillance.

TARGET RESOLUTION– A process to ensure that correlated radar targets do not touch. Target resolution must be applied as follows:

a. Between the edges of two primary targets or the edges of the ASR-9/11 primary target symbol.

b. Between the end of the beacon control slash and the edge of a primary target.

c. Between the ends of two beacon control slashes.

Note 1: Mandatory traffic advisories and safety alerts must be issued when this procedure is used.

Note 2: This procedure must not be used when utilizing mosaic radar systems or multi–sensor mode.

TARGET SYMBOL
(See TARGET.)
(See ICAO term TARGET.)

TARMAC DELAY– The holding of an aircraft on the ground either before departure or after landing with no opportunity for its passengers to deplane.

TARMAC DELAY AIRCRAFT– An aircraft whose pilot–in–command has requested to taxi to the ramp, gate, or alternate deplaning area to comply with the Three–hour Tarmac Rule.

TARMAC DELAY REQUEST– A request by the pilot–in–command to taxi to the ramp, gate, or alternate deplaning location to comply with the Three–hour Tarmac Rule.

TAS–
(See TERMINAL AUTOMATION SYSTEMS.)

TAWS–
(See TERRAIN AWARENESS WARNING SYSTEM.)

TAXI– The movement of an airplane under its own power on the surface of an airport (14 CFR Section 135.100 [Note]). Also, it describes the surface movement of helicopters equipped with wheels.
(See AIR TAXI.)
(See HOVER TAXI.)
(Refer to 14 CFR Section 135.100.)
(Refer to AIM.)

TAXI PATTERNS– Patterns established to illustrate the desired flow of ground traffic for the different runways or airport areas available for use.

TBM–
(See TIME–BASED MANAGEMENT.)

TBO–
(See TRAJECTORY–BASED OPERATIONS.)

TCAS–
(See TRAFFIC ALERT AND COLLISION AVOIDANCE SYSTEM.)

TCH–
(See THRESHOLD CROSSING HEIGHT.)

TDLS–
(See TERMINAL DATA LINK SYSTEM.)

TDZE–
(See TOUCHDOWN ZONE ELEVATION.)

TEMPORARY FLIGHT RESTRICTION (TFR)− A TFR is a regulatory action issued by the FAA via the U.S. NOTAM System, under the authority of United States Code, Title 49. TFRs are issued within the sovereign airspace of the United States and its territories to restrict certain aircraft from operating within a defined area on a temporary basis to protect persons or property in the air or on the ground. While not all inclusive, TFRs may be issued for disaster or hazard situations such as: toxic gas leaks or spills, fumes from flammable agents, aircraft accident/incident sites, aviation or ground resources engaged in wildfire suppression, or aircraft relief activities_following a disaster. TFRs may also be issued in support of VIP movements, for reasons of national security; or when determined necessary for the management of air traffic in the vicinity of aerial demonstrations or major sporting events. NAS users or other interested parties should contact a FSS for TFR information. Additionally, TFR information can be found in automated briefings, NOTAM publications, and on the internet at http://www.faa.gov. The FAA also distributes TFR information to aviation user groups for further dissemination.

TERMINAL AREA− A general term used to describe airspace in which approach control service or airport traffic control service is provided.

TERMINAL AREA FACILITY− A facility providing air traffic control service for arriving and departing IFR, VFR, Special VFR, and on occasion en route aircraft.
(See APPROACH CONTROL FACILITY.)
(See TOWER.)

TERMINAL AUTOMATION SYSTEMS (TAS)− TAS is used to identify the numerous automated tracking systems including STARS and MEARTS.

TERMINAL DATA LINK SYSTEM (TDLS)− A system that provides Digital Automatic Terminal Information Service (D−ATIS) both on a specified radio frequency and also, for subscribers, in a text message via data link to the cockpit or to a gate printer. TDLS also provides Pre−departure Clearances (PDC), at selected airports, to subscribers, through a service provider, in text to the cockpit or to a gate printer. In addition, TDLS will emulate the Flight Data Input/Output (FDIO) information within the control tower.

TERMINAL FLIGHT DATA MANAGER (TFDM)− An integrated tower flight data automation system to provide improved airport surface and terminal airspace management. TFDM enhances traffic flow management data integration with Time−Based Flow Management (TBFM) and Traffic Flow Management System (TFMS) to enable airlines, controllers, and airports to share and exchange real−time data. This improves surface traffic management and enhances capabilities of TFMS and TBFM. TFDM assists the Tower personnel with surface Traffic Flow Management (TFM) and Collaborative Decision Making (CDM) and enables a fundamental change in the Towers from a local airport−specific operation to a NAS−connected metering operation. The single platform consolidates multiple Tower automation systems, including: Departure Spacing Program (DSP), Airport Resource Management Tool (ARMT), Electronic Flight Strip Transfer System (EFSTS), and Surface Movement Advisor (SMA). TFDM data, integrated with other FAA systems such as TBFM and TFMS, allows airlines, controllers, and airports to manage the flow of aircraft more efficiently through all phases of flight from departure to arrival gate.

TERMINAL RADAR SERVICE AREA− Airspace surrounding designated airports wherein ATC provides radar vectoring, sequencing, and separation on a full-time basis for all IFR and participating VFR aircraft. The AIM contains an explanation of TRSA. TRSAs are depicted on VFR aeronautical charts. Pilot participation is urged but is not mandatory.

TERMINAL SEQUENCING AND SPACING (TSAS)− Extends scheduling and metering capabilities into the terminal area and provides metering automation tools to terminal controllers and terminal traffic management personnel. Those controllers and traffic management personnel become active participants in time−based metering operations as they work to deliver aircraft accurately to Constraint Satisfaction Points within terminal airspace to include the runway in accordance with scheduled times at those points. Terminal controllers are better able to utilize efficient flight paths, such as Standard Instrument Approach Procedures (SIAPs) that require a Navigational Specification (NavSpec) of RNP APCH with Radius−to−Fix (RF) legs, or Advanced RNP

(A–RNP), through tools that support the merging of mixed–equipage traffic flows. For example, merging aircraft flying RNP APCH AR with RF, A–RNP, and non–RNP approach procedures. Additional fields in the flight plan will identify those flights capable of flying the RNP APCH with RF or A–RNP procedures, and those flights will be scheduled for those types of procedures when available. TSAS will schedule these and the non–RNP aircraft to a common merge point. Terminal traffic management personnel have improved situation awareness using displays that allow for the monitoring of terminal metering operations, similar to the displays used today by center traffic management personnel to monitor en route metering operations.

TERMINAL VFR RADAR SERVICE– A national program instituted to extend the terminal radar services provided instrument flight rules (IFR) aircraft to visual flight rules (VFR) aircraft. The program is divided into four types service referred to as basic radar service, terminal radar service area (TRSA) service, Class B service and Class C service. The type of service provided at a particular location is contained in the Chart Supplement.

a. Basic Radar Service– These services are provided for VFR aircraft by all commissioned terminal radar facilities. Basic radar service includes safety alerts, traffic advisories, limited radar vectoring when requested by the pilot, and sequencing at locations where procedures have been established for this purpose and/or when covered by a letter of agreement. The purpose of this service is to adjust the flow of arriving IFR and VFR aircraft into the traffic pattern in a safe and orderly manner and to provide traffic advisories to departing VFR aircraft.

b. TRSA Service– This service provides, in addition to basic radar service, sequencing of all IFR and participating VFR aircraft to the primary airport and separation between all participating VFR aircraft. The purpose of this service is to provide separation between all participating VFR aircraft and all IFR aircraft operating within the area defined as a TRSA.

c. Class C Service– This service provides, in addition to basic radar service, approved separation between IFR and VFR aircraft, and sequencing of VFR aircraft, and sequencing of VFR arrivals to the primary airport.

d. Class B Service– This service provides, in addition to basic radar service, approved separation of aircraft based on IFR, VFR, and/or weight, and sequencing of VFR arrivals to the primary airport(s).

(See CONTROLLED AIRSPACE.)
(See TERMINAL RADAR SERVICE AREA.)
(Refer to AIM.)
(Refer to CHART SUPPLEMENT U.S.)

TERMINAL-VERY HIGH FREQUENCY OMNIDIRECTIONAL RANGE STATION (TVOR)– A very high frequency terminal omnirange station located on or near an airport and used as an approach aid.

(See NAVIGATIONAL AID.)
(See VOR.)

TERRAIN AWARENESS WARNING SYSTEM (TAWS)– An on–board, terrain proximity alerting system providing the aircrew 'Low Altitude warnings' to allow immediate pilot action.

TERRAIN FOLLOWING– The flight of a military aircraft maintaining a constant AGL altitude above the terrain or the highest obstruction. The altitude of the aircraft will constantly change with the varying terrain and/or obstruction.

TETRAHEDRON– A device normally located on uncontrolled airports and used as a landing direction indicator. The small end of a tetrahedron points in the direction of landing. At controlled airports, the tetrahedron, if installed, should be disregarded because tower instructions supersede the indicator.

(See SEGMENTED CIRCLE.)
(Refer to AIM.)

TF–

(See TERRAIN FOLLOWING.)

TFDM–

(See TERMINAL FLIGHT DATA MANAGER.)

TGUI–

(See TIMELINE GRAPHICAL USER INTERFACE.)

THAT IS CORRECT– The understanding you have is right.

THA–
(See TRANSITIONAL HAZARD AREA.)

THE RECREATIONAL UAS SAFETY TEST (TRUST)– The electronically administered free test required for all recreational UAS operators referred to as the aeronautical knowledge and safety test, under 49 USC §44809 (g).

THREE–HOUR TARMAC RULE– Rule that relates to Department of Transportation (DOT) requirements placed on airlines when tarmac delays are anticipated to reach 3 hours.

360 OVERHEAD–
(See OVERHEAD MANEUVER.)

THRESHOLD– The beginning of that portion of the runway usable for landing.
(See AIRPORT LIGHTING.)
(See DISPLACED THRESHOLD.)

THRESHOLD CROSSING HEIGHT– The theoretical height above the runway threshold at which the aircraft's glideslope antenna would be if the aircraft maintains the trajectory established by the mean ILS glideslope or the altitude at which the calculated glidepath of an RNAV or GPS approaches.
(See GLIDESLOPE.)
(See THRESHOLD.)

THRESHOLD LIGHTS–
(See AIRPORT LIGHTING.)

TIE-IN FACILITY– The FSS primarily responsible for providing FSS services, including telecommunications services for landing facilities or navigational aids located within the boundaries of a flight plan area (FPA). Three-letter identifiers are assigned to each FSS/FPA and are annotated as tie-in facilities in the Chart Supplement and FAA Order JO 7350.9, Location Identifiers. Large consolidated FSS facilities may have many tie-in facilities or FSS sectors within one facility.
(See FLIGHT PLAN AREA.)
(See FLIGHT SERVICE STATION.)

TIME–BASED FLOW MANAGEMENT (TBFM)– A foundational Decision Support Tool for time–based management in the en route and terminal environments. TBFM's core function is the ability to schedule aircraft within a stream of traffic to reach a defined constraint point (e.g., meter fix/meter arc) at specified times, creating a time–ordered sequence of traffic. The scheduled times allow for merging of traffic flows, efficiently utilizing airport and airspace capacity while minimizing coordination and reducing the need for vectoring/holding. The TBFM schedule is calculated using current aircraft estimated time of arrival at key defined constraint points based on wind forecasts, aircraft flight plan, the desired separation at the constraint point and other parameters. The schedule applies spacing only when needed to maintain the desired separation at one or more constraint points. This includes, but is not limited to, Single Center Metering (SCM), Adjacent Center Metering (ACM), En Route Departure Capability (EDC), Integrated Departure/Arrival Capability (IDAC), Ground–based Interval Management–Spacing (GIM–S), Departure Scheduling, and Extended/Coupled Metering.

TIME–BASED MANAGEMENT (TBM)– A methodology for managing the flow of air traffic through the assignment of time at specific points for an aircraft. TBM applies time to manage and condition air traffic flows to mitigate demand/capacity imbalances and enhance efficiency and predictability of the NAS. Where implemented, TBM tools will be used to manage traffic even during periods when demand does not exceed capacity. This will sustain operational predictability and assure the regional/national strategic plan is maintained. TBM uses capabilities within TFMS, TBFM, and TFDM. These programs are designed to achieve a specified interval between aircraft. Different types of programs accommodate different phases of flight.

TIME GROUP– Four digits representing the hour and minutes from the Coordinated Universal Time (UTC) clock. FAA uses UTC for all operations. The term "ZULU" may be used to denote UTC. The word "local" or the time zone equivalent shall be used to denote local when local time is given during radio and telephone communications. When written, a time zone designator is used to indicate local time; e.g., "0205M" (Mountain). The local time may be based on the 24-hour clock system. The day begins at 0000 and ends at 2359.

TIMELINE GRAPHICAL USER INTERFACE (TGUI)– A TBFM display that uses timelines to display the Estimated Time of Arrival and Scheduled Time of Arrival of each aircraft to specified constraint points. The TGUI can also display pre–departure and scheduled aircraft.

TIS–B–
(See TRAFFIC INFORMATION SERVICE–BROADCAST.)

TMI–
(See TRAFFIC MANAGEMENT INITIATIVE.)

TMPA–
(See TRAFFIC MANAGEMENT PROGRAM ALERT.)

TMU–
(See TRAFFIC MANAGEMENT UNIT.)

TOD–
(See TOP OF DESCENT.)

TODA–
(See TAKEOFF DISTANCE AVAILABLE.)
(See ICAO term TAKEOFF DISTANCE AVAILABLE.)

TOI–
(See TRACK OF INTEREST.)

TOP ALTITUDE– In reference to SID published altitude restrictions, the charted "maintain" altitude contained in the procedure description or assigned by ATC.

TOP OF DESCENT (TOD)– The point at which an aircraft begins the initial descent.

TORA–
(See TAKEOFF RUN AVAILABLE.)
(See ICAO term TAKEOFF RUN AVAILABLE.)

TORCHING– The burning of fuel at the end of an exhaust pipe or stack of a reciprocating aircraft engine, the result of an excessive richness in the fuel air mixture.

TOS–
(See TRAJECTORY OPTIONS SET)

TOTAL ESTIMATED ELAPSED TIME [ICAO]– For IFR flights, the estimated time required from takeoff to arrive over that designated point, defined by reference to navigation aids, from which it is intended that an instrument approach procedure will be commenced, or, if no navigation aid is associated with the destination aerodrome, to arrive over the destination aerodrome. For VFR flights, the estimated time required from takeoff to arrive over the destination aerodrome.
(See ICAO term ESTIMATED ELAPSED TIME.)

TOUCH-AND-GO– An operation by an aircraft that lands and departs on a runway without stopping or exiting the runway.

TOUCH-AND-GO LANDING–
(See TOUCH-AND-GO.)

TOUCHDOWN–

a. The point at which an aircraft first makes contact with the landing surface.

b. Concerning a precision radar approach (PAR), it is the point where the glide path intercepts the landing surface.

(See ICAO term TOUCHDOWN.)

TOUCHDOWN [ICAO]− The point where the nominal glide path intercepts the runway.

Note: Touchdown as defined above is only a datum and is not necessarily the actual point at which the aircraft will touch the runway.

TOUCHDOWN RVR−

(See VISIBILITY.)

TOUCHDOWN ZONE− The first 3,000 feet of the runway beginning at the threshold. The area is used for determination of Touchdown Zone Elevation in the development of straight-in landing minimums for instrument approaches.

(See ICAO term TOUCHDOWN ZONE.)

TOUCHDOWN ZONE [ICAO]− The portion of a runway, beyond the threshold, where it is intended landing aircraft first contact the runway.

TOUCHDOWN ZONE ELEVATION− The highest elevation in the first 3,000 feet of the landing surface. TDZE is indicated on the instrument approach procedure chart when straight-in landing minimums are authorized.

(See TOUCHDOWN ZONE.)

TOUCHDOWN ZONE LIGHTING−

(See AIRPORT LIGHTING.)

TOWER− A terminal facility that uses air/ground communications, visual signaling, and other devices to provide ATC services to aircraft operating in the vicinity of an airport or on the movement area. Authorizes aircraft to land or takeoff at the airport controlled by the tower or to transit the Class D airspace area regardless of flight plan or weather conditions (IFR or VFR). A tower may also provide approach control services (radar or nonradar).

(See AIRPORT TRAFFIC CONTROL SERVICE.)
(See APPROACH CONTROL FACILITY.)
(See APPROACH CONTROL SERVICE.)
(See MOVEMENT AREA.)
(See TOWER EN ROUTE CONTROL SERVICE.)
(See ICAO term AERODROME CONTROL TOWER.)
(Refer to AIM.)

TOWER EN ROUTE CONTROL SERVICE− The control of IFR en route traffic within delegated airspace between two or more adjacent approach control facilities. This service is designed to expedite traffic and reduce control and pilot communication requirements.

TOWER TO TOWER−

(See TOWER EN ROUTE CONTROL SERVICE.)

TRACEABLE PRESSURE STANDARD− The facility station pressure instrument, with certification/calibration traceable to the National Institute of Standards and Technology. Traceable pressure standards may be mercurial barometers, commissioned ASOS or dual transducer AWOS, or portable pressure standards or DASI.

TRACK− The actual flight path of an aircraft over the surface of the earth.

(See COURSE.)
(See FLIGHT PATH.)
(See ROUTE.)
(See ICAO term TRACK.)

TRACK [ICAO]− The projection on the earth's surface of the path of an aircraft, the direction of which path at any point is usually expressed in degrees from North (True, Magnetic, or Grid).

TRACK OF INTEREST (TOI)– Displayed data representing an airborne object that threatens or has the potential to threaten North America or National Security. Indicators may include, but are not limited to: noncompliance with air traffic control instructions or aviation regulations; extended loss of communications; unusual transmissions or unusual flight behavior; unauthorized intrusion into controlled airspace or an ADIZ; noncompliance with issued flight restrictions/security procedures; or unlawful interference with airborne flight crews, up to and including hijack. In certain circumstances, an object may become a TOI based on specific and credible intelligence pertaining to that particular aircraft/object, its passengers, or its cargo.

TRACK OF INTEREST RESOLUTION– A TOI will normally be considered resolved when: the aircraft/object is no longer airborne; the aircraft complies with air traffic control instructions, aviation regulations, and/or issued flight restrictions/security procedures; radio contact is re–established and authorized control of the aircraft is verified; the aircraft is intercepted and intent is verified to be nonthreatening/nonhostile; TOI was identified based on specific and credible intelligence that was later determined to be invalid or unreliable; or displayed data is identified and characterized as invalid.

TRAFFIC–

a. A term used by a controller to transfer radar identification of an aircraft to another controller for the purpose of coordinating separation action. Traffic is normally issued:

1. In response to a handoff or point out,

2. In anticipation of a handoff or point out, or

3. In conjunction with a request for control of an aircraft.

b. A term used by ATC to refer to one or more aircraft.

TRAFFIC ADVISORIES– Advisories issued to alert pilots to other known or observed air traffic which may be in such proximity to the position or intended route of flight of their aircraft to warrant their attention. Such advisories may be based on:

a. Visual observation.

b. Observation of radar identified and nonidentified aircraft targets on an ATC radar display, or

c. Verbal reports from pilots or other facilities.

Note 1: The word "traffic" followed by additional information, if known, is used to provide such advisories; e.g., "Traffic, 2 o'clock, one zero miles, southbound, eight thousand."

Note 2: Traffic advisory service will be provided to the extent possible depending on higher priority duties of the controller or other limitations; e.g., radar limitations, volume of traffic, frequency congestion, or controller workload. Radar/ nonradar traffic advisories do not relieve the pilot of his/her responsibility to see and avoid other aircraft. Pilots are cautioned that there are many times when the controller is not able to give traffic advisories concerning all traffic in the aircraft's proximity; in other words, when a pilot requests or is receiving traffic advisories, he/she should not assume that all traffic will be issued.

(Refer to AIM.)

TRAFFIC ALERT (aircraft call sign), TURN (left/right) IMMEDIATELY, (climb/descend) AND MAINTAIN (altitude).

(See SAFETY ALERT.)

TRAFFIC ALERT AND COLLISION AVOIDANCE SYSTEM (TCAS)– An airborne collision avoidance system based on radar beacon signals which operates independent of ground-based equipment. TCAS-I generates traffic advisories only. TCAS-II generates traffic advisories, and resolution (collision avoidance) advisories in the vertical plane.

TRAFFIC INFORMATION–

(See TRAFFIC ADVISORIES.)

TRAFFIC INFORMATION SERVICE–BROADCAST (TIS–B)– The broadcast of ATC derived traffic information to ADS–B equipped (1090ES or UAT) aircraft. The source of this traffic information is derived from ground–based air traffic surveillance sensors, typically from radar targets. TIS–B service will be available throughout the NAS where there are both adequate surveillance coverage (radar) and adequate broadcast coverage from ADS–B ground stations. Loss of TIS–B will occur when an aircraft enters an area not covered by the GBT network. If this occurs in an area with adequate surveillance coverage (radar), nearby aircraft that remain within the adequate broadcast coverage (ADS–B) area will view the first aircraft. TIS–B may continue when an aircraft enters an area with inadequate surveillance coverage (radar); nearby aircraft that remain within the adequate broadcast coverage (ADS–B) area will not view the first aircraft.

TRAFFIC IN SIGHT– Used by pilots to inform a controller that previously issued traffic is in sight.

(See NEGATIVE CONTACT.)
(See TRAFFIC ADVISORIES.)

TRAFFIC MANAGEMENT INITIATIVE (TMI)– Tools used to manage demand with capacity in the National Airspace System (NAS.) TMIs can be used to manage NAS resources (e.g., airports, sectors, airspace) or to increase the efficiency of the operation. TMIs can be either tactical (i.e., short term) or strategic (i.e., long term), depending on the type of TMI and the operational need.

TRAFFIC MANAGEMENT PROGRAM ALERT– A term used in a Notice to Air Missions (NOTAM) issued in conjunction with a special traffic management program to alert pilots to the existence of the program and to refer them to a special traffic management program advisory message for program details. The contraction TMPA is used in NOTAM text.

TRAFFIC MANAGEMENT UNIT– The entity in ARTCCs and designated terminals directly involved in the active management of facility traffic. Usually under the direct supervision of an assistant manager for traffic management.

TRAFFIC NO FACTOR– Indicates that the traffic described in a previously issued traffic advisory is no factor.

TRAFFIC NO LONGER OBSERVED– Indicates that the traffic described in a previously issued traffic advisory is no longer depicted on radar, but may still be a factor.

TRAFFIC PATTERN– The traffic flow that is prescribed for aircraft landing at, taxiing on, or taking off from an airport. The components of a typical traffic pattern are upwind leg, crosswind leg, downwind leg, base leg, and final approach.

a. Upwind Leg– A flight path parallel to the landing runway in the direction of landing.

b. Crosswind Leg– A flight path at right angles to the landing runway off its upwind end.

c. Downwind Leg– A flight path parallel to the landing runway in the direction opposite to landing. The downwind leg normally extends between the crosswind leg and the base leg.

d. Base Leg– A flight path at right angles to the landing runway off its approach end. The base leg normally extends from the downwind leg to the intersection of the extended runway centerline.

NOTE–
ATC may instruct a pilot to report a "2–mile left base" to Runway 22. This instruction means that the pilot is expected to maneuver their aircraft into a left base leg that will intercept a straight–in final 2 miles from the approach end of Runway 22 and advise ATC.

REFERENCE–
Pilot's Handbook of Aeronautical Knowledge, FAA–H–8083–25, Chapter 14, Airport Operations, Traffic Patterns.

e. Final Approach– A flight path in the direction of landing along the extended runway centerline. The final approach normally extends from the base leg to the runway. An aircraft making a straight-in approach VFR is also considered to be on final approach.

NOTE–
ATC may instruct a pilot to report "5–mile final" to Runway 22. This instruction means that the pilot should maneuver their aircraft onto a straight–in final and advise ATC when they are five miles from the approach end of Runway 22.

REFERENCE–
Pilot's Handbook of Aeronautical Knowledge, FAA–H–8083–25, Chapter 14, Airport Operations, Traffic Patterns.
(See STRAIGHT-IN APPROACH VFR.)
(See TAXI PATTERNS.)
(See ICAO term AERODROME TRAFFIC CIRCUIT.)
(Refer to 14 CFR Part 91.)
(Refer to AIM.)

TRAFFIC SITUATION DISPLAY (TSD)– TSD is a computer system that receives radar track data from all 20 CONUS ARTCCs, organizes this data into a mosaic display, and presents it on a computer screen. The display allows the traffic management coordinator multiple methods of selection and highlighting of individual aircraft or groups of aircraft. The user has the option of superimposing these aircraft positions over any number of background displays. These background options include ARTCC boundaries, any stratum of en route sector boundaries, fixes, airways, military and other special use airspace, airports, and geopolitical boundaries. By using the TSD, a coordinator can monitor any number of traffic situations or the entire systemwide traffic flows.

TRAJECTORY– A EDST representation of the path an aircraft is predicted to fly based upon a Current Plan or Trial Plan.
(See EN ROUTE DECISION SUPPORT TOOL.)

TRAJECTORY–BASED OPERATIONS (TBO)– An Air Traffic Management method for strategically planning and managing flights throughout the operation by using Time–Based Management (TBM), information exchange between air and ground systems, and the aircraft's ability to fly trajectories in time and space. Aircraft trajectory is defined in four dimensions – latitude, longitude, altitude, and time.

TRAJECTORY MODELING– The automated process of calculating a trajectory.

TRAJECTORY OPTIONS SET (TOS)– A TOS is an electronic message, submitted by the operator, that is used by the Collaborative Trajectory Options Program (CTOP) to manage the airspace captured in the traffic management program. The TOS will allow the operator to express the route and delay trade-off options that they are willing to accept.

TRANSFER OF CONTROL– That action whereby the responsibility for the separation of an aircraft is transferred from one controller to another.
(See ICAO term TRANSFER OF CONTROL.)

TRANSFER OF CONTROL [ICAO]– Transfer of responsibility for providing air traffic control service.

TRANSFERRING CONTROLLER– A controller/facility transferring control of an aircraft to another controller/facility.
(See ICAO term TRANSFERRING UNIT/CONTROLLER.)

TRANSFERRING FACILITY–
(See TRANSFERRING CONTROLLER.)

TRANSFERRING UNIT/CONTROLLER [ICAO]– Air traffic control unit/air traffic controller in the process of transferring the responsibility for providing air traffic control service to an aircraft to the next air traffic control unit/air traffic controller along the route of flight.
Note: See definition of accepting unit/controller.

TRANSITION– The general term that describes the change from one phase of flight or flight condition to another; e.g., transition from en route flight to the approach or transition from instrument flight to visual flight.

TRANSITION POINT– A point at an adapted number of miles from the vertex at which an arrival aircraft would normally commence descent from its en route altitude. This is the first fix adapted on the arrival speed segments.

TRANSITIONAL AIRSPACE– That portion of controlled airspace wherein aircraft change from one phase of flight or flight condition to another.

TRANSITIONAL HAZARD AREA (THA)– Used by ATC. Airspace normally associated with an Aircraft Hazard Area within which the flight of aircraft is subject to restrictions.
(See AIRCRAFT HAZARD AREA.)
(See CONTINGENCY HAZARD AREA.)
(See REFINED HAZARD AREA.)

TRANSMISSOMETER– An apparatus used to determine visibility by measuring the transmission of light through the atmosphere. It is the measurement source for determining runway visual range (RVR).
(See VISIBILITY.)

TRANSMITTING IN THE BLIND– A transmission from one station to other stations in circumstances where two-way communication cannot be established, but where it is believed that the called stations may be able to receive the transmission.

TRANSPONDER– The airborne radar beacon receiver/transmitter portion of the Air Traffic Control Radar Beacon System (ATCRBS) which automatically receives radio signals from interrogators on the ground, and selectively replies with a specific reply pulse or pulse group only to those interrogations being received on the mode to which it is set to respond.
(See INTERROGATOR.)
(See ICAO term TRANSPONDER.)
(Refer to AIM.)

TRANSPONDER [ICAO]– A receiver/transmitter which will generate a reply signal upon proper interrogation; the interrogation and reply being on different frequencies.

TRANSPONDER CODES–
(See CODES.)

TRANSPONDER OBSERVED – Phraseology used to inform a VFR pilot the aircraft's assigned beacon code and position have been observed. Specifically, this term conveys to a VFR pilot the transponder reply has been observed and its position correlated for transit through the designated area.

TRIAL PLAN– A proposed amendment which utilizes automation to analyze and display potential conflicts along the predicted trajectory of the selected aircraft.

TRSA–
(See TERMINAL RADAR SERVICE AREA.)

TRUST–
(See THE RECREATIONAL UAS SAFETY TEST.)

TSAS–
(See TERMINAL SEQUENCING AND SPACING.)

TSD–
(See TRAFFIC SITUATION DISPLAY.)

TURBOJET AIRCRAFT– An aircraft having a jet engine in which the energy of the jet operates a turbine which in turn operates the air compressor.

TURBOPROP AIRCRAFT– An aircraft having a jet engine in which the energy of the jet operates a turbine which drives the propeller.

TURBULENCE– An atmospheric phenomenon that causes changes in aircraft altitude, attitude, and or airspeed with aircraft reaction depending on intensity. Pilots report turbulence intensity according to aircraft's reaction as follows:

a. Light – Causes slight, erratic changes in altitude and or attitude (pitch, roll, or yaw).

b. Moderate– Similar to Light but of greater intensity. Changes in altitude and or attitude occur but the aircraft remains in positive control at all times. It usually causes variations in indicated airspeed.

c. Severe– Causes large, abrupt changes in altitude and or attitude. It usually causes large variations in indicated airspeed. Aircraft may be momentarily out of control.

d. Extreme– The aircraft is violently tossed about and is practically impossible to control. It may cause structural damage.

(See CHOP.)
(Refer to AIM.)

TURN ANTICIPATION– (maneuver anticipation).

TVOR–
(See TERMINAL-VERY HIGH FREQUENCY OMNIDIRECTIONAL RANGE STATION.)

TWO-WAY RADIO COMMUNICATIONS FAILURE–
(See LOST COMMUNICATIONS.)

U

UAM–
(See URBAN AIR MOBILITY.)

UAS FACILITY MAP (UASFM)– Defined grid squares showing maximum altitudes around airports where the FAA may authorize Part 107 sUAS operations without additional safety analysis. The maps should be consulted prior to conducting UAS operations (Part 91, Part 107 or Section 44809) in controlled airspace. The UASFM will aid in determining if the airspace authorization or waivers are necessary. UASFM(s) are charted on the UAS Data Delivery System (UDDS) at the following website address: https://faa.maps.arcgis.com/apps/webappviewer/index.html?id=9c2e4406710048e19806ebf6a06754ad.

UAS TEST SITE– Independently owned UAS test & research sites, recognized by the FAA.

UAS TRAFFIC MANAGEMENT (UTM)–The unmanned aircraft traffic management ecosystem that will allow multiple low altitude BVLOS operations and which is separate from, but complementary to, FAA's Air Traffic Control System.

UASFM–
(See UAS FACILITY MAP.)

UHF–
(See ULTRAHIGH FREQUENCY.)

ULTRAHIGH FREQUENCY (UHF)– The frequency band between 300 and 3,000 MHz. The bank of radio frequencies used for military air/ground voice communications. In some instances this may go as low as 225 MHz and still be referred to as UHF.

ULTRALIGHT VEHICLE– A single-occupant aeronautical vehicle operated for sport or recreational purposes which does not require FAA registration, an airworthiness certificate, or pilot certification. Operation of an ultralight vehicle in certain airspace requires authorization from ATC.
(Refer to 14 CFR Part 103.)

UNABLE– Indicates inability to comply with a specific instruction, request, or clearance.

UNASSOCIATED– A radar target that does not display a data block with flight identification and altitude information.
(See ASSOCIATED.)

UNCONTROLLED AIRSPACE– Airspace in which aircraft are not subject to controlled airspace (Class A, B, C, D, or E) separation criteria.

UNDER THE HOOD– Indicates that the pilot is using a hood to restrict visibility outside the cockpit while simulating instrument flight. An appropriately rated pilot is required in the other control seat while this operation is being conducted.
(Refer to 14 CFR Part 91.)

UNFROZEN– The Scheduled Time of Arrival (STA) tags, which are still being rescheduled by the time–based flow management (TBFM) calculations. The aircraft will remain unfrozen until the time the corresponding estimated time of arrival (ETA) tag passes the preset freeze horizon for that aircraft's stream class. At this point the automatic rescheduling will stop, and the STA becomes "frozen."

UNICOM– A nongovernment communication facility which may provide airport information at certain airports. Locations and frequencies of UNICOMs are shown on aeronautical charts and publications.
(See CHART SUPPLEMENT.)
(Refer to AIM.)

UNMANNED AIRCRAFT (UA)- A device used or intended to be used for flight that has no onboard pilot. This device can be any type of airplane, helicopter, airship, or powered-lift aircraft. Unmanned free balloons, moored balloons, tethered aircraft, gliders, and unmanned rockets are not considered to be a UA.

UNMANNED AIRCRAFT SYSTEM (UAS)- An unmanned aircraft and its associated elements related to safe operations, which may include control stations (ground, ship, or air based), control links, support equipment, payloads, flight termination systems, and launch/recovery equipment. It consists of three elements: unmanned aircraft, control station, and data link.

UNPUBLISHED ROUTE– A route for which no minimum altitude is published or charted for pilot use. It may include a direct route between NAVAIDs, a radial, a radar vector, or a final approach course beyond the segments of an instrument approach procedure.
(See PUBLISHED ROUTE.)
(See ROUTE.)

UNRELIABLE (GPS/WAAS)– An advisory to pilots indicating the expected level of service of the GPS and/or WAAS may not be available. Pilots must then determine the adequacy of the signal for desired use.

UNSERVICEABLE (U/S)
(See OUT OF SERVICE/UNSERVICEABLE.)

UPWIND LEG–
(See TRAFFIC PATTERN.)

URBAN AIR MOBILITY (UAM)– A subset of Advanced Air Mobility (AAM), referring to an air transportation system utilizing highly automated aircraft to transport passengers or cargo in urban/suburban areas.

URGENCY– A condition of being concerned about safety and of requiring timely but not immediate assistance; a potential distress condition.
(See ICAO term URGENCY.)

URGENCY [ICAO]– A condition concerning the safety of an aircraft or other vehicle, or of person on board or in sight, but which does not require immediate assistance.

USAFIB–
(See ARMY AVIATION FLIGHT INFORMATION BULLETIN.)

UTM–
(See UAS TRAFFIC MANAGEMENT.)

VASI–
(See VISUAL APPROACH SLOPE INDICATOR.)

VCOA–
(See VISUAL CLIMB OVER AIRPORT.)

VDP–
(See VISUAL DESCENT POINT.)

VECTOR– A heading issued to an aircraft to provide navigational guidance by radar.
(See ICAO term RADAR VECTORING.)

VERIFY– Request confirmation of information; e.g., "verify assigned altitude."

VERIFY SPECIFIC DIRECTION OF TAKEOFF (OR TURNS AFTER TAKEOFF)– Used by ATC to ascertain an aircraft's direction of takeoff and/or direction of turn after takeoff. It is normally used for IFR departures from an airport not having a control tower. When direct communication with the pilot is not possible, the request and information may be relayed through an FSS, dispatcher, or by other means.
(See IFR TAKEOFF MINIMUMS AND DEPARTURE PROCEDURES.)

VERTICAL NAVIGATION (VNAV)– A function of area navigation (RNAV) equipment which calculates, displays, and provides vertical guidance to a profile or path.

VERTICAL SEPARATION– Separation between aircraft expressed in units of vertical distance.
(See SEPARATION.)

VERTICAL TAKEOFF AND LANDING AIRCRAFT (VTOL)– Aircraft capable of vertical climbs and/or descents and of using very short runways or small areas for takeoff and landings. These aircraft include, but are not limited to, helicopters.
(See SHORT TAKEOFF AND LANDING AIRCRAFT.)

VERY HIGH FREQUENCY (VHF)– The frequency band between 30 and 300 MHz. Portions of this band, 108 to 118 MHz, are used for certain NAVAIDs; 118 to 136 MHz are used for civil air/ground voice communications. Other frequencies in this band are used for purposes not related to air traffic control.

VERY HIGH FREQUENCY OMNIDIRECTIONAL RANGE STATION–
(See VOR.)

VERY LOW FREQUENCY (VLF)– The frequency band between 3 and 30 kHz.

VFR–
(See VISUAL FLIGHT RULES.)

VFR AIRCRAFT– An aircraft conducting flight in accordance with visual flight rules.
(See VISUAL FLIGHT RULES.)

VFR CONDITIONS– Weather conditions equal to or better than the minimum for flight under visual flight rules. The term may be used as an ATC clearance/instruction only when:

a. An IFR aircraft requests a climb/descent in VFR conditions.

b. The clearance will result in noise abatement benefits where part of the IFR departure route does not conform to an FAA approved noise abatement route or altitude.

c. A pilot has requested a practice instrument approach and is not on an IFR flight plan.

Note: All pilots receiving this authorization must comply with the VFR visibility and distance from cloud criteria in 14 CFR Part 91. Use of the term does not relieve controllers of their responsibility to separate aircraft in

Class B and Class C airspace or TRSAs as required by FAA Order JO 7110.65. When used as an ATC clearance/instruction, the term may be abbreviated "VFR;" e.g., "MAINTAIN VFR," "CLIMB/DESCEND VFR," etc.

VFR FLIGHT–
(See VFR AIRCRAFT.)

VFR MILITARY TRAINING ROUTES (VR)– Routes used by the Department of Defense and associated Reserve and Air Guard units for the purpose of conducting low-altitude navigation and tactical training under VFR below 10,000 feet MSL at airspeeds in excess of 250 knots IAS.

VFR NOT RECOMMENDED– An advisory provided by a flight service station to a pilot during a preflight or inflight weather briefing that flight under visual flight rules is not recommended. To be given when the current and/or forecast weather conditions are at or below VFR minimums. It does not abrogate the pilot's authority to make his/her own decision.

VFR-ON-TOP– ATC authorization for an IFR aircraft to operate in VFR conditions at any appropriate VFR altitude (as specified in 14 CFR and as restricted by ATC). A pilot receiving this authorization must comply with the VFR visibility, distance from cloud criteria, and the minimum IFR altitudes specified in 14 CFR Part 91. The use of this term does not relieve controllers of their responsibility to separate aircraft in Class B and Class C airspace or TRSAs as required by FAA Order JO 7110.65.

VFR TERMINAL AREA CHARTS–
(See AERONAUTICAL CHART.)

VFR WAYPOINT–
(See WAYPOINT.)

VHF–
(See VERY HIGH FREQUENCY.)

VHF OMNIDIRECTIONAL RANGE/TACTICAL AIR NAVIGATION–
(See VORTAC.)

VIDEO MAP– An electronically displayed map on the radar display that may depict data such as airports, heliports, runway centerline extensions, hospital emergency landing areas, NAVAIDs and fixes, reporting points, airway/route centerlines, boundaries, handoff points, special use tracks, obstructions, prominent geographic features, map alignment indicators, range accuracy marks, and/or minimum vectoring altitudes.

VISIBILITY– The ability, as determined by atmospheric conditions and expressed in units of distance, to see and identify prominent unlighted objects by day and prominent lighted objects by night. Visibility is reported as statute miles, hundreds of feet or meters.
(Refer to 14 CFR Part 91.)
(Refer to AIM.)

a. Flight Visibility– The average forward horizontal distance, from the cockpit of an aircraft in flight, at which prominent unlighted objects may be seen and identified by day and prominent lighted objects may be seen and identified by night.

b. Ground Visibility– Prevailing horizontal visibility near the earth's surface as reported by the United States National Weather Service or an accredited observer.

c. Prevailing Visibility– The greatest horizontal visibility equaled or exceeded throughout at least half the horizon circle which need not necessarily be continuous.

d. Runway Visual Range (RVR)– An instrumentally derived value, based on standard calibrations, that represents the horizontal distance a pilot will see down the runway from the approach end. It is based on the sighting of either high intensity runway lights or on the visual contrast of other targets whichever yields the greater visual range. RVR, in contrast to prevailing or runway visibility, is based on what a pilot in a moving aircraft should see looking down the runway. RVR is horizontal visual range, not slant visual range. It is based on the measurement of a transmissometer made near the touchdown point of the instrument runway and is reported in hundreds of feet. RVR, where available, is used in lieu of prevailing visibility in determining minimums for a particular runway.

1. Touchdown RVR– The RVR visibility readout values obtained from RVR equipment serving the runway touchdown zone.

2. Mid-RVR– The RVR readout values obtained from RVR equipment located midfield of the runway.

3. Rollout RVR– The RVR readout values obtained from RVR equipment located nearest the rollout end of the runway.

(See ICAO term FLIGHT VISIBILITY.)
(See ICAO term GROUND VISIBILITY.)
(See ICAO term RUNWAY VISUAL RANGE.)
(See ICAO term VISIBILITY.)

VISIBILITY [ICAO]– The ability, as determined by atmospheric conditions and expressed in units of distance, to see and identify prominent unlighted objects by day and prominent lighted objects by night.

a. Flight Visibility– The visibility forward from the cockpit of an aircraft in flight.

b. Ground Visibility– The visibility at an aerodrome as reported by an accredited observer.

c. Runway Visual Range [RVR]– The range over which the pilot of an aircraft on the centerline of a runway can see the runway surface markings or the lights delineating the runway or identifying its centerline.

VISUAL APPROACH– An approach conducted on an instrument flight rules (IFR) flight plan which authorizes the pilot to proceed visually and clear of clouds to the airport. The pilot must, at all times, have either the airport or the preceding aircraft in sight. This approach must be authorized and under the control of the appropriate air traffic control facility. Reported weather at the airport must be: ceiling at or above 1,000 feet, and visibility of 3 miles or greater.

(See ICAO term VISUAL APPROACH.)

VISUAL APPROACH [ICAO]– An approach by an IFR flight when either part or all of an instrument approach procedure is not completed and the approach is executed in visual reference to terrain.

VISUAL APPROACH SLOPE INDICATOR (VASI)–
(See AIRPORT LIGHTING.)

VISUAL CLIMB OVER AIRPORT (VCOA)– A departure option for an IFR aircraft, operating in visual meteorological conditions equal to or greater than the specified visibility and ceiling, to visually conduct climbing turns over the airport to the published "climb–to" altitude from which to proceed with the instrument portion of the departure. VCOA procedures are developed to avoid obstacles greater than 3 statute miles from the departure end of the runway as an alternative to complying with climb gradients greater than 200 feet per nautical mile. Pilots are responsible to advise ATC as early as possible of the intent to fly the VCOA option prior to departure. These textual procedures are published in the 'Take–Off Minimums and (Obstacle) Departure Procedures' section of the Terminal Procedures Publications and/or appear as an option on a Graphic ODP.

(See AIM.)

VISUAL DESCENT POINT– A defined point on the final approach course of a nonprecision straight-in approach procedure from which normal descent from the MDA to the runway touchdown point may be commenced, provided the approach threshold of that runway, or approach lights, or other markings identifiable with the approach end of that runway are clearly visible to the pilot.

VISUAL FLIGHT RULES– Rules that govern the procedures for conducting flight under visual conditions. The term "VFR" is also used in the United States to indicate weather conditions that are equal to or greater than minimum VFR requirements. In addition, it is used by pilots and controllers to indicate type of flight plan.

(See INSTRUMENT FLIGHT RULES.)
(See INSTRUMENT METEOROLOGICAL CONDITIONS.)
(See VISUAL METEOROLOGICAL CONDITIONS.)
(Refer to 14 CFR Part 91.)
(Refer to AIM.)

VISUAL HOLDING– The holding of aircraft at selected, prominent geographical fixes which can be easily recognized from the air.
(See HOLDING FIX.)

VISUAL LINE OF SIGHT (VLOS)– Condition of operations wherein the operator maintains continuous, unaided visual contact with the unmanned aircraft.

VISUAL METEOROLOGICAL CONDITIONS– Meteorological conditions expressed in terms of visibility, distance from cloud, and ceiling equal to or better than specified minima.
(See INSTRUMENT FLIGHT RULES.)
(See INSTRUMENT METEOROLOGICAL CONDITIONS.)
(See VISUAL FLIGHT RULES.)

VISUAL OBSERVER (VO)– A person who is designated by the remote pilot in command to assist the remote pilot in command and the person operating the flight controls of the small UAS (sUAS) to see and avoid other air traffic or objects aloft or on the ground.

VISUAL SEGMENT–
(See PUBLISHED INSTRUMENT APPROACH PROCEDURE VISUAL SEGMENT.)

VISUAL SEPARATION– A means employed by ATC to separate aircraft in terminal areas and en route airspace in the NAS. There are two ways to effect this separation:

a. The tower controller sees the aircraft involved and issues instructions, as necessary, to ensure that the aircraft avoid each other.

b. A pilot sees the other aircraft involved and upon instructions from the controller provides his/her own separation by maneuvering his/her aircraft as necessary to avoid it. This may involve following another aircraft or keeping it in sight until it is no longer a factor.
(See SEE AND AVOID.)
(Refer to 14 CFR Part 91.)

VLF–
(See VERY LOW FREQUENCY.)

VMC–
(See VISUAL METEOROLOGICAL CONDITIONS.)

VOICE SWITCHING AND CONTROL SYSTEM (VSCS)– A computer controlled switching system that provides air traffic controllers with all voice circuits (air to ground and ground to ground) necessary for air traffic control.
(Refer to AIM.)

VOR– A ground-based electronic navigation aid transmitting very high frequency navigation signals, 360 degrees in azimuth, oriented from magnetic north. Used as the basis for navigation in the National Airspace System. The VOR periodically identifies itself by Morse Code and may have an additional voice identification feature. Voice features may be used by ATC or FSS for transmitting instructions/information to pilots.
(See NAVIGATIONAL AID.)
(Refer to AIM.)

VOR TEST SIGNAL–
(See VOT.)

VORTAC– A navigation aid providing VOR azimuth, TACAN azimuth, and TACAN distance measuring equipment (DME) at one site.
(See DISTANCE MEASURING EQUIPMENT.)
(See NAVIGATIONAL AID.)
(See TACAN.)
(See VOR.)
(Refer to AIM.)

VORTICES− Circular patterns of air created by the movement of an airfoil through the air when generating lift. As an airfoil moves through the atmosphere in sustained flight, an area of area of low pressure is created above it. The air flowing from the high pressure area to the low pressure area around and about the tips of the airfoil tends to roll up into two rapidly rotating vortices, cylindrical in shape. These vortices are the most predominant parts of aircraft wake turbulence and their rotational force is dependent upon the wing loading, gross weight, and speed of the generating aircraft. The vortices from medium to super aircraft can be of extremely high velocity and hazardous to smaller aircraft.

(See AIRCRAFT CLASSES.)
(See WAKE TURBULENCE.)
(Refer to AIM.)

VOT− A ground facility which emits a test signal to check VOR receiver accuracy. Some VOTs are available to the user while airborne, and others are limited to ground use only.

(See CHART SUPPLEMENT.)
(Refer to 14 CFR Part 91.)
(Refer to AIM.)

VR−
(See VFR MILITARY TRAINING ROUTES.)

VSCS−
(See VOICE SWITCHING AND CONTROL SYSTEM.)

VTOL AIRCRAFT−
(See VERTICAL TAKEOFF AND LANDING AIRCRAFT.)

WA–
(See AIRMET.)
(See WEATHER ADVISORY.)

WAAS–
(See WIDE-AREA AUGMENTATION SYSTEM.)

WAKE RE–CATEGORIZATION (RECAT)– A set of optimized wake separation standards, featuring an increased number of aircraft wake categories, in use at select airports, which allows reduced wake intervals.
(See WAKE TURBULENCE.)

WAKE TURBULENCE– A phenomenon that occurs when an aircraft develops lift and forms a pair of counter–rotating vortices.
(See AIRCRAFT CLASSES.)
(See VORTICES.)
(Refer to AIM.)

WARNING AREA–
(See SPECIAL USE AIRSPACE.)

WAYPOINT– A predetermined geographical position used for route/instrument approach definition, progress reports, published VFR routes, visual reporting points or points for transitioning and/or circumnavigating controlled and/or special use airspace, that is defined relative to a VORTAC station or in terms of latitude/longitude coordinates.

WEATHER ADVISORY– In aviation weather forecast practice, an expression of hazardous weather conditions not predicted in the Aviation Surface Forecast, Aviation Cloud Forecast, or area forecast, as they affect the operation of air traffic and as prepared by the NWS.
(See AIRMET.)
(See GRAPHICAL AIRMEN'S METEOROLOGICAL INFORMATION.)
(See SIGMET.)

WEATHER RADAR PRECIPITATION INTENSITY– Existing radar systems cannot detect turbulence, however, there is a direct correlation between turbulence intensity and precipitation intensity. Controllers must issue all precipitation displayed on their user display systems. When precipitation intensity is not available, controllers will report intensity as UNKNOWN. When precipitation intensity levels are available, they will be described as follows:

a. LIGHT (< 26 dBZ)

b. MODERATE (26 to 40 dBZ)

c. HEAVY (> 40 to 50 dBZ)

d. EXTREME (> 50 dBZ)

WEATHER RECONNAISSANCE AREA (WRA)– A WRA is airspace with defined dimensions and published by Notice to Air Missions, which is established to support weather reconnaissance/research flights. Air traffic control services are not provided within WRAs. Only participating weather reconnaissance/research aircraft from the 53rd Weather Reconnaissance Squadron and National Oceanic and Atmospheric Administration Aircraft Operations Center are permitted to operate within a WRA. A WRA may only be established in airspace within U.S. Flight Information Regions outside of U.S. territorial airspace.

WHEN ABLE–

a. In conjunction with ATC instructions, gives the pilot the latitude to delay compliance until a condition or event has been reconciled. Unlike "pilot discretion," when instructions are prefaced "when able," the pilot is expected to seek the first opportunity to comply.

b. In conjunction with a weather deviation clearance, requires the pilot to determine when he/she is clear of weather, then execute ATC instructions.

c. Once a maneuver has been initiated, the pilot is expected to continue until the specifications of the instructions have been met. "When able," should not be used when expeditious compliance is required.

WIDE-AREA AUGMENTATION SYSTEM (WAAS)– The WAAS is a satellite navigation system consisting of the equipment and software which augments the GPS Standard Positioning Service (SPS). The WAAS provides enhanced integrity, accuracy, availability, and continuity over and above GPS SPS. The differential correction function provides improved accuracy required for precision approach.

WIDE AREA MULTILATERATION (WAM)– A distributed surveillance technology which may utilize any combination of signals from Air Traffic Control Radar Beacon System (ATCRBS) (Modes A and C) and Mode S transponders, and ADS-B transmissions. Multiple geographically dispersed ground sensors measure the time-of-arrival of the transponder messages. Aircraft position is determined by joint processing of the time-difference-of-arrival (TDOA) measurements computed between a reference and the ground stations' measured time-of-arrival.

WILCO– I have received your message, understand it, and will comply with it.

WIND GRID DISPLAY– A display that presents the latest forecasted wind data overlaid on a map of the ARTCC area. Wind data is automatically entered and updated periodically by transmissions from the National Weather Service. Winds at specific altitudes, along with temperatures and air pressure can be viewed.

WIND SHEAR– A change in wind speed and/or wind direction in a short distance resulting in a tearing or shearing effect. It can exist in a horizontal or vertical direction and occasionally in both.

WIND SHEAR ESCAPE– An unplanned abortive maneuver initiated by the pilot in command (PIC) as a result of onboard cockpit systems. Wind shear escapes are characterized by maximum thrust climbs in the low altitude terminal environment until wind shear conditions are no longer detected.

WING TIP VORTICES–
(See VORTICES.)

WORDS TWICE–

a. As a request: "Communication is difficult. Please say every phrase twice."

b. As information: "Since communications are difficult, every phrase in this message will be spoken twice."

WS–
(See SIGMET.)
(See WEATHER ADVISORY.)

WST–
(See CONVECTIVE SIGMET.)
(See WEATHER ADVISORY.)

Made in the USA
Las Vegas, NV
04 December 2024